A QUEST FOR GLORY

A Quest for Glory

Major General
Robert Howe and the
American Revolution

Charles E. Bennett / *Donald R. Lennon*

The University of North Carolina Press Chapel Hill & London

© 1991 The University of North
Carolina Press
All rights reserved
Library of Congress
Cataloging-in-Publication Data
Bennett, Charles E., 1910–
A quest for glory : Major General Robert
Howe and the American Revolution / by
Charles E. Bennett and Donald R. Lennon.
p. cm.
Includes bibliographical references and
index.
ISBN 0-8078-1982-4 (alk. paper)
1. Howe, Robert, 1732–1786. 2. Generals
—United States—Biography. 3. United
States. Continental Army—Biography.
4. United States—History—Revolution,
1775–1783—Campaigns. I. Lennon,
Donald R. II. Title.
E207.H85B44 1991
973.7′092—dc20
[B] 91-7825
CIP

Some passages in this book have been
previously published in Donald R. Lennon,
" 'The Graveyard of American
Commanders': The Continental Army's
Southern Department, 1776–1778." *North
Carolina Historical Review* 67 (April 1990):
133–58.

The paper in this book meets the guidelines
for permanence and durability of the
Committee on Production Guidelines for
Book Longevity of the Council on Library
Resources.

Manufactured in the United States of
America
95 94 93 92 91
5   4   3   2   1

TO OUR WIVES

Jean Bennett & Billie Royall Lennon

CONTENTS

ILLUSTRATIONS

PREFACE

*R*obert Howe, descendant of a wealthy North Carolina planter family, was the product of a colonial aristocracy that by privilege of birth assumed the right and the responsibility of leadership. For more than a decade, Howe vocally participated in the public life of colonial North Carolina. He was considered one of the most effective legislators in the provincial assembly; and when the breach with the mother country began to develop he moved easily into the forefront of the Revolutionary War movement in North Carolina. He rose from militia colonel to major general in the Continental Army and became one of the few elite general officers who attained the distinction of serving for the entire war. He was one of twenty-nine men to wear the blue ribbon of the major general, and by the war's end he stood seventh in seniority among the major generals of the Continental Army. Howe held an independent post as commander of the Southern Department and subsequently served as commanding officer of Fort West Point and division commander in General Washington's main army. His greatest strength as a patriot—and probably his greatest weakness as a military commander—was his abiding faith in the concept of civilian rule. He constantly espoused the sacred trust in civil authority and the inalienable rights of the citizenry. As a military officer, he found himself irresistibly drawn into a quest for glory, but he was never willing to subvert the Whig principle of civilian rule in order to attain the glory he sought.

Unlike most of his associates in the fight for independence, General Howe has never been the subject of full biographical treatment. The few published accounts of his life primarily have focused on his unhappy military command in Georgia and/or his amorous personal life. Undoubtedly, the lack of documentation has been a major factor in the lack of interest in the general. No body of personal papers has survived. Although there are an abundance of Howe letters in such major collections as the Papers of the Continental Congress, the George Washington Papers, and the William Heath Papers, Howe's handwriting constitutes a herculean barrier to the historian. In many cases, his "hieroglyphics" must be deciphered one word at a time, a process not conducive to large-scale research.

In preparing this work, there are numerous acknowledgments that must be made. From East Carolina University and the Southern Regional Education Board in Atlanta, Georgia, we received financial support to help defray research expenses. We also express sincere appreciation to L. Van Loan Naisawald for his valuable contributions to and involvement in an earlier version of the Robert Howe biography. Also, we must thank the staff of Joyner Library at East Carolina University, especially the staff of its Archives and Manuscripts Department. A particular debt of gratitude is due to Susan R. Midgette and Morgan J. Barclay, who went far beyond the call of duty, and to Martha G. Elmore and Kim F. Krize for their valuable assistance. For his artistic talents in preparing draft versions of the maps, we thank Roger E. Kammerer. Finally, to our colleagues in the historical and archival professions, we express our appreciation for their assistance throughout the project.

A QUEST FOR GLORY

Major General Robert Howe (From the Preston R. Davie Collection, #3406, Southern Historical Collection, Library of the University of North Carolina at Chapel Hill)

CHAPTER I

A CAROLINA

ARISTOCRACY

When, in June 1773, Josiah Quincy of Massachusetts passed through southeastern North Carolina, he found a genial and articulate company of men with whom to associate. For this young scion of a prominent New England family, the Cape Fear society provided a high point of his tour north from Charleston. Quincy was highly impressed with William Hooper and Cornelius Harnett, with whom he dined and discussed politics at length; but it was Robert Howe, a militia colonel, legislator, and planter from Brunswick County, who caught the imagination of the visitor. In him Quincy found "a most happy compound of the man of sense, sentiment and dignity, with the man of the world, the sword, the senate, and the buck. A truly surprising character." In his journal Quincy wrote, "This gentleman is a very extraordinary character. Formed by nature and his education to shine in the senate and the field—in company of the philosopher and libertine—a favorite of the man of sense and the female world. He has faults and vices—but alas who is without them? His faults are those of high spirits—his vices those of a man of feeling." [1]

Quincy, more than any contemporary commentator, captured the essence of what Robert Howe envisioned himself to be. "Man of the world, the sword, the senate, and the buck" would serve as a most gratifying postscript to the life of a man who served with distinction in the colonial legislature of North Carolina, who was in the forefront of the revolutionary movement as it took form in his native province, and who ultimately became the highest ranking revolutionary war general from the states south of Virginia.

Robert Howe was born around 1732 into a wealthy Cape Fear River planter family that had recently migrated from South Carolina. His great-grandfather, Job Howes, had come to Charleston from England during the early 1680s. Although Job Howes's background is obscure, he was the right age to have been the son of Job Howes, "gentleman of the city of London," who married Margaret Haughton at St. Mary Magdalene on Old Fish Street in London in 1646. It is known that Robert's great-grandfather Job was in South Carolina by 1683, when he settled a 290-acre plantation on Foster's Creek, in what became St. James–Goose Creek Precinct, west of Charles Town. In addition to this Howe Hall Plantation, he owned other properties on Goose Creek. He joined with other Englishmen and Barbadians, such as James Moore, Maurice Matthews, and Arthur Middleton, to form the notorious "Goose Creek men." Most members of this powerful political faction were Anglican in background, and during the 1680s and much of the 1690s they stridently opposed the proprietary rule in South Carolina. Job Howes led the provincial Parliament in 1687 in passing the Charter Bill, which denied the legality of the proprietors' Fundamental Constitutions of Carolina and declared the royal charter of 1665 to be the only legal foundation of government. Howes's political acumen in the 1690 Parliament led one critic to refer to him as "prolocutor or dictator in our last senat [*sic*] and the Transcriber of the Salvo Act." This opponent, who claimed to have challenged Howes on one occasion with swords, contended that his enemy had once been a linkboy (and then a barber) in London. Like the linkboys—who walk through puddles and mire carrying the light so that travelers may walk behind them clean and dry—Howes, it was suggested, had soiled himself in order to lead the way in the South Carolina legislature.[2]

Howes represented Berkeley and Craven counties in the South Carolina Commons from 1696 until his death, serving as speaker of the Lower House during the final six years. He was credited with paving the way for the formal establishment of the Anglican Church in South Carolina by forcing passage of the Exclusion Act of 1704,

which barred dissenters from service in the assembly. He also sponsored a 1700 law that provided government support for a provincial
library. Prior to his death from yellow fever during the summer of
1706, Job Howes had served as deputy lords proprietor and sur-
veyor general of Carolina. He had been one of six Goose Creek men
who dominated the political life of South Carolina for more than a
decade.[3]

Job Howes married Sarah Middleton, widow of Edward Middleton and mother of South Carolina council president Arthur Middleton. Their only son, Robert, inherited most of the Howes fortune and
retained the position of a wealthy planter in the Goose Creek community. Robert married Mary Moore, daughter of Governor James
Moore and sister of James, Maurice, Roger, and Nathaniel Moore.
The Goose Creek men, now including Robert Howes, continued to
influence South Carolina government and economy, bringing fear
and frustration to proprietary officials, who felt the constant sting
of their opposition to "oppressive" policy. Robert served as a parish
vestryman, tax inquisitor, and representative in the South Carolina
Assembly. When he died in 1724, his only son, Job, was still a minor.
Job presumably grew up in the company of the Moores at the very
time that plans for a Cape Fear settlement were reaching fruition.[4]

As late as 1725, the Cape Fear River valley remained a com
plete wilderness, unoccupied except for a scattered Indian population. James and Maurice Moore had passed through the area during
the Tuscarora and Yamassees Indian wars of a decade earlier, and
Maurice had remained in North Carolina to marry the daughter of
Alexander Lillington—thus becoming tied to the influential Lillington, Moseley, Porter, and Swann families of this province. It was
Maurice, with the support and collusion of the erratic North Carolina governor George Burrington, who initiated the settlement of the
Cape Fear. Burrington explored the area during 1724 and 1725 and
circumvented proprietary restrictions on settlement by issuing land
patents directly from his office. Maurice Moore was living on the
river by 1726 and his brothers arrived soon thereafter. It is uncertain when the young Job Howes moved to the Cape Fear wilderness;
but, since he was a kinsman of Maurice, Roger, and James Moore,
it is apparent that he was among the earliest settlers of southeastern
North Carolina. His widowed mother had married Thomas Clifford,

a leading planter who represented the St. James–Goose Creek Precinct from 1731 to 1733. It appears that Job attained legal age in 1731, at which time he received eight hundred acres on Goose Creek from his father's estate. Obviously, Job had been on the Cape Fear prior to this date; by 1734 his mother and stepfather had joined him in North Carolina and were actively developing plantations along the river.[5]

The early Cape Fear settlers attempted to replicate the life-style that had been enjoyed by the South Carolina Low-Country aristocracy. Although vast marshlands held the promise for major rice production (as in South Carolina), the early planters were also attracted to forest products—such as timber and naval stores, grain crops, and livestock—and experimentation in such exotic undertakings as silk and indigo production. Huge estates took form along the river and its tributaries as the Moores, Allens, Porters, and Swanns laid claim to thousands of acres of the finest lands the area had to offer. Imaginative and exotic names, such as Orton, Kendal, Blue Banks, Lilliput, Pleasant Oaks, Spring Garden, and Stag Park, adorned plantations stretching for miles up the Cape Fear. Brunswick Town was laid off in 1726 by Job Howes's uncle, Maurice Moore, and it became the first seat of New Hanover County. Even after the rival community of Newtown (Wilmington) began to take form during the 1730s, the Moore—Allen—Porter—Swann "family" continued to reign supreme in the political and social life of the region. Fifteen men, most related by marriage or blood, claimed more than eighty thousand acres of land along the river, with Roger and Maurice Moore alone owning twenty-five thousand acres each.[6]

As a nephew of the Moore brothers, Job Howes was a part of the "family" and its endeavors. By 1731 he was selling the Goose Creek plantations that were inherited from his father. Prior to 1732, he had taken up a tract of land on New Topsail Sound, opposite Barren Inlet on the coast northeast of the future town of Wilmington. This plantation, which subsequently was known as Howe's Point, became his principal residence. Presumably it was here at Howe's Point that the Robert Howe of this study was born. In 1735 Job purchased a one-thousand-acre plantation opposite Mount Misery on the west bank of the Cape Fear River. This property stretched from Indian Creek to Gabourel Bluff, and it would appear that the Howes family inhabited the house on this plantation at least part of the time.[7]

In addition to Robert, Job fathered four other sons and two daughters, but the household was a result of three marriages. As North Carolinians, the family dropped the "s" from their name, giving it the spelling that was to become famous in colonial politics. Job Howe (formerly Job Howes), while still a young Cape Fear region planter, had married Martha Jones, daughter of North Carolina chief justice Frederick Jones of Chowan County. Jones held vast estates in North Carolina and Virginia, including seventeen thousand acres in Chowan County. Following Martha's early death, Job married Elizabeth Watters, the daughter of a prominent Cape Fear planter. Twice widowed, he then married a lady named Jane. From these three unions, Job fathered not only Robert but also Elizabeth, Job, Jr., Thomas Clifford, Arthur, Joseph, and Mary. Robert (and perhaps Job, Jr.) may have been the only children born to Martha Howe before her early death, with the result that the remaining children were half brothers and half sisters with whom Robert did not closely relate. Although several of his brothers were active in provincial affairs, there is no evidence that "Bob" and his brothers shared a family relationship. It is obvious, however, that Robert was a favorite of his grandmother, for she provided him with slaves, real estate, and money as he developed into manhood.[8]

The specifics of Robert Howe's early life are sketchy and largely undocumented. It is apparent from his high degree of literacy and his intimate knowledge of English literature that he was well educated. A tradition exists that Robert attended school in England, but documentation is lacking to give substance to the claim. It is unknown whether he received plantation schooling on the Cape Fear, found education among kinsmen in Charleston, or indeed did enroll in an English school. It is certain that he had a love for Shakespeare and other major English writers, a fluency with the English language, and an air of breeding and confidence that was a part of his general demeanor. He was not conversant with French, and his penmanship was so deplorable that he frequently referred to his writing as "hieroglyphics." Whether this was a reflection on his education or indicated an unrecorded limitation remains hidden from the modern viewer.[9]

The young Robert Howe, perhaps as early as 1751, married Sarah Grange, daughter of Thomas Grange of Bladen County. The newlyweds took up residence on Grange property where Beaver Dam and

Kendal Plantation, home of Major General Robert Howe (From Leslie's Illustrated Newspaper, 26 October 1866, p. 72. Print courtesy of the North Carolina Division of Archives and History)

Waymans creeks flow into the Cape Fear River in modern Columbus County. Around 1754 Robert became a captain in the Bladen County militia, in 1756 he was appointed a justice of the peace, and during the spring of 1760 he was elected for the first time to represent Bladen County in the General Assembly. Except for the period between 1762 and 1764, Howe served in every session of the provincial legislature until he took formal command of the Second North Carolina Regiment in 1775. By 1764 Howe had moved from Bladen County—presumably to some location on Old Town Creek below Brunswick Town, where he had purchased several plantations during 1763—or to the plantation opposite Mount Misery that he had inherited from his father. It was not until after 1770 that he finally obtained Kendal, which was on the Cape Fear adjoining Orton Plantation. This well-known rice plantation, which had originated as a part of Roger Moore's 1726 grant, was Howe's home throughout the remainder of his life. Kendal contained approximately 400 acres, 180 acres of which were excellent rice-field marshes.[10]

It appears that Howe, as a planter and businessman, was less than successful. As early as 1754 he had received slaves from his grandmother, and in 1759 he inherited from his father the one-thousand-acre plantation opposite Mount Misery. In the years that followed, he purchased substantial lands, primarily in the Old Town Creek area of what was to become Brunswick County. By 1766, however, the purchases had turned into sales; and, during practically every year between 1766 and 1775, Howe sold and/or mortgaged land or slaves. During the latter year, as he awaited appointment to the command of one of North Carolina's regiments, Howe was forced to mortgage Kendal Plantation for £214 3s. 5d. At this late date, it is impossible to determine the causes of these financial reversals. One critic complained that Howe starved his wife and children so that he could make a good appearance annually at the races in Virginia and Maryland. In the same vein, Governor Josiah Martin accused Howe of misapplication of public money, as "he had inherited a good fortune but had wrecked it." [11] The actual record is blank on this score, but his excessive involvement in public affairs as a legislator, judge, and military commander obviously infringed upon any time for business enterprises that would have benefited him financially. Later in life, he was to comment that, since he had been "born to affluence, I have been bred to no trade or profession." [12]

In his personal life, Robert Howe apparently achieved numerous conquests but few lasting attachments. In an age where divorce was virtually unknown, he and his wife Sarah were legally separated in 1772. The agreement stipulated that the couple would live separately and that Howe would transfer ownership of sixteen slaves to her brothers John and Thomas Grange, who were acting as trustees in her behalf. Howe was to retain possession of the slaves and pay £100 annually for use of the property. All debts incurred by Sarah would be paid from the income. No mention is made of arrangements for their children. Information is even contradictory as to the number of children produced by the union, but Sarah in her will specifically names Robert, Jr., Mary Moore, and Ann Goodlet Daniel. [13] There is no indication of where Sarah and the children resided after the separation, but she did remain in Brunswick County until her death in 1804.

Numerous contemporary accounts portrayed Howe as a man of charm, sophistication, and imagination. He was active in the Masonic Order, loved to dance, and was most impressive in the midst of social activities. He was generally known as "Bob," and, as a grudging admirer and critic recorded, "he had that general polite gallantry, which every man of good breeding ought to have." Other contemporaries commented that his "imagination fascinated," his "repartee overpowered," and his "conversation was enlivened by strains of exquisite raillery." [14]

A revealing glimpse of Bob Howe's social graces can be seen in an incident that followed a militia review in Wilmington in June of 1775. A group of the officers, including Howe, had been invited to dine in the home of one of the Wilmington residents. During the evening, Howe wandered into an adjoining room and returned carrying an open book of Shakespeare's works, which a lady guest had been reading. When she chided him for taking such a liberty, the gallant Bob bowed, admitted his fault, and offered to accept any punishment that she should inflict. The lady, who was avidly pro-British, promptly sentenced him to read aloud to the group a passage that she would designate from the book. Much to Howe's chagrin, she opened the volume to act 4, scene 2 of "The First Part of King Henry the Fourth." Howe instantly recognized the passage in which Falstaff admitted that he was ashamed of his ragamuffin army. The militia colonel "coloured like scarlet" when he realized that he was being outwitted and humiliated. He quickly recovered his composure and proceeded to read the passage in which Falstaff described his army as "tattered prodigals lately come from swine-keeping" and as "scarecrows." Howe shortly thereafter whispered in the lady's ear: "You will certainly get yourself tarred and feathered; shall I apply to be executioner?" [15]

Robert Howe's character elicited numerous negative impressions, however, particularly with regard to his personal and romantic entanglements. These flaws have tended to overshadow the positive attributes. An unidentified Cape Fear writer on the eve of the Revolution characterized Howe as "the shell of patriotism without its kernal[,] a carcass without a heart, a scabby sheep that would damn a Myriad in gloomy Sable"—the latter reference obviously intended as criticism of Howe's attitude toward his slave holdings. A visitor to the region in 1774 wrote that "he is deemed a horrid animal, a sort of womaneater that devours every thing that comes in his way, . . . no woman can withstand him." [16] This weakness for romantic conquests appears to explain the legal separation from his wife and the attitude that he displayed toward women throughout his life.

CHAPTER 2

COLONIAL

LAWMAKER

*T*he enthusiasm and persuasive charm of young Robert Howe obviously was better suited to public life than to the pursuits of a coastal planter. Upon taking his seat as a representative from Bladen County, Howe immediately immersed himself in the work of the General Assembly. His early interest in military affairs, and his captaincy of the Bladen County militia, resulted in an assignment to a committee selected to prepare legislation for the better regulation of the militia. The French and Indian War was then in progress, and the need of forces and funds for the support of the wartime effort was of prime concern to Governor Arthur Dobbs and to most legislators. In 1760 Howe not only was involved in legislation to put the militia on a more efficient footing, but he likewise served on a committee to provide finances for the governor's war effort, sat on the public claims committee that examined and approved all expenditures of public funds to individuals, and helped prepare an address of response to the governor. It would appear that the Bladen County representative had a productive term, especially since he was a freshman legislator.[1]

Subsequent sessions of the General Assembly witnessed the increasing influence and involvement of Representative Howe. In April 1761 Howe, along with William Dry and, later, John Sampson, brought in bills—to be used by His Majesty during the war—for granting funds to raise and clothe five hundred men. The legislation

9

as passed provided for the expenditure of £20,000 "proclamation money" to provide a military force to be employed as directed by the commander in chief of His Majesty's forces in America or by the governor of North Carolina. The act also provided for pay and subsistence for the fifty men and officers then in garrison and for the appointment of an agent to represent North Carolina in England. The expenditure was funded by printing bills of credit in the prescribed amount with a two-shilling poll-tax levy, beginning on 1 January 1764, to redeem the bills of credit.[2]

During the 1761 session, Howe presented a bill designed to prevent sheriffs and other officers from exacting illegal and exorbitant fees. Local officials received no salaries but were authorized to charge specified fees for their services. Although the amount legitimately charged was stipulated in the laws, no regulation existed to make sheriffs and other officers of the court accountable to the public for the fees. Residents of the backcountry repeatedly accused sheriffs and other local government officials of charging exorbitant fees far in excess of those permitted by law. Howe's bill, when enacted, called for a £10 fine from any official who failed to specifically endorse all executions he processed with the amount of fees charged. This endorsement was to be entered by the clerk on the execution docket. The sheriff also was required to prepare a bill of his fees for every action or suit and to itemize separately all clerk's and attorney's fees, along with any other fees. This receipt was to be submitted to the party against whom the execution was issued. The fine for violation was to be divided between the county and the individual who brought charges against the sheriff. Had this legislation been enforced by the county courts across the piedmont of North Carolina during the 1760s, it could have diffused a major complaint of backcountry citizens and thus constituted a significant factor in preventing the Regulator uprising that swept the area between 1765 and 1771.[3]

Although it is known that Howe participated in the French and Indian War that raged across the frontier of America between 1754 and 1763, it is uncertain when he joined military forces who were combating the threat from the French and their allies. Militia forces and independent companies from North Carolina, recruited specifically for the crisis, intermittently marched west to face the foe. A Captain Howe was with Col. Hugh Waddell at an encampment at Bigg Island on the Holston River in present-day Tennessee on 23 October 1761, but it is uncertain whether this was Robert or his brother Arthur, who also served in the war. Robert's whereabouts between April 1761 and late 1762 are undocumented. Hugh Waddell and William Bartram represented Bladen County in the fall Assembly session of 1762, and no session was held during 1763. From land transactions undertaken during January 1763, it is obvious that Robert Howe was in the Cape Fear region before the war's official conclusion in February, thus leaving the months between April 1761 and January 1763 largely unaccounted for—as are his activities before 1760. The nature and extent of Howe's service is unknown. It was reported in 1775 that he had served several campaigns as captain of an independent North Carolina company in conjunction with Virginia regiments, and one contemporary from Virginia later made note that he had served with Howe on the Holstein River during the "past war." North Carolina governor William Tryon at one time also referred to Howe as a veteran of the Indian war.[4]

In 1764 Howe represented Bladen County in the Assembly for the last time. During the previous year, he had purchased plantations on Town Creek, and he subsequently acquired nearby Kendal Plantation above Brunswick Town at the mouth of Orton Creek. As an assemblyman, he sponsored legislation in 1764 that created Brunswick County out of Bladen and New Hanover counties. Howe served on the commission that determined the bounds of the new county; and when the 1765 Assembly convened he took his seat as a representative of the newly formed county. Interestingly, the western boundary for the new county began on the Cape Fear River at the John Grange plantation that Howe had occupied on Beaver Dam Creek and ran south to Lake Waccamaw and thence to the South Carolina line.[5]

It is unfortunate that Howe's reputation rests so exclusively in the military arena, as he was an energetic and effective legislator whose skills in drafting legislation and in verbalizing the collective feelings of the House placed him in the forefront of the legislative leadership. Historian Jack P. Greene rated Robert Howe in the top rank of effective North Carolina legislators between 1770 and 1774 and in the second plateau of the leadership prior to that time.[6] Throughout his legislative career, Howe—whenever an address, letter, resolution, or other written declamation was required—inevitably was assigned to the committee responsible for preparing the document.

Aside from his interest in military preparedness and local issues, Howe's legislative talents embraced a significant cross section of provincial problems. His influence was particularly strong with regard to issues surrounding the lack of an acceptable circulating currency with which the residents could pay taxes and conduct business activities. Along with John Ashe and Edmund Fanning, Howe prepared in 1766 an address to His Majesty George III, expressing appreciation for repeal of the Stamp Act.[7] A second address written by the same committee requested the king's permission for North Carolina to emit paper currency to relieve the dire shortage of a circulating medium for the colony. This petition is indicative of Howe's concern for a currency situation that crippled business, stymied commerce, and frustrated the inhabitants. The British government attempted to prevent the printing of paper money in the colony, and the absence of specie left the people heavily dependent on a credit system. In 1768 Cornelius Harnett and Maurice Moore joined Howe in a new appeal on the subject, and at the same time these three legislators petitioned the governor with a demand for an emission of paper currency equal to £100,000 proclamation money. In a further effort to alleviate the problem, Howe prepared a bill for making specific commodities legal tender in the payment of debts. Agricultural commodities had been designated for this purpose early in the province's development. By the mid-eighteenth century, however, such limitations were placed on the procedure that the practice survived only in some eastern counties where provincial warehouses and inspectors were available to examine the goods and issue inspector's notes. These notes in turn were acceptable for taxes or trade. Neither warehouses nor inspectors were made available to the rapidly developing backcountry, thus further aggravating the currency shortage in the piedmont. Howe's commodity bill failed to survive the legislative process, as did a 1771 bill he introduced for establishing two loan offices in the province. Also during the 1771 term, Howe, Harnett, and Moore once again appealed to the king for repeal of the anti–paper currency law, at the same time forwarding a copy of their petition to the members of Parliament.[8]

Other important legislation introduced by the Brunswick County representative reflects his interests and stature in the General Assembly. In 1767 he led the move for establishing a new system of court laws and subsequently served on the committee that divided the province into five superior court districts and undertook to better regulate the proceedings of the court. He also authored legislation to regulate pilotage on the Cape Fear River by requiring pilots to put to sea on orders from the captain of Fort Johnston and by prohibiting pilots from combining to share revenue. Howe drafted bills to institute new militia laws, amend a law on free Negroes, pardon the former Regulators, reform election laws, establish triennial assemblies, protect slaves from injuries, more easily recover debts, settle the boundary with South Carolina, control the hunting of deer, and regulate issuance of marriage licenses.[9]

Committee responsibilities constitute the lifeblood of the legislative process, and the General Assembly in colonial North Carolina was no exception. Not only did Howe serve frequently on the committees on public accounts and public claims, but also his presence was felt on the committee of correspondence with North Carolina's agent in England, the committee on privilege and elections, and the joint committee to settle decorum—to say nothing of the innumerable special committees created to expedite particular items of legislation.[10]

With the death of Arthur Dobbs in 1764, William Tryon assumed the office of governor for the province. Tryon, a descendant of British nobility, held the rank of lieutenant colonel in the British army, was a veteran of the Seven Years' War, and could point with pride to a wound that he suffered in the evacuation of St. Cas Bay in 1758. His past experience should have prepared him to judge the capabilities of those with whom he associated. The new governor quickly made friends with Robert Howe and depended on his influence within the legislature. The governor admitted that he was in need of someone who could provide spirited support for Crown measures in the General Assembly and that the Brunswick County representative seemed "well inclined to give his aid, consistent with the interests of his constituents."[11]

On numerous occasions, Howe introduced bills in the General Assembly that supported the new administration. At the request of Governor Tryon, Howe drafted legislation in 1768 to prevent persons from enticing seamen to desert from Royal naval vessels. During the same session, he introduced a bill to provide the king with a duty on the tonnage of ships and other vessels entering the province. Two years later, he helped prepare legislation to grant funds to the Crown, and in 1771 he wrote a bill to facilitate the collection of His Majesty's quit rents.[12] As a military officer and a legislator, he supported the governor in the dispute with the Regulators of the backcountry. An entry in the House minutes for 22 December 1770 reads: "On motion of Mr. Howe, Resolved that in case the Insurgents should be insolent and desperate enough to make any attempt against the honor and dignity of Government or the peace and safety of the community that this House will, to the utmost of their power, support His Excellency in any measure he should think necessary to take on such an important occasion."[13]

The rapport that Howe developed with Tryon tended to serve him well. Howe already was serving as associate justice of the superior court for the Wilmington district as early as 1763, and in January 1766 Tryon appointed him to the office of chief baron of the Court of Exchequer. Apparently Howe avoided a role of conspicuous local leadership in the Stamp Act confrontation at Wilmington and Brunswick in 1765–66. Even though the Lower Cape Fear was the center of Stamp Act protests for North Carolina and most local leaders were directly involved, the name of Robert Howe is noticeably absent from all records of the incident. As early as May of 1765, the governor was supporting Howe as a candidate to replace Capt. John Dalrymple as commander of Fort Johnston at the mouth of the Cape Fear River. Tryon represented Dalrymple as an unsavory character who had been arrested by the former governor, Arthur Dobbs; Howe, in comparison, was portrayed as a man "whose spirit, diligence and integrity I entertain a good opinion of."[14] Upon receiving word of Captain Dalrymple's death, Tryon quickly commissioned his protégé as commandant of Fort Johnston. After Howe had served in that capacity for a year, Capt. John Collet arrived on the scene with a ministry commission that preempted the North Carolinian's appointment to command the fort. When Collet left North Carolina in 1769, Tryon reinstated Howe in the Fort Johnston post. During the ensuing years, Captain Howe proceeded to repair and improve the fort, increasing the garrison to twenty-five men by 1773.[15]

Fort Johnston constituted the primary defense for the Cape Fear and its port towns of Brunswick and Wilmington. In addition, it provided a measure of control for commerce entering and departing the river and maintained an arsenal for use in emergencies throughout the province. The fort was a small, poorly constructed, rectangular structure featuring four bastions joined by curtains. It had been undertaken originally as a reaction to Spanish raids along the coast during the 1740s. Efforts had been made during Arthur Dobbs's administration to strengthen the post by covering the pine planks of the bastions and curtains facing the river with a wall of tapia made from oyster shells, lime, and sand. Although this mixture had a reputation for hardening into a concretelike substance, the finish as completed in 1764 (under contract with William Dry) was so poorly mixed that it crumbled whenever the guns were fired. During his command of the fort, Howe labored to improve the facility and the living quarters of the garrison, as well as to increase the number of troops assigned to man the works. Despite improvements, travelers who sailed past were prone to disparage the installation as a "timber-bush" with "guns peeping thro' the sticks." [16]

As the backcountry protests—known as the Regulator Movement —began to develop into violence in the late 1760s, the governor depended upon Howe for support from Fort Johnston. Gunpowder, swivel guns, cannonballs, and other armament were transferred from the fort to New Bern for protection of the capital. By 1768 the situation had reached such a crisis point that Governor Tryon traveled to Hillsborough to persuade the insurgents to obey the laws. Howe was a member of the governor's large entourage of attendants. When violence was predicted for the upcoming session of Orange County superior court, some 1,461 militiamen were called into service. Tryon held a council of war to plan government strategy, at which time Howe was made a major of brigade with the rank of colonel. Bloodshed was avoided during this July 1768 confrontation, but the grievances continued to fester. In the spring of 1771, Tryon once again ordered the militia into Regulator territory. Approximately 1,000 troops, including 151 officers, marched to Great Alamance Creek, west of Hillsborough, where they faced about 2,000 unorganized and poorly armed Regulators. On 16 May the battle of Alamance was fought: the insurgents were defeated and the movement crushed. In this engagement, Howe commanded a corps of artillery and served as quartermaster general for the army.[17]

Tryon's departure from North Carolina in 1771, and Josiah Martin's arrival as governor of the province, marked a significant change in direction for Howe. He did not develop a working relationship with Martin, and they clashed repeatedly on major issues facing the colony. The new governor contended that Howe's dual positions as commandant of Fort Johnston and baron of the Court of Exchequer constituted a conflict of interest and thereupon removed him from the Exchequer post. Shortly thereafter, John Collet returned to North Carolina and Martin used him to replace Howe as commander of the fort. The governor thus deprived Howe of both offices that had been awarded by the previous governor.[18]

Of primary concern to North Carolinians at this juncture was the renewal of laws regulating the civil courts of the province. As early as 1746, the legislature had included in the court laws a clause that allowed creditors to attach property owned in North Carolina by nonresidents of the province—the British, in other words—in order to satisfy their debts. The British Board of Trade ignored the clause until 1770, when a newly appointed legal advisor raised objections to certain aspects of the attachment provision. The board thereupon took the position that attachment as specified in the North Carolina legislation violated acceptable legal practice. The British ministry in 1770 urged the governor to "induce" the colonial assembly to amend the foreign attachment clause or to omit it entirely from the court law. Martin, shortly after he replaced the more diplomatic Tryon, took the attachment clause issue as a matter of principle. He was convinced that the provincial government favored colonists at the expense of the British and that this clause was proof of the impropriety of their views.[19]

North Carolina lawmakers were determined that the attachment clause would be retained regardless of the governor's opposition, and this issue became a crucial factor around which anti-British sentiment developed in North Carolina. After a confrontation between the governor and the House, Governor Martin offered what he considered a compromise: he would allow attachment of up to £20 of personal property when it could be shown that the individual had actually fled the colony to prevent legal action. The attachment of real property would not be permitted. Martin emphasized that these were the same

rules governing attachment in commercial cities of England and in other parts of Europe. The House reacted to Martin's offer with what the governor considered an "intemperate" and "indecent" response. Without the clause, North Carolina creditors would be forced to undergo the expense and inconvenience of suing in English courts to gain satisfaction for debts owed by non–North Carolinians; and the impracticality of such a procedure was more than they were willing to accept. In the event of bankruptcy, suit in England was not even an option, since, under parliamentary statutes of bankruptcy, British law did not permit nonresidents of Great Britain to recover debts. To North Carolinians, attachment was too important as a legal tool, and as a principle, to be compromised away.[20]

Robert Howe quickly moved to the forefront of the attachment confrontation. Ten days after Martin offered his "compromise," Howe prepared a resolution that called for the House to appeal to the king and to write to former governor William Tryon in New York, requesting his intercession and representation before His Majesty. It must have been galling to Martin to read the resolution, which spoke in glowing terms of Tryon, "who happily for this Country for many years presided over it."[21] The House, acting on the resolution, appointed Howe to the committee charged with writing to the New York governor. Governor Martin subsequently charged that Howe and Isaac Edwards had engineered the move in the General Assembly out of spite for him. He pointed to Howe's removal from the Exchequer and Fort Johnston posts as motivation for the action and accused Howe of misapplication of public money in an effort to salvage his own personal fortune. "He is a man of lively parts and good understanding, but in other respects and character of no account or consideration in the present desperate state of his affairs."[22]

The relationship between the governor and Howe had steadily declined over a period of months, and it would seem that the attachment controversy was a significant factor in the eruption. As to Martin's contention that Howe's opposition stemmed from his removal as commander of Fort Johnston, a contemporary writing several months before Howe's replacement commented that he was "hot and zealous in the cause of America."[23]

It is obvious that the attachment controversy was an issue of principle deeply rooted in North Carolina legal thought of that day. Despite Martin's contention, the question went far beyond individual personalities and struck at what public-spirited colonists considered a basic right. Governor Tryon had a better understanding of the people of the province, and in December 1774 he actually visited London and talked with the legal counsel to the Board of Trade. Tryon apparently supported the colonists and suggested that some gentlemen in England owned large tracts of land in America that they wished exempted from attachment.[24]

By the spring of 1775, the Board of Trade was responsive to memorials presented by North Carolina agents in London. The fact that all the other colonies utilized foreign attachments without being challenged was a major consideration, as were promises that North Carolina legislators would modify the language in its attachment legislation. By this juncture, however, Royal government in North Carolina had collapsed, the governor was no longer in control of the province, and the issue was lost in the rush toward revolution.[25]

CHAPTER 3

"PATRON OF

REVOLT AND

ANARCHY"

*J*t is apparent that the attachment clause controversy consti
tuted a major factor in the alienation of Gov. Josiah Martin from the political leadership of North Carolina. Robert
Howe's role in this confrontation fully aligned him with the Sons
of Liberty, who had led the Stamp Act protests during the 1760s,
and provides the earliest concrete evidence of his Whig tendencies.
In addition to Howe and Isaac Edwards, the committee, which was
assigned the task of preparing the petition to the king, consisted of
Speaker John Harvey, Samuel Johnston, William Hooper, John Ashe,
Cornelius Harnett, and Joseph Hewes. These men, without exception, remained in the forefront of the revolutionary movement in
North Carolina; and Howe, as a member of this group, had assumed
a position of leadership for the confrontation that lay ahead.[1]

During the midst of the attachment controversy, Josiah Quincy of
Massachusetts visited the colony on his trip north from Charleston.
Quincy, who had graduated from Harvard in 1763, was considered a
brilliant lawyer and an ardent patriot. He was closely associated with
John Adams in the early revolutionary maneuvers in Massachusetts,
and his premature death in 1775 deprived that state and the entire

movement of one of its most promising leaders. Quincy spent five days in the Lower Cape Fear region from 26 March to 31 March 1773. During that time, he met repeatedly with the local aristocracy, which included Howe, William Dry, William Hooper, William Hill, John Burgwin, and Cornelius Harnett. Although Quincy graduated from Harvard the same year that Hooper received a Master of Arts degree from that institution, Quincy appears less than certain of his schoolmate's revolutionary tendencies. In his journal he noted that Hooper was "apparently in the Whig interest" and was being "caressed by the Whigs." The visitor identified more readily with Harnett and Howe, and it was with them that he held discussions regarding a plan for Continental correspondence. Quincy recorded that Howe was "hot and zealous in the cause of America," and he styled Harnett as "the Samuel Adams of North Carolina." It intrigued the Bostonian that these men had agreed to maintain ledgers in which they would document the activities of those loyal to the British ministry because their actions could be used against them in the future. Before Quincy's departure from the Cape Fear, Howe pledged to promote the scheme for Continental correspondence and to write his visitor "by the first opportunity." [2]

When the General Assembly convened in the fall of 1773, the attachment controversy and the need for better communication among the colonies were uppermost in the minds of North Carolina legislators. Howe, Harnett, and Samuel Johnston were appointed to respond to letters received from Massachusetts, Virginia, Rhode Island, Connecticut, and Delaware; and the Lower House proceeded to discuss the concept of regular communication among the colonies. On 8 December a "standing committee of correspondence and Enquiry" was named, consisting of John Harvey, Robert Howe, Cornelius Harnett, William Hooper, Richard Caswell, Edward Vail, John Ashe, Joseph Hewes, and Samuel Johnston. It is of interest that, of the nine members selected for the committee, four lived on the Cape Fear and four were from the Albemarle Sound, leaving only Richard Caswell as a resident of other areas of the colony. The committee specifically was charged with the responsibility "to obtain the most early and authentick Intelligence of all such Acts and Resolutions of the British Parliament, or proceedings of Administration as may relate to or effect the British Colonies in America and to keep up and maintain

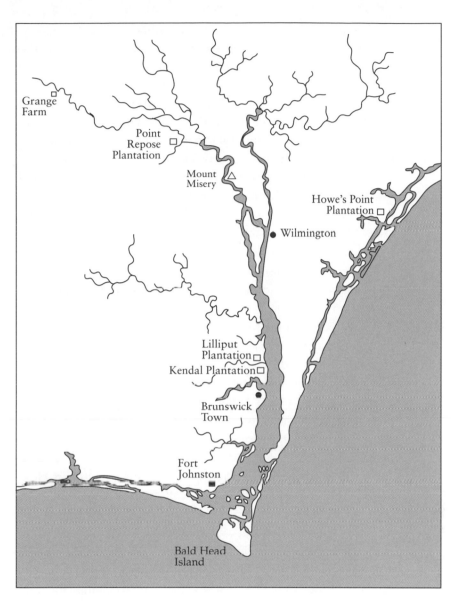

Lower Cape Fear Region

a Correspondence and Communication with our Sister Colonies respecting these important Considerations and the Result of such, their proceedings from time to time, to lay before this House."[3]

Events in Boston at this time, and the subsequent reaction in London, propelled the North Carolinians toward an ultimate showdown with Royal authority. On 16 December, after a mass meeting of eight thousand people at Boston's Old South Church, a group of men disguised as Mohawk Indians boarded the merchant ship *Dartmouth*, docked at Griffin's Wharf, and proceeded to dump 342 chests of tea into Boston harbor. The British Crown was furious over this blatant outrage against lawful authority, and during the following spring a series of laws designed to punish the wayward colony was passed by Parliament. The Boston Port Bill closed the port of Boston and moved the customhouse to Salem. Commerce, the lifeblood for Massachusetts's chief city, came to a standstill; no ships were allowed to enter or leave that port.

Rather than isolating Massachusetts by making it an example and a warning to other troublesome colonies, these "Coercive Acts" succeeded in drawing the colonies together in a common cause. North Carolinians joined with other colonists in rallying around the beleaguered Bostonians; and ships loaded with peas, corn, flour, and pork were dispatched from Wilmington, New Bern, Pitt County, and Edenton to help relieve the crisis. On the Cape Fear, a committee composed of James Moore, George Hooper, Robert Howe, Archibald Maclaine, William Hooper, John Ancrum, Robert Hogg, and Francis Clayton supervised the collection of 2,096 bushels of corn, 22 barrels of flour, and 17 barrels of pork, which were loaded on Parker Quince's *Penelope* and transported to Marblehead.[4]

The situation in Massachusetts had deteriorated to the point that a show of colonial unity was necessary. During May and June, calls for a Continental Congress went out from several colonies, including a 17 June resolution by the Massachusetts legislature suggesting that a congress convene in Philadelphia in September. Governor Martin was determined to forestall his colony's representation at such a congress. He therefore refused to convene the session of the General Assembly that earlier had been prorogued until 26 July, thus denying the Whigs a convenient forum for selecting delegates. The governor's action brought a swift and heated rebuke from the provincial leadership. When Martin communicated to House Speaker John Harvey of Perquimans County that the session would not reconvene on schedule, Harvey was livid. He proclaimed that the "people will convene one themselves" and began to confer with associates around the province as to the best means to circumvent the governor's obstruction. Samuel Johnston reported that Harvey was in a "very violent mood" and declared that he would issue handbills for the meeting over his own name.[5]

The Committee of Correspondence was actively functioning during this period, keeping other colonies informed and encouraging their participation in a unified resistance. In a letter to the South Carolina committee on 10 June, the North Carolinians proclaimed that "the cause of the town of Boston [is] the cause of America in general."[6] The letter called for a meeting by delegates of the several colonies and proclaimed that, if the governors failed to cooperate, the colonies should follow the example of Virginia, where House of Burgesses members met and formed an association to elect delegates. In similar letters to Virginia, the North Carolinians applauded the leadership of that colony and pledged to "use the best means to obtain" authorization to speak for the people of North Carolina. They would see that representatives of the people met to deliberate. "We have the fullest confidence that the share which they may take in this important controversy will not be unworthy of men who have ever been sacredly retentive of their Constitutional Rights, and desirous to hand them unimpaired to posterity."[7]

At the instigation of the Committee of Correspondence, a public meeting convened in Wilmington on 21 July. This gathering, which was presided over by William Hooper, appointed a committee to prepare a circular letter calling for a provincial congress for North Carolina. Robert Howe, along with James Moore, John Ancrum, Frederick Jones, Samuel Ashe, Robert Hogg, Francis Clayton, and Archibald Maclaine, served on the committee. The circular urged each county to elect representatives to meet at Johnston County courthouse to elect delegates to a general congress. The site subsequently was moved to New Bern, where the governor was witness to their actions. Governor Martin responded by issuing a proclamation against this assembly ordering "all and every His Majesty's Subjects, to forbear to attend at any such illegal meetings."[8]

When the First Provincial Congress of North Carolina convened in New Bern on 25 August, Howe took his seat as a representative of Brunswick County. This congress expressed loyalty to the Crown yet condemned British misrule for its illegal demands of taxation. Among the resolutions were declarations of the rights of Englishmen without abridgment and the right not to be taxed without their consent or that of their legal representative. The Boston Port Bill and the acts of Parliament that imposed duties on the colonies were condemned, and the conduct of the people of Massachusetts was endorsed. A resolution against the exportation of tobacco, pitch, tar, turpentine, or other articles to England and the importation of British tea after a specific future date was approved; and William Hooper, Joseph Hewes, and Richard Caswell were elected to represent North Carolina in Philadelphia.[9]

The Continental Congress that convened in Philadelphia on 5 September was composed of delegates from all colonies except Georgia. Several schemes for redressing the grievances against British misrule were debated before the Declaration and Resolves were finally adopted on 14 October, denouncing Parliament's action toward America as unjust, cruel, and unconstitutional. Congress subsequently approved the Continental Association, which was devised to put an end to all commerce between Britain and the thirteen colonies. Nonexportation, nonimportation, and nonconsumption were to be enforced by means of local committees of safety elected by every municipality and county throughout the continent. Violators were to be punished by publicity and boycott, with the element of public ridicule and harassment serving as a potent weapon in the hands of a zealous committee.

The Lower Cape Fear, with the vocal leadership it possessed, was not long in acting upon the resolutions of Congress. On 23 November, less than a month after the Philadelphia meeting had adjourned and long before the colony could act upon the measure, Wilmington voters gathered to discuss the proposal. They promptly elected a committee to implement the Association. Later that same day, the Wilmington Committee of Safety convened to investigate the arrival of the brig *Sally*, carrying a cargo of tea. Howe, as a resident of Brunswick County, was not directly involved in the proceedings of the Wilmington committee; and it is unknown when the Brunswick

Committee of Safety was formed. No records of that group have survived, but Howe did represent Brunswick County at district meetings in Wilmington and coauthored several letters with Harnett and John Ashe on behalf of the Wilmington District. On 16 June 1775 Governor Martin issued a proclamation from Fort Johnston in which he angrily condemned "sundry ill disposed persons" who are "going about the County of Brunswick and other counties of the Province, industriously propagating false, seditious and scandalous reports." He accused these "desperate, unprincipled, ignorant and abandoned men" of using their committees to threaten and intimidate loyal subjects and urged the citizenry to reject these "wicked . . . fools of faction." At a general meeting of the several committees of the Wilmington District on 20 June, the proclamation was read, and Howe, Archibald Maclaine, and Samuel Ashe were appointed to prepare an answer to the proclamation.[10]

The response declared that Martin, by his proclamation and the tenor of his conduct, "discovered himself to be an enemy to the happiness of this Colony in particular & to the freedom, rights, & privileges of America in General." The committee rejected the claim that they had used threats and intimidation, contending that all signers of the Association had done so of their own volition. The resolution further attacked the Lord Frederick North ministry and Parliament and accused them of "a low, base, flagitiously wicked attempt to entrap America into slavery."[11]

By early 1775 Robert Howe had begun training Brunswick County militia. Although Governor Martin scoffed that he was "very sure little danger is to be apprehended from him in a military character,"[12] Martin on several occasions identified Howe as one of the colony's most dangerous men. In July the governor requested of the Earl of Dartmouth that Howe, Harnett, John Ashe, and Abner Nash be proscribed for "their unremitted labours to promote sedition and rebellion here from the beginning of the discontents in America, to this time, that they stand foremost among the patrons of revolt and anarchy."[13] Again, in August, Martin issued a proclamation against Howe and John Ashe for training the militia without his commission.[14] It is obvious, from the attention given to the Brunswick County militia "colonel," that the governor perceived a danger that he was not willing to admit.

A brief glimpse of the training of local troops is available from the journal of Janet Schaw, who spent most of 1775 on the Cape Fear. Miss Schaw, of Edinburgh, Scotland, was appalled by the treasonous action she beheld on every hand in North Carolina; and, shortly after her arrival in the spring, she was quick to recognize the explosive situation that was developing. She reported that "Bob" Howe was a candidate for the command of the army—"for an army certainly is raising." Miss Schaw warned that, if a "proper exertion" was not undertaken immediately to crush the rebellion, it would "devour" them. Her reaction to a military review in Wilmington, in which Howe participated, aptly reflects the situation in 1775:

> Their exercise was that of bush-fighting, but it appeared so confused and so perfectly different from any thing I ever saw, I cannot say whether they performed it well or not; but this I know that they were heated with rum till capable of committing the most shocking outrages. . . . They at last . . . assembled on a plain field, and I must really laugh while I recollect their figure: 2000 men in their shirts and trousers, preceded by a very ill beat-drum and a fiddler, who was also in his shirt with a long sword and a cue at his hair, who played with all his might. They made indeed a most unmartial appearance. But the worst figure there can shoot from behind a bush and kill even a General Wolfe.[15]

The frustration of Governor Martin at this time was at such a level that he repeatedly railed against the treacherous outrages of Howe, John Ashe, and Harnett. Martin fled from the governor's palace in New Bern on 24 May, after spiking the palace cannon and hiding his supply of ammunition. Traveling overland to Cross Creek, he conferred with the loyal Highlander element before taking refuge in Fort Johnston at the mouth of the Cape Fear River. After learning of a planned attack on the fort, he boarded the British sloop-of-war *Cruizer*, which was standing by just inside the bar. Local Whigs, in an apparent ruse to capture the fugitive governor, invited him to meet with them on shore. The offer was declined and, during the weeks that followed, Capt. John Collet, commander of Fort Johnston, warned Martin that the fort was indefensible with the few men at his disposal.[16]

The governor ordered Collet to dismantle all cannon and move

them to a position on the riverfront where they could be protected by
the *Cruizer*. Rumors were circulating among local Whigs that Collet planned to enlarge and reinforce the fort to the point that it would be impregnable to rebel forces. Accordingly, a letter was delivered to Martin, from the "People" of the Cape Fear, protesting the removal of the weapons that had been mounted in the fort for the defense of the province. The letter informed Martin that the militia intended to march on the fort and reclaim the guns, which would be kept safely for their king. Collet also was charged in the letter with seizing corn from local residents and encouraging slaves to rebel against their masters.[17]

During the night of 18 July, Martin was awakened to watch red flames leaping into the heavens as the fort and its buildings were put to the torch. A throng of men could be observed from the ship, prowling through the fort and spreading the flames from building to building. Approximately five hundred local militia remained on the site for much of the following day, inspecting the ruins and observing the warship. The dismantled guns were out of reach, under the protection of the *Cruizer*. Martin accused John Ashe and Harnett of executing this blatant attack upon Crown property, but Robert Howe had been en route to the scene with forces as early as 15 July, and there are indications that Howe had been involved on several occasions in previous efforts to capture the governor.[18]

With Josiah Martin clearly in flight, the Whig leadership saw the need for immediate action to stabilize the government. Since House Speaker John Harvey had died subsequent to the Second Provincial Congress, it fell to Samuel Johnston of Edenton to call a new congress. Johnston delayed taking action; and in May and June Howe, Harnett, and John Ashe, on behalf of the Wilmington Committee of Safety, wrote Johnston at least three times urging him to convene the congress.[19]

The Third Provincial Congress finally met at Hillsborough on 20 August. Immediately after the session was convened, Howe, who once more represented Brunswick County, was appointed to a committee to prepare a "test" to be signed by all members of the congress. The committee, which was composed of William Hooper, Thomas Burke, Willie Jones, Maurice Moore, Allen Jones, and John Penn— in addition to Robert Howe—presented their test oath on 23 August, and it was signed by the members. After declaring allegiance to the king, the signers did "solemnly profess, testify and declare that we do absolutely believe that neither the Parliament of Great Britain, nor any Member of or Constituent Branch thereof, have a right to impose Taxes upon these Colonies to regulate the internal police thereof; and that all attempts by fraud or force to establish and exercise such claims and powers are Violations of the peace and Security of the people and ought to be resisted to the utmost."[20]

The delegates meeting at Hillsborough were deeply concerned with military preparedness. Across the continent, the storm clouds of war had continued to gather during the summer of 1775. The Continental Congress had named George Washington as commander in chief of the Continental Army on 15 June, and he had taken command of the troops around Boston in early July—two weeks after the bloody British assault on Breed's Hill (Bunker Hill), which overlooked the city. In August Congress authorized Gen. Philip Schuyler to invade Canada and seize any points that were vital to colonial security. The Continental Congress called upon all the colonies for troops to meet the British threat, and in North Carolina it became the responsibility of the Provincial Congress to raise men, money, and supplies in preparation for war. The Hillsborough congress authorized two regiments of Continental Line forces to contain five hundred men each. Four hundred men from the first regiment were to be stationed in the Wilmington District. The second regiment, along with the final one hundred men from the first, were to be distributed equally between the districts of Salisbury, New Bern, and Edenton. Six battalions of minutemen were authorized, and the individual counties were instructed to provide for the training of their local militia. James Moore and Robert Howe were given the rank of colonel and appointed on 1 September to command the two North Carolina regiments. Serving with Howe in the Second North Carolina Regiment were Lt. Col. Alexander Martin, Maj. John Patten, Dr. John White (adjutant), nine captains, and ten lieutenants. By late November the regiments were taken over by the Continental Congress, and Moore and Howe became a part of the Continental command.[21]

It would appear that Colonel Howe located the headquarters for his Second North Carolina Regiment in or near New Bern during the fall of 1775. In October he was there acquiring guns and powder for

his regiment and unspiking the cannon incapacitated by Governor
Martin prior to his flight the previous May.[22] In his new command,
Howe was primarily responsible for the northern half of the province, and his recruiting efforts extended throughout the Albemarle
region and to the common border with Virginia.

The situation in Virginia was of great concern to Colonel Howe,
and he obviously remained alert to the threat posed by Virginia Loyalists. Virginia's governor, Lord Dunmore—like his Royal neighbor
to the south—had failed in efforts to hold his capital of Williamsburg for the Crown. He had fled to the British man-of-war, *Fowery*,
in the York River, from whence he initiated raiding parties against
Virginia communities. During the fall of 1775, Dunmore's Loyalists
occupied Norfolk, which they used as a base for plundering the entire
region. The merchant population of the city contained a significant
contingent of loyal Highland Scots, with the result that Norfolk was
dominated by an unusually large Loyalist element. Dunmore thus
pressured residents to align themselves with his cause. Apparently, he
also encouraged slaves to rebel against their masters, and both Virginians and North Carolinians were appalled that he had organized a
black regiment to fight against the colonists. There also were rumors
that he planned to arm Indians along the frontier. Virginia dispatched
Col. William Woodford with a detachment of minutemen and militia to drive the deposed governor from the state. Reports reached
North Carolina that Dunmore was recruiting Albemarle Loyalists
and planned to march into the region with his forces. Howe's Continental Line, along with Edenton minutemen, moved into Pasquotank
and Currituck counties, and Howe extended an offer to Virginia's
Colonel Woodford that he would march his troops into Virginia to
aid Woodford's army if needed. It would appear that the ambitious
North Carolinian saw in the Virginia crisis an opportunity for glory
and military action—the latter being a necessity before the former
could become a reality. Woodford initially declined Howe's proposal,
until the Virginia Convention instructed him to "embrace the offer
of assistance."[23]

Before the North Carolina Continentals could reach the scene,
Colonel Woodford was forced to face Dunmore's army at Great
Bridge, Virginia, on 9 December. Dunmore, marching the twelve
miles from Norfolk to Great Bridge, had occupied a fortification con-

structed at the east end of a long causeway leading to the city. Woodford built a redoubt at the opposite end of the causeway and stationed his little army on a hill to the rear, leaving only about ninety troops to man the breastworks. The Tory forces, many of whom were blacks, set fire to houses near the rebel encampment, destroyed buildings on their own side of the bridge, and reportedly destroyed houses of rebel supporters throughout the countryside. Dunmore, concerned about the anticipated arrival of North Carolina reinforcements, ordered a frontal assault down the narrow causeway. The attack proved disastrous for the British, resulting in the loss of sixty-two men and a complete routing of his army. This was the first encounter between colonists and British since Bunker Hill, and the Whig victory left Dunmore and his followers badly shaken. Upon hearing of the defeat, the Royal governor "raved like the madman he is." The Tory troops retreated once more into Norfolk, where frantic preparations got under way for a precipitous evacuation.[24]

Col. Edward Vail and 250 North Carolina militia arrived at the rebel camp on 10 December, and Colonel Howe and his North Carolina troops joined the Virginians at Great Bridge two days later. As Dunmore and his Tories abandoned Norfolk for the safety of their warships, the rebels took up positions along the city's waterfront. At a conference between Howe and Woodford (with whom Howe had served in the French and Indian War), it was determined that the North Carolinian was the ranking officer and thus commander of all troops in Norfolk. Woodford appears to have accepted his supersession without complaint and worked closely with Howe during the trying weeks that followed.[25]

Woodford and Howe were in complete agreement with respect to Norfolk and the inhabitants of Norfolk and Prince Anne counties. Howe described the local people as "the most contemptible lot of wretches," and Woodford reported that the inhabitants of the area were "in general our Enemys." The Virginia colonel assured his state convention that "the Town of Norfolk deserves no favour." The argument of both commanders was that the region was overwhelmingly Tory and that the rebels could not defend Norfolk without a permanent force of five thousand men stationed in the city. Strategically, it provided an ideal base for a navally superior enemy: it offered command of the waterways of the Chesapeake Bay; comfortable housing

for six thousand to seven thousand troops; easy access for invasion
of Virginia and North Carolina; and a ready and abundant store of pork and grain in the nearby North Carolina counties of Pasquotank, Perquimans, and Currituck. The only options identified by Howe and Woodford were to maintain a superior army in Norfolk on a permanent basis or to destroy the city. Howe personally felt that the best defensive strategy would be to fortify Great Bridge, maintain an outpost at Kemp's Landing, and headquarter the rebel defensive force at Portsmouth. "I think Norfolk cannot be maintained with any troops you can place there, against an attack by sea & land." [26]

Responding to the immediate situation, Colonel Howe took command of Norfolk and put the town on a wartime footing. At the same time, he proceeded to cut off supplies to the enemy ships anchored nearby. He communicated with Dunmore on a variety of topics and refused to be cowered by the demands and threats of His Lordship. Dunmore requested an exchange of prisoners, insisting that rank be equal between British officers and American militia. Howe was quick to inform the governor that this was unacceptable and that, if His Lordship were ignorant of such matters, Howe would inform him that a militia officer was considered as one rank below a minuteman officer and two ranks below a regular officer. "We can, by no means, submit to place the officers and soldiers of the army, who have been taken in battle, upon a footing with those officers of militia and the peasants that you have thought proper to deprive of their liberty. . . . I shall consent to no exchange but such as equity shall warrant." [27]

As provisions aboard the ships became increasingly short, tempers flared. The British demanded the right to purchase food for themselves and the multitude of sympathizers that crowded their decks. Dunmore threatened to send raiding parties to seize what they needed if they were denied the privilege of provisioning. He also objected to the men in arms against their government having the "audacity" to make themselves visible to the women and children that were aboard ship. Howe proved to be an unyielding negotiator on provisions, exchange of prisoners, and treatment of Norfolk residents. To add to the friction, American soldiers on several occasions fired upon the British vessels in the harbor from buildings near the water. As the British returned the fire, American soldiers stood on the wharf jeering and making obscene gestures, which infuriated the British even more. By 24 December Dunmore issued the ultimatum that he would put raiding parties ashore to burn buildings and seize provisions from the local inhabitants if Howe did not agree to his demands. Howe and Woodford were convinced that Norfolk must be destroyed as a defensive measure, yet they consulted with the Virginia Convention before responding to the British threat to do the deed for them. The American commanders felt that the Convention should be party to the events that obviously were to follow.[28]

By late December the Americans were prepared for an attack. The total American force stood at 1,258 men, including 376 men in Howe's own Second North Carolina Regiment. The remaining 882 men belonged to four Virginia units that were on the scene. Howe warned the Virginia Convention that a permanent occupation force for Norfolk would be necessary if they were to maintain the town intact. He repeatedly emphasized the strategic importance of Norfolk if it were to fall once more into enemy hands. To the North Carolina Provincial Council he observed: "Every circumstance conspires to demonstrate this colony will be the seat of war and Norfolk a place of Arms. To those who have command of Navigation, it is the most advantageous situation I ever saw . . . I look upon it that Virginia and North Carolina must stand or fall together, and then if they fall Norfolk will be the cause of it."[29]

On 29 December Capt. Henry Bellew of HMS *Liverpool* maneuvered the large frigate into position and, with two mortars and four thousand stands of arms aboard a store ship, he began to menace the waterfront. During the night, the British opened fire on an occupied guardhouse, but no one was injured. At the same time, another "large" vessel and "several less vessels" arrived with more than three hundred soldiers on board. As Howe reported, "Everything here wears the Face of Action."[30]

Around 3:15 P.M. on 1 January 1776, the British commenced a bombardment of the city. Four British ships mounting over sixty guns bombarded the waterfront for seven hours. British landing parties repeatedly came ashore during the cannonade and undertook to torch buildings near the waterfront. North Carolina and Virginia troops stood their ground despite the billowing flames, and the British landing parties were driven back to their boats without gaining a foothold. The British continued their artillery fire until 2:00 A.M. on

2 January, and the fire continued to burn for two days. Witnesses
later testified that the Americans not only failed to combat the flames, but also that some troops reportedly spread the fire to other nearby Tory-owned buildings and proceeded to loot as they burned. Under instructions from the Convention, American detachments were dispatched to destroy the pumps and well at the distillery and to burn a building identified as "Hill house," a windmill, and other sources of supplies or sustenance that were vulnerable to the enemy. Once the smoke had cleared, four-fifths of Virginia's largest city lay in ashes. During the action, Colonel Howe was struck in the thigh by a spent musket ball, but apparently the wound was so slight that the colonel hardly noticed it. As late as 21 January, the British warships *Liverpool* and *Otter* continued to shell the city, and an enemy detachment was beaten back from Town Point Wharf, where it had attempted to torch houses that escaped the earlier conflagration. The American command recommended to the Virginia Convention that the remaining houses in Norfolk be destroyed due to the suitability of the town as a British base and the impracticality of maintaining American troops there on a permanent basis. With the concurrence of the Convention, the remainder of Norfolk was put to the torch. The fact that Norfolk was widely perceived as a "nest of Tories" undoubtedly salved the feelings of government officials in Williamsburg toward the loss of such an important port.[31]

The Whig leadership of Virginia was effusive in its praise of Robert Howe and his forces at Norfolk. On 10 January 1776 the Virginia Convention president Edmund Pendleton wrote of Howe: "If it may not seem unnecessary to speak of this worthy officer to you, Gent., we can with equal truth and pleasure assure, he has in everything conducted himself like a brave, prudent & spirited commander and given general Satisfaction to the Country and Army." The North Carolina Provincial Congress joined the praise by passing a resolution thanking Howe "for his manly, generous and warlike conduct in these unhappy times; more especially for the reputation which our Provincial troops acquired under him at the conflagration of Norfolk."[32]

Once the danger of Norfolk was past, Howe split his forces and stationed detachments at Kemp's Landing, Great Bridge, and Suffolk. He personally reported to the Virginia Convention in Williamsburg on 13 January, where he was questioned with regard to the action at Norfolk. Four days later, Howe was still in attendance at the Convention, but he shortly thereafter established his command at Suffolk. By early February concern was growing over a threatened Tory uprising in North Carolina. Highland Scots and former Regulators reportedly were rallying to the Royal standard, and information arrived to indicate that Sir Henry Clinton and a British fleet had left England en route to the Cape Fear River. The Virginia Convention thereupon relieved the North Carolinians of responsibilities in the peninsula and assigned Virginia militia to accompany Colonel Howe's forces in their efforts to counter the British threat to their own state. It appears, however, that Howe remained in Suffolk rather than accept the Virginia Convention offer. The anticipated Regulator uprising failed to materialize, and the Highlanders were crushed at the battle of Moores Creek Bridge on 27 February, thus relieving the immediate alarm for North Carolina. Howe continued to pursue defensive measures for tidewater Virginia until Maj. Gen. Charles Lee arrived in Williamsburg on 29 March as commander of the Southern Department.[33]

CHAPTER 4

DEFENDING

THE SOUTHERN

DEPARTMENT

*A*s events of early 1776 made obvious to all but the most hesitant patriots, a military solution to problems with the mother country had become a necessity. Although events in New England and New York held the attention of most observers, the Southern colonies were deeply concerned with their own vulnerability. The activities of Lord Dunmore in Virginia spread fears that a British invasion of that colony was imminent. In North Carolina, Royal governor Martin had unfolded to William Legge, the earl of Dartmouth, a grand scheme that called for a British invasion to complement and augment an uprising of Scots Highlanders and former Regulators. Farther south, South Carolinians had confronted Tory bands in the "Snow Campaign," and Georgia had experienced the first of innumerable raids from East Florida along its unprotected frontier.

In the establishment of the infant Continental Army, Congress had concentrated on the immediate threat to New England and the Middle colonies. During the fall of 1775, however, increasing concern from the Southern provinces directed attention to that region. On 1 January 1776, a congressional committee recommended that North

Carolina, South Carolina, and Georgia undertake to seize the British fortress at St. Augustine, Florida. Congress also recommended that delegations from these three colonies meet in Charleston to confer upon matters relative to their own defense and security. By February Southern delegates were clamoring for a defensive force that would assure the safety of their region. As relations with England continued to deteriorate, the need for organizing the colonies into military departments had become increasingly apparent. Therefore, a congressional committee on 17 February recommended that—since Northern and Eastern departments were already in place—New York, New Jersey, Pennsylvania, and the lower counties of Delaware and Maryland should be formed into a Middle Department with one major general and two brigadiers; and that Virginia, North Carolina, South Carolina, and Georgia should compose a Southern Department under the command of one major general and three brigadiers. The Southern Department would be responsible for the defense of the entire region, operating directly under the provenance of Congress without direction from General Washington as the supreme commander.[1]

The overwhelming choice for the Southern command was Maj. Gen. Charles Lee. Lee, who was to become the most enigmatic and controversial officer in the American camp, was at this point of his career its most popular general officer. As second in command to General Washington, he was considered his superior in ability and a future replacement for the commander in chief. His choice on 1 March 1776—to take command of forces in Virginia, the Carolinas, and Georgia—came only ten days after Congress had instructed him to invade Canada. In informing Lee of his appointment, congressional president John Hancock reported that "after a warm contest, occasioned by the high Estimation the Members of the Congress have of your worth and abilities, every one wishing to have you where he had most at stake, the Congress . . . determined . . . that you shall take the command of the Continental forces in the Southern Department."[2]

In establishing the new departments, Congress appointed six brigadier generals, four (rather than three, as recommended) of whom would serve under Lee's command in the South. In order of appointment, they were John Armstrong, William Thompson, Andrew

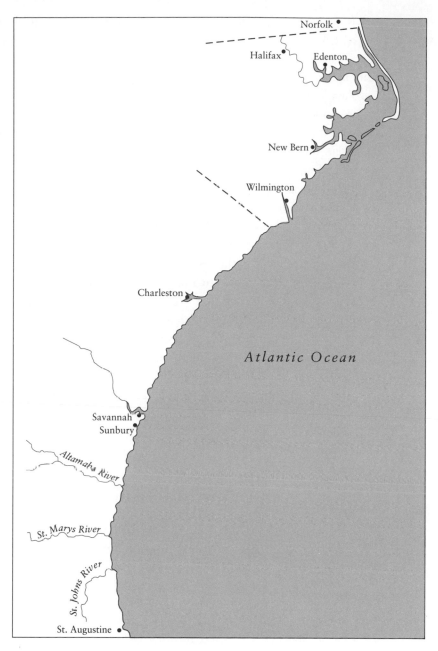

Norfolk

Halifax
Edenton

New Bern

Wilmington

Charleston

Atlantic Ocean

Savannah
Sunbury

Altamaha River

St. Marys River

St. Johns River

St. Augustine

Southern Department

Lewis, James Moore, William Alexander (Lord Stirling), and Robert
Howe. Lewis and Howe were instructed to take command of Continental forces in Virginia until receipt of further orders, Moore was to
command in North Carolina, and Armstrong was to repair to South
Carolina.[3] Howe was headquartered at Williamsburg when news of
his promotion arrived, and in his acknowledgment he assured John
Hancock that he was "devoted to the cause of America. I feel no wish
so ardent, no ambition so strong, as to be able to contribute to its
service and support."[4]

When General Lee arrived in Williamsburg on 28 March, he
quickly became convinced of the impending danger to that province.
The numerous navigable rivers left Virginia vulnerable to attack, and
the capture of Williamsburg and Yorktown would provide a base
for the control of much of the province. Although others argued that
Wilmington, Charleston, or Savannah would suffer the brunt of a
British invasion, Lee insisted that Williamsburg would be the target;
and the continuous flood of contradictory reports left him frustrated.
Just prior to Lee's arrival, Howe had moved his forces to Edenton, North Carolina, for recruiting purposes. In a letter of 5 April,
the Southern commander expressed to Howe this frustration: "My
own situation is extremely disagreeable from an uncertainty of the
enemies designs. I know not where to turn me, where to fix myself."[5]

The Fourth Provincial Congress of North Carolina convened at
Halifax on 4 April, and it was obvious from the outset that the
delegates were prepared to take the ultimate political plunge and
support a separation from the mother country. The presiding officer,
Samuel Johnston, noted that "all our people here are up for independence." A committee of seven, headed by Cornelius Harnett, was
appointed to consider the "usurpations" and "violences" attempted
against America by the king and Parliament and to recommend measures to counter these actions. The committee, on 12 April, offered a
resolution that would empower North Carolina delegates to the Continental Congress to "concur with the delegates of the other Colonies
in declaring Independence, and forming foreign alliances." These
"Halifax Resolves" constituted the first official provincial action for
independence in America.[6]

By 10 April Howe had moved on to Halifax, where he served as
military advisor to the North Carolina Provincial Congress. He was

Major General Charles Lee (From Benson J. Lossing, The Pictorial Field-Book of the Revolution *[1859])*

in attendance at the time that the Halifax Resolves were adopted, and he observed that "independence seems to be the word. I know not one dissenting voice."[7] As Congress proceeded to deal with the difficult question of raising additional regiments and providing necessary provisions and equipment, Howe was available to offer expert counsel. The North Carolinian encouraged Lee to meet him in Halifax, and the delegates expected his arrival, but the Southern commander was more concerned with preparations for the anticipated British invasion of Virginia. Brigadier General Armstrong, however, did stop in Halifax en route to his new post in Charleston and was amazed to find "in these lesser deserts of Arabia" men of "so much good sense & politeness" as William Hooper, John Penn, and Robert Howe.[8]

While Howe attempted to influence the North Carolinians in support of increased defensive measures, Lee was facing a multitude of difficulties that were to become all too familiar to his successors in the South. Although Congress regularly appropriated funds to support the war effort in the South, those appropriations were totally inadequate for the defense of so widespread an area. Moreover, the appropriations were directed to officials of the provincial governments, not to the Continental commanders. Individual states controlled funds for the support of troops enlisted for their regiments, and the Continental commanders were at the mercy of provincial (and, later, state) governments for troops, equipment, armament, and every necessity of war. Militia forces called into service in time of emergency frequently were not subject to military justice and were under Continental command only to the extent designated by state officials. Continental commanders frequently complained that the state troops were "soldiers rather from Courtesy, than Compulsion, and consequently are not much to be depended upon."[9]

General Lee found himself without cannon, extra arms, or entrenching tools for construction of fieldworks. Arms were in such short supply that he dispatched men into the backcountry of Virginia in an effort to buy rifles from the citizenry. To add to the confusion, the Virginia Committee of Safety had assigned their battalions in such a fashion that two regiments each were assigned to widely scattered locations between each of the major rivers of the tidewater. The rationale for this action was that, "since the expense is equal, the security ought to be equal." In a letter to Howe, Lee commented, "I wonder they did not carry it still further, and post one or two men by way of general security in every individual's house." To General Washington, Lee mused that the members of the New York Provincial Congress were "angels of decision when compared with your countrymen."[10]

As April progressed, the news from Wilmington became more

alarming. Portions of a British fleet arrived in the Cape Fear River on
18 April, and by 3 May the entire fleet had assembled there. Reports
indicated that Sir Henry Clinton had landed redcoats on Battery
Island near the mouth of the Cape Fear River, where he was training them in street-firing tactics. While in Halifax, Howe learned that
William Dry's home in Brunswick Town had been burned and that
his own Kendal Plantation had been ravaged. Nine hundred enemy
troops landed at Howe's plantation at 3:00 A.M. on a Sunday morning, in an effort to surprise a small detachment of Americans stationed there. Several women living in the house were "mistreated,"
and all of Howe's chairs, tables, glasses, china, and plates were taken.
"It is reported that they destroyed all my private letters and accounts,
as if determined to injure me without Benefit to themselves or to
their cause." [11]

Even with sixty to seventy topsail vessels in the Cape Fear River
and seventeen hundred British troops encamped near the ruins of
Fort Johnston, Lee refused to believe that North Carolina was the
target. Like Howe, the Southern commanding general saw peninsula
Virginia as the most likely seat of war in the South. Lee witnessed
the same Tory domination of Portsmouth that Howe and William
Woodford had experienced in Norfolk: "For even the Women and
Children had learn'd the art and practic'd with address the Office of
Spies." It was Lee's intention to remove without exception all people
out of Portsmouth, and he recommended to the Virginia Convention
that the town be destroyed totally to keep it out of enemy hands.
He actually proceeded to demolish the houses of "some of the most
notorious Traitors," as a means of intimidating the neighborhood.
A Mr. Hopkins, who had "prevaricated and perjur'd himself very
handsomely," was forced to stand and watch his house burn to the
ground after American troops removed the furnishings. [12]

Without concealing their deep foreboding for the safety of Virginia, Lee and Howe felt compelled to react to the British presence
below Wilmington. They departed Virginia on 12 May en route to
Halifax and from there progressed to North Carolina's Tarboro,
New Bern, and Wilmington. North Carolina and Virginia troops
made up their forces, although the Eighth Virginia Regiment was so
unruly and mutinous as to delay the departure from Halifax. This
backcountry regiment consisted largely of "refactory-spirited" [sic]

Irishmen who continuously deserted and contaminated the orderliness of the other troops. Lee and Howe finally succeeded in getting "this Banditta out of the Town" and on their way south. In New Bern the people turned out in a public ceremony to welcome the army and to present a formal welcoming address to Lee. Despite a total British force of some thirty-two hundred troops at Cape Fear, it became apparent that eastern North Carolina indeed was not the ultimate object of attack. The defeat of the Highlanders at Moores Creek Bridge on 27 February thwarted the British scheme to invade through the Cape Fear valley. Without a friendly force to augment their own troops, North Carolina became a much less attractive target. On 5 May, Sir Henry Clinton, aboard his ship *Pallisser* in the Cape Fear River, issued a proclamation offering to pardon all North Carolinians who would lay down their arms and submit to the laws— "excepting only from the benefit of such pardon Cornelius Harnett and Robert Howes [*sic*]." [13] To the British ministry, Robert Howe had become an outlaw.

By 4 June the British fleet appeared off Charleston, and South Carolina president John Rutledge dashed off an emotional note: "For God's sake lose not a moment. There are fifty sail at anchor off the bar, within sight of the town." [14] Brigadier General Armstrong had been in Charleston since 3 May, but his efforts to prepare the area for an attack had resulted in numerous frustrations. He found that the South Carolina military was completely under the control of the state president and was not answerable to Continental commands. The question of ultimate authority had been referred to the Continental Congress, but South Carolina officials insisted that Armstrong await a ruling from Congress with regard to his authority over South Carolina troops. [15]

The Charleston harbor was protected by Sullivan's and James islands, which formed a natural barrier from the dangers of the sea. A deep but relatively narrow channel separates the islands, both of which were backed by shallow marshlands. South Carolina officials had concentrated their defenses on the two barrier islands, depending primarily upon a palmetto-log fortification being constructed on Sullivan's Island under the direct supervision of Col. William Moultrie.

As the Continental forces marched into South Carolina, Lee ap-

pealed to Congress to dispatch two thousand Pennsylvania and
Maryland troops to Virginia to replace regiments that he was ordering south from that colony. The Southern commander was now convinced that South Carolina and Georgia had become the focus of
the enemy's war effort. On the morning of 9 June, Lee, Howe, and
their retinue arrived at Charleston, where President Rutledge turned
over all South Carolina troops to Lee's command. Before entering
the town, the generals rode immediately to Haddrell's Point in the
harbor and examined fortifications there and on Sullivan's and James
islands. By 10 June work was under way to complete the defenses
already begun by the South Carolinians. Buildings on the wharf were
pulled down, entrenchments were thrown up around the town, and
barricades were constructed in the major streets. Everyone was urged
to "take to pick axe and spade" to prepare the city for an attack
that appeared inevitable. A 9:00 P.M. curfew was enforced and sen-
tries were stationed throughout the city to control local traffic. Lee
(wearing a blue ribbon as a badge of his rank), along with Howe
and Armstrong (who wore the pink markings of brigadiers), supervised the urgent preparation as the hours and days slipped by and the
enemy hovered just outside the harbor, examining its prey. Within a
matter of days, the city was enclosed by lines, trenches, and redoubts,
and the streets were securely barricaded. The wharves were cleared
and batteries were constructed at landings above the town.[16]

From the very beginning, General Lee was convinced that Fort
Sullivan was indefensible and should be abandoned. He argued that
Colonel Moultrie and the South Carolina troops on Sullivan's Island
would be cut off from retreat, with the result that the fort would
become a "slaughter pen." Moultrie had complete confidence in his
handiwork, and President Rutledge, who had final authority over
South Carolina troops, supported Moultrie's position. Lee could do
no more than protest and try to prepare for every eventuality. He did
insist on the construction of a bridge from the island, but it proved
less than satisfactory as a means for withdrawal. Since Lee envisioned
that the British fleet would sail harmlessly past Sullivan's Island to
attack Charleston proper, he viewed the city as the focal point for the
invasion. Howe was assigned to command at Charleston and Armstrong was stationed at Haddrell's Point. The South Carolinians were
left to defend the island positions: Moultrie at Fort Sullivan, Colonel

Thompson at the east end of Sullivan's Island (to prevent a British land attack on the fort), and Col. Christopher Gadsden across the harbor at Fort Johnson on James Island. A regiment of North Carolina Regulars under Colonel Thomas Clark was assigned to support Moultrie on Sullivan's Island.[17]

For a week before the battle actually got under way, the British fleet of fifty topsail vessels maneuvered off the Charleston bar. Observers expressed amazement that the enemy would dawdle away the prime monthly tides for moving into the river and at the same time allow precious days to pass during which the rebels improved their defenses. About 10:30 A.M. on 28 June, the *Thunder*, a bomb ship of six guns and two mortars, finally began to throw shells on Fort Sullivan. As the battle progressed, it appeared that the British planned to execute the maneuver anticipated by Lee. While the *Active* (28 guns), *Bristol* (50 guns), *Experiment* (50 guns), and *Solebay* (28 guns) unleashed a barrage of heavy fire against the fort, the *Sphinx* (20 guns), *Acteon* (28 guns), and *Syren* (28 guns) moved up the channel in order to navigate past the fort and into the harbor. Fortunately for the Americans, the ships ran aground on a shoal and for hours lay exposed to American artillery fire. The British ships continued to pound Moultrie's fort; but the cannon fire harmlessly embedded itself in the soft palmetto logs of the fort, and the defenders suffered little damage. By evening the British had had enough. Two of the stranded frigates floated free on the rising tide, but the *Acteon* was destroyed and abandoned. The British suffered scores of casualties and several of their ships were badly damaged. The *Bristol*, flagship for Sir Peter Parker, reportedly had at least seventy cannonballs fired through her, destroying her mizzenmast and mainmast in the process. General Howe, due to the concentration of the conflict on Sullivan's Island, did not participate in the actual combat and thus could serve only as a spectator to the glorious victory proclaimed by the Americans. The South Carolinians, and Colonel Moultrie in particular, claimed the laurels for their successful defense of Charleston.[18]

Once the immediate threat of invasion had subsided, the Continental command in Charleston was faced with a multitude of decisions that demanded their attention. It was widely believed that the British would return for a second venture, probably in the fall. To counter this, the forts in the harbor required additional attention, works near

Haddrell's Point were needed, and the bridge from Sullivan's Island
to the mainland received high priority. Lee experienced repeated frustrations in efforts to improve the Charleston defenses. He discovered that the quartermaster general took orders from the state rather than the Continental command, he had no access to the building where tools were kept, and gunpowder was sent to the various posts without his knowledge. To further compound the problems, palmetto logs promised for the fortifications had not arrived weeks after they were promised, and tools for the work were nowhere to be seen despite repeated assurances from South Carolina officials. In disgust, Lee complained that they were "playing at Duke & No Duke, and throwing everything into confusion and anarchy."[19]

While Charleston looked to the east with foreboding, the frontier settlements of the backcountry were faced with warfare of a slightly different complexion. The Cherokee nation had seized the opportunity during the spring of 1776 to strike at white encroachments into their hunting grounds. A joint expedition from Virginia, North Carolina, and South Carolina broke the power of the Cherokees during the summer of 1776, but Creek tribes along the frontier of Georgia continued to be a concern. Continental commanders in the Southern Department repeatedly sought to draw the Creeks into a relationship with the United States, or at least into neutrality, but the influence of the British post at St. Augustine, Florida, was great among the Creeks.[20]

Without question, the most formidable challenge to the Southern command was Georgia's inability to develop any defensive posture. The state constituted a buffer to the Creek Indians on the frontier and to the British in East Florida. The small population was torn between Loyalist and patriot elements, and even those who supported the revolution were caught in intractable factional cliques that precluded all efforts for aggressive military action. The political cleavage between the Savannah elite and the yeomen resulted in constant friction, bitter confrontations, and a fatal duel, which pitted the Continental Army against the civil government. Georgia was a virtual storehouse of cattle, rice, and other food products, which made raids from East Florida lucrative for the enemy—to say nothing of the military advantages of harassment and debilitation of the southernmost colony. The northern border of East Florida stretched to the St. Marys River, where the British had constructed Fort Tonyn as an outpost for raids into Georgia. Georgians on the Sea Islands—and northward to the Altamaha River—were vulnerable to raids by Florida Rangers, Indians, British Regulars, and the multitude of Southern Tories who had fled into Florida from Georgia and South Carolina. Underpopulated, disunited, and economically unable to finance a substantial defensive effort, Georgia constituted a weak—but vital—link in the Southern defensive structure.[21]

Even with the British fleet still arrayed off Charleston harbor, reports were pouring into the Continental command that British Regulars, Tories, and Indians were raiding across the St. Marys River, kidnapping families, seizing cattle, and bringing terror to the region. Georgians assured General Lee that St. Augustine was militarily weak and overrun with refugees to the extent that a detachment could easily seize East Florida. Lee promptly promised Georgia president Archibald Bulloch and the state's lone Continental commander, Col. Lachlan McIntosh, that a battalion of troops would be dispatched once the threat to South Carolina had ended. With Brigadier General Armstrong in command of Continental forces stationed in Charleston, Lee began to plan for a Southern expedition. Armstrong, finding himself totally unsuited to the situation in Charleston, used the opportunity to plead for his own replacement in command. Although Armstrong outranked Howe, the Pennsylvanian urged Lee to allow them to exchange assignments. "Genl. Howe has a thousand qualifications for this meridian . . . he is able to wash off all the dryness incidental as it was, with half a dozen of Madeira, or a single dance with the ladies will shake it off as we do the dust from our feet. . . . Can he wish a more respectable command? . . . I think Howe a genius amongst our American best." He implored Lee to give Howe the command of Charleston and permit himself to follow the commander for further orders. Lee was not amenable to such a change in command and proceeded with his officers in place as originally assigned.[22]

Much to the general's chagrin, the South Carolina Council attempted to interfere with the use of South Carolina troops in Georgia. Lee heatedly pointed out that Virginia and North Carolina had stripped their states of troops in order to defend Charleston, and that he could see no merit to their arguments against marching South

Carolina troops to the defense of Georgia. After a confrontation with
President Rutledge, an accord was reached that permitted the use
of some South Carolina troops in cooperation with regiments from
North Carolina and Virginia. By 8 August the Southern commander
had ridden south, leaving to General Howe and Colonel Moultrie
the responsibility for dispatching troops, field pieces, and the various
necessities of war. As these details were being completed, an express
arrived from Philadelphia, announcing the signing of the Declaration
of Independence. Robert Howe, with great enthusiasm, described the
occasion as "indeed important and teeming with Event" and called
for a union as the only way to "Effect the Glorious Establishment we
are struggling for." [23]

By 10 August Howe had seen to all of the details of march and
was on his way to join his commander. It appears that Howe even
had personal custody of at least four of General Lee's ever-present
dogs as he prepared to depart Charleston. The American force that
marched into Georgia was estimated to contain some 1,500 men. Included were Virginia and North Carolina Continentals, detachments
of 78 men and officers from the First and Second South Carolina
battalions, 130 men from South Carolina's Third (Ranger) Battalion,
and 30 men from the South Carolina Artillery.[24]

The problems in Georgia were of such herculean proportions that
they probably were beyond the capabilities of the most competent
Continental officers. The potential importance of Georgia was obvious from the numerous natural advantages and resources contained
within its borders. Its rivers and harbors, mild winters; and prodi-
gious quantities of rice, cattle, and lumber were qualities to be nur-
tured. The defense of the province at that time consisted of a Georgia
battalion under the command of Colonel McIntosh, an independent
artillery company consisting of twenty-six men, and about twenty-
five hundred militia in whom "very little confidence can be placed."
Georgia officials were quick to admit their lack of military resources;
they petitioned Lee for the Continental Congress to provide six battalions of troops for the defense of Georgia, to be recruited outside
the state and paid for by Congress. In addition, it was expected that
Congress would provide money for fortifications and guard boats, as
well as for funds to pay the frontier Indians to maintain neutrality.
The inability of the state to defend itself, and the expectations of Con-

gress that they could, combined to form an insoluble problem for the Continental command in the South. Lee, like succeeding commanders, recognized the need and appealed to Congress for one thousand cavalry to defend the South. General Washington agreed that the request was justified, but it never translated into mounted troops provided by Congress. All Lee could do was explain to state officials that he had no means to defend them beyond troops provided by the states themselves.[25]

Among the numerous crises faced by the Continental forces was widespread profiteering by merchants, mechanics, farmers, and planters who dealt with the army. Prices for everything necessary for the operation of the army were at such a premium that the Continental command accused the sellers of practicing extortion in their pricing of food, clothing, drugs, wagons, and other commodities. The situation was equally bad in Charleston and Savannah—to the point that General Lee suggested that North Carolina and Virginia soldiers might refuse to defend Charleston if it were once again attacked.[26]

Equally frustrating to the army were the attitudes and expectations of the civil officials of Georgia, who were determined that an attack on East Florida was the panacea for all problems. In a conference with the Georgia Council of Safety, Lee outlined the difficulty of attacking St. Augustine without sufficient forces. The lack of cannon and the impossibility of transporting a significant quantity of cannon, ammunition, and provisions through the wasteland between the St. Marys and the St. Johns rivers constituted a handicap too great for the meager resources of the Continental command. The Georgia council unrealistically responded with the opinion that the garrison at St. Augustine would surrender at the approach of the American army, that the country along the way abounded in provisions that could be taken as the need arose, and that rice to supplement the troops' diet could be sent by boat to meet the army at various places along the way. The Georgia authorities were so insistent on an invasion that the Continental commander concurred, despite his opinion that "the whole will . . . conclude in an incursion of insult."[27] General Lee's view of the Georgia civil authorities is best related in a letter to General Armstrong on 27 August:

> The People here are if possible more harum skarum than their sister colony. They will propose anything, and after they have

proposed it, discover that they are incapable of performing the
least. They have propos'd securing their Frontiers by constant
patroles of horse Rangers, when the scheme is approv'd of they
scratch their heads for some days, and at length inform you that
there is a small difficulty in the way; that of the impossibility
to procure a single horse—their next project is to keep their inland Navigation clear of Tenders by a numerous fleet of Guarda
Costa arm'd boats, when this is agreed to, they recollect that
they have not a single boat—Upon the whole I shou'd not be
surprized if they were to propose mounting a body of Mermaids
on Alligators.[28]

At the beginning of September, a courier arrived in Savannah with
a dispatch for General Lee. He was to leave at once for Philadelphia,
where he would be reassigned to assist General Washington in the defense of New York and New Jersey. The order, dated 8 August, made
no reference to a replacement for Lee in the Southern Department—
and thereupon hinged the potential for future controversy. Without
a major general in the department, the chain of command logically
evolved upon the ranking brigadier. John Armstrong, first in rank but
ailing and anxious to return to his native Pennsylvania, was stationed
at Charleston; James Moore, second in appointment, was in North
Carolina seeing to the defense of the Cape Fear; Andrew Lewis remained in command of Continental forces in Virginia; and Robert
Howe, the fourth brigadier, was in Georgia carrying on defensive
measures for that state.[29]

General Lee had ordered some of the Virginia and North Carolina
troops to follow him northward, and Georgia was unable to provide
additional troops to compensate for the losses. The remaining Continentals, encamped at Sunbury and elsewhere on the south Georgia
rivers, sickened in the late summer heat. Robert Howe remained in
Georgia until 20 September, attempting to pacify Georgia officials
and their expectations of a Florida conquest. Without medical supplies or reinforcements, South Carolina began to recall her troops,
forcing the remaining Continentals to postpone all ambitions of an
East Florida invasion. The main body of troops progressed no farther
south than Sunbury, but an advance guard did reach the St. Johns
River. There is evidence that Howe may have been present on this
expedition, in which a scouting party captured a small detachment

of the enemy. Substantial property damage resulted from the expedition as the Americans destroyed buildings, fences, and provisions belonging to suspected Tories between the St. Marys and the St. Johns rivers. This foray forced the British temporarily to remove Loyalist troops stationed on the Georgia border to the safer positions south of the St. Johns. British colonel Augustine Prevost reported on 9 September that "the party which was on the St. Marys has been obliged by a strong one of the rebels to abandon that river and to retire on the south side of St. Johns River. They took lately a sergant [sic] and 5 men of the party reinforced to 100 men."[30]

When General Howe repaired to Charleston in September, he found himself the ranking officer in the state. Armstrong, upon hearing of Howe's pending return, departed for the north, pleading poor health and an inability to cope with the Southern climate. Howe immediately began work on the defenses of the South Carolina capital. He outlined to the state president and council his plans for defending the city by strengthening the forts, constructing row-galleys, and providing minutemen, wagons, and ferry flats for use in the event of invasion. The South Carolina legislature agreed to every major point of Howe's recommendation, but the appropriation of funds necessary to realize the measures went beyond the call of most legislators. Much of the time during the fall of 1776 was occupied with the training and discipline of troops, the oversight of local defenses, and efforts to overcome chronic arms shortages both in South Carolina and Georgia.[31]

In his efforts to maintain the defensive readiness of both states, Howe returned to Georgia for several weeks during November and December. The general was highly displeased with the condition of Continental troops upon his arrival in Savannah. During his absence, discipline had deteriorated; soldiers appeared "slovenly" and "indecent," and civilians complained of soldiers injuring their property. Howe immediately reprimanded officers for allowing "the uncombed, unshaved and dirty condition of many soldiers," initiated policies of strictest discipline, and warned that violations would be "punished with the utmost Severity."[32]

Early in 1777, Florida Rangers and Indians invaded Georgia, and on 18 February Fort McIntosh—just north of the Satilla River—surrendered to the foe. When Howe was notified of the threat to the

border, he ordered Continental troops south under Colonels Thomas
Sumter and Isaac Motte, with instructions for Lt. Col. Francis Marion
to proceed by water to join them in Savannah. As Howe assembled his
troops in the Georgia capital, the enemy raiders retreated once more
into their East Florida sanctuary. Upon his return to Charleston in
April, he lamented his "fatiguing, fruitless, expedition to Georgia."[33]

It was not until the spring of 1777 that Howe succeeded to the
command of the Southern Department. The command had passed
to James Moore upon Armstrong's departure, and in late November
this son of the founder of Brunswick Town repaired to Charleston,
in keeping with congressional orders. Moore retained the Southern
command until February, when he was ordered to move his North
Carolina regiments north to join General Washington's army. Moore
was delayed in Wilmington due to a lack of money for supplies, and
there he sickened and died. Although Moore's death on 9 April pre-
maturely ended a promising career, his departure from Charleston
left his cousin, Robert Howe, as ranking officer in the South.[34]

CHAPTER 5

SOUTHERN

POLITICS AND

CONTINENTAL

COMMAND

*T*he military aspect of the American Revolution was a limited and somewhat subordinate facet of the overall effort to forge a new nation. American political culture of the eighteenth century was dominated by a localist world view and a deep distrust of the military. Whig ideology, deeply rooted in a conspiracy mentality heralding back to the Cromwellian era, feared the excessive power of a standing army and, thus, took great pains to see that the military was under sufficient civil control to prevent abuses of power. This attitude inevitably hindered military operations and prolonged the war, at the same time assuring a government dominated by civil authority. Distrust of the military apparatus so necessary to win independence was reflected in continuous efforts to restrain the military establishment of the new nation. Most Continental officers, from General Washington down, recognized their own subordinate role but at the same time chafed under the numerous restrictions emanating from Continental and state civil authorities. One of the great strengths of Washington was his appreciation for civil control, although his effectiveness as a commander was limited by the lack of command authority. Repeatedly, the collective judgment of the Continental Congress, with its Board of War, took precedence over the obvious dictates of effective military strategy. From the assignment of general officers to the placement of armies, the military establishment regularly yielded to the dictates of politicians.[1]

The Southern Department of the Continental Army suffered the twofold frustration of congressional controls compounded by an attitude of state supremacy on the provincial level. Southern states, particularly during the first three years of warfare, viewed their sovereignty as preeminent in all matters, both civil and military, that occurred within their borders. The unwillingness of states to overcome their localist view and the inability of Congress to grapple with the problem created a command devoid of power. Since the department operated directly under the provenance of Congress, without direction from or consultation with the supreme commander, disputes with state governments were referred to Congress for resolution. The delays inherent in the deliberative process of legislative command, to say nothing of the distances and uncertainties of communication, severely hindered the Southern commanders in determining the perimeters of their authority.

When Gen. John Armstrong arrived in Charleston in May 1776, he discovered that South Carolina troops were not a part of the Continental establishment. He therefore had no army at his disposal and served for all intent and purposes as a spectator to the events swirling about him during this critical period. Charles Lee subsequently observed that "it cou'd never be the intention of Congress to order Brigadier Armstrong to Charlestown for his health or merely to see the country."[2] On 28 June, the day of the British attack, South Carolina placed five of its regiments on the Continental establishment, but South Carolina president John Rutledge was slow to relinquish complete authority.[3]

General Lee pushed for Continental control of all regiments, and he and President Rutledge soon became involved in a struggle that had potentially dire consequences for the ability of the Southern command to function. During July 1776, as Lee and Howe prepared for an expedition in relief of Georgia, Rutledge denied the right of the

Continental command to march South Carolina troops beyond her borders. Although Congress had authorized the removal of one-third of the army, Rutledge resorted to creative interpretation to pursue his argument. Lee pointed to the role of North Carolina and Virginia troops in the defense of Charleston and hinted at the possibility of a direct challenge to civil authority by ordering the troops to Georgia contrary to the president's wishes. "Shou'd the President and myself have so little regard for the Public Welfare as to make a Tryal [*sic*] of our respective authority, I believe I shou'd be obey'd by three fourths, His Excellency by one, but thank God I believe we have both too much grace to make the experiment."[4]

Robert Howe, as Southern commander, faced similar challenges, for which he pursued a less direct means of resolution. Howe continuously acknowledged an abiding commitment to civil dominance, and by yielding to the vacillations of political influence he undoubtedly sacrificed much of his effectiveness as a commander. In the repeated confrontations with South Carolina and Georgia authorities over appointments and the line of command, he referred issues to the Continental Congress, invariably with the long delays inherent in poor communication and legislative debate. Time and again, the determination of South Carolina and Georgia governors to exert control over military matters created confusion and contradiction within the Southern command. A case in point evolved around the source of authority for appointment of staff officers. Congress in its wisdom had reserved to itself the right to appoint general officers, leaving to the individual states the authority to appoint field officers and junior officers to command the state's Continental regiments. Howe felt that staff officers (i.e., deputy quartermaster general, adjutant, mustermaster) who served in a multistate capacity and constituted an integral part of the commander's inner circle should be appointed by the commander with the confirmation of Congress. Since President Rutledge insisted on South Carolina's prerogative here, intensive debate raged on the issue. The Southern commander pleaded for a resolution of the problem: "For the sake of service & for the honour of your country, . . . fix the Line between Civil and Military Arrangements in such a manner that designing men may not have room to Cavil, or have an opportunity of promoting their own private views under the cover of publick confusion."[5]

As late as the summer and fall of 1778, the Continental command
in the South continued to face repeated frustrations in contending with state civil authorities. While Howe was in Georgia planning an expedition toward Florida, William Moultrie had assumed command in South Carolina. It was Moultrie's responsibility to dispatch men, armament, and provisions for the expedition. The South Carolina hero, however, was unsuccessful in procuring funds from his own state's treasury to support provincial troops, on the grounds that the state auditor had not examined the Continental accounts for past expenditures. Moultrie contended that the quartermaster's books were transmitted monthly to the congressional Board of War and to Q.M. Gen. Thomas Mifflin for auditing and that state auditors had no business with the accounts of the Continental Army, nor were they competent to judge the correctness of the accounts. The president of South Carolina defiantly refused to convene the council to approve funds for the expedition south. He also claimed the right to suspend Col. Francis Huger, the Southern command's deputy quartermaster general for South Carolina, although Moultrie protested that Huger held a commission directly from Congress. Ironically, when Congress did rule on the issue, they supported South Carolina president Rawlins Lowndes and ruled that he acted with propriety in withholding money to Colonel Huger until he accounted for funds already expended. While military and civil authorities awaited action from Congress, the logistical support, without which the Southern army could not move, remained beyond the grasp of the military command.[6]

Efforts to adequately maintain a fighting force were repeatedly frustrated by the recalcitrant nature of state government. When Georgia failed to provide clothing for her own Continental troops, Howe appointed Maj. Raymond Demere to purchase clothes for the soldiers, using drafts on the Continental clothier general. Congress refused to honor the drafts under the contention that Georgia would provide clothing for the men and that Major Demere's action interfered with the state's procurement program. Howe pointed to his efforts to relieve the "absolute wretchedness" of an army with three-fourths of its soldiers "without rags to cover their nakedness." Realizing the incapability of Georgia to provide for its forces, Howe continued to plead for congressional support of the army.[7]

Perhaps more frustrating was the refusal of Georgia governors to relinquish command of their militia during military engagements. The Georgia constitution had made the governor captain-general and commander in chief over all military and naval forces belonging to the state. Allured by the glory of military conquest, the governors in succession appeared determined to command and argued that within Georgia they must remain supreme. Howe insisted that a single military command was vital to an effective operation. Unless he was free to decide on the movements of Continentals and militia alike, the prospects for success were dim. Although Congress supported Howe and ruled that he indeed bore the responsibility for all troops during a military expedition, Georgia governor Button Gwinnett and his successor John Houstoun chose to ignore the dictates of Congress. Gwinnett demanded that Howe be subordinate to him during the proposed 1777 invasion of East Florida, and Houstoun refused to release troops to Howe's authority during the 1778 expedition.[8] The inability of the Southern command to exert influence over civil authorities eroded its potential for success and, coupled with the failure of Congress to provide substantive funding for defensive and offensive goals, placed the command at the mercy of forces it could not control.

Both South Carolina and Georgia were plagued by divergent political factions. The internecine bitterness of the cleavage, particularly in Georgia, created a political climate that directly affected the performance of the Southern command. Political resistance to General Howe in South Carolina centered on the question of Continental rank in the state and first became evident after the promotion of Christopher Gadsden to brigadier general on 1 October 1776. Gadsden began to question the right of the North Carolinian to command in South Carolina. The issue was based primarily on the desire of Gadsden for the command that he, as senior South Carolinian, felt to be rightfully his own. Several times—at Fort Moultrie in April 1777, in a gathering at the president's residence during August, and during a dinner at the plantation of Lt. Col. William Cattel on the Ashley River—Gadsden demanded to know of Howe his authority to command in South Carolina. His contention was that Howe had been left in Georgia by the departing General Lee in September 1776 and that, without a written order from Lee or from Congress direct-

ing him to repair to Charleston, the senior brigadier had no choice
but to remain in Georgia. Howe countered that he had received verbal instructions from Lee to return and that, by the departure of Lee, Armstrong, and Moore, the command evolved on him as senior officer. Such an explanation was unacceptable to Gadsden, and in August 1777 he prevailed upon his political cronies to bring the matter before the state legislature. South Carolina chief justice William Henry Drayton moved in the House that an inquiry be initiated into Howe's right to command. The motion, which empowered the legislature to send for all persons, records, and papers pertinent to the matter, was seconded by future governor Rawlins Lowndes. A heated and prolonged debate ensued, which resulted in the overwhelming defeat of the measure. Even those who disliked Howe had no delusions as to his authority. As one local commented: "I don't know what can be said on the subject, it seems a plain case he is a senior officer. I am not blinded by partiality, you know Genl. Howe is no favorite of mine." [9]

Gadsden blamed this defeat in the legislature on direct intervention by Howe, who was in attendance at the session. Humiliated by his defeat, Gadsden stripped the riband (or "Bauble," as he called it) from his uniform and tendered his commission directly to his foe. Howe attempted to decline the resignation, whereupon Gadsden threw it into the general's hat. Although Gadsden thus resigned his commission in the Continental Army, his friends pledged to continue the fight to unseat Howe.[10]

The political turmoil was of such proportions that Howe realized some definite resolution was necessary. He had not been included in the promotion lists in February, and his disappointment at being passed over was at least partially attributable to the command controversy. A promotion to major general would resolve the issue and defuse Gadsden and his allies. Often, during the summer of 1777, he pleaded with Henry Laurens in Congress to rescue him: "For God's Sake get me out of the Brigadiers list, or at least tell me what is to become of me & assure me that I shall not be superseded in the future. Save me from a future contest like that which happened lately in this State." [11] Laurens attempted to assuage his friend's feelings by assuring him that it was far better to have an independent command as he did in the South than to be a general with the main army without a specific command. Despite his advice to the contrary, Laurens offered a resolution to Congress calling for Howe's transfer out of the Southern Department; but when an opportunity developed in October for Howe's promotion in rank, the South Carolina delegate withdrew his resolution in favor of the promotion.[12]

There rested the issue until June 1778, when Gadsden learned of a letter Howe had written to Congress eleven months earlier, in which the differences between himself and Gadsden had been detailed. Drayton had prepared and sent to Gadsden a copy of the correspondence; and, although Gadsden had earlier demanded that the issue be laid before Congress, he was furious because his adversary had not provided a copy for his advance approval. A detailed paragraph-by-paragraph rebuttal was prepared, which Gadsden requested Drayton circulate and present to Congress. Apparently, Drayton took no action on the matter, much to the chagrin of the former general. The South Carolinian even appealed to Gen. Charles Lee; but, like others, Lee expressed indifference to Gadsden's contention. Howe had considered his letter to Congress a private matter, but when Gadsden persisted in circulating his rebuttal and talking of it publicly, Howe felt the entire question had become a public affair and a question of honor. Gadsden had attacked Howe's integrity in his letter by referring to his "downright low cunning, Jockeying and sharping, . . . none but a Man determined at any rate to wedge himself into Command would stoop to it, the effect of low Ambition indeed." [13]

Col. Charles Cotesworth Pinckney delivered a letter from Howe, demanding an apology or an opportunity for personal satisfaction. Several letters, in which Howe made assurances that he had never meant to reflect upon or injure Gadsden, passed between the foes. If he had failed to fulfill any promises to Gadsden, it was due to a "fault of understanding" and not a lack of integrity. Gadsden's friends, Bernard Elliott and Peter Horry, advised him that Howe's statement was a great concession and warranted an apology on his part, but the South Carolinian refused to budge.[14]

The "Éclaircissement en Militaire" was set for 30 August under the Liberty Tree, with pistols. It was a Sunday, and when the combatants arrived at 11:00 A.M. they discovered that a large crowd had assembled to watch the proceedings. Some spectators had even climbed the tree for a better view. Gadsden and Howe agreed to move to a

GEN. GADSDEN

Christopher Gadsden (Courtesy of the South Carolina Historical Society)

more private location on Reverend William Percy's land. Gadsden and his second, Colonel Elliott, traveled by carriage; Howe and his second, Pinckney, rode on horseback. They faced each other at only "eight very small paces," urged each other to fire first, and stared at each other through the sights of their pistols as seconds ticked away. Howe finally fired wide of his target and Gadsden responded by firing over his left arm at right angles with Howe. Colonel Elliott commented that Gadsden could not have made a handsomer apology or Howe shown a higher degree of honor. Gadsden informed Howe that he did not apologize for challenging Howe's right to command in South Carolina, only for his use of abusive language. The two men shook hands and parted. Despite the public honor they preserved, Gadsden continued to harbor resentment. In a 22 September letter to Drayton, he complained: "Besides having a Stranger introduced to Command us without proper Authority, *can* anything be farther if possible more humiliating unless it be to bind Georgia about our Necks in the Manner it is." [15]

The Howe-Gadsden affair received widespread attention throughout the continent. The British adjutant, Maj. John André, a man of letters who subsequently lost his life during the Benedict Arnold treason, penned an eighteen-stanza poem about the duel.

. . . .

G. went before, with Colonel E.,
    Together in a carriage;
On horseback followed H. and P.
    As if to steal a marriage.

On chosen ground they now alight,
    For battle duly harnessed;
A shady place, and out of sight:
    It shew'd they were in earnest.
. . . .

Quoth H. to G.,—"Sir, please to fire;"
    Quoth G.,—"No, pray begin, Sir:"
And truly, we must needs admire
    The temper they were in, Sir.
. . . .

They paused awhile, these gallant foes,
    By turns, politely grinning;

'Till, after many *cons* and *pros*,
    H. made a brisk beginning.

H. missed his mark, but not his aim;
    The shot was well directed.
It saved them both from hurt and shame;
    What more could be expected?

Then, G., to shew he meant no harm,
    But hated jars and jangles,
His pistol fired across his arm:
    From H., almost at angles.[16]

.   .   .   .   .   .

    Aside from the Gadsden faction, Howe probably had better rela-
tions with South Carolina politicians than Georgia politicians. The
bitter internal struggle for power in this frontier state was such
that lines were finely drawn. After the sudden death of Governor
Archibald Bulloch in February 1777, Button Gwinnett ascended to
the office. Gwinnett was enamored with the thought of military as
well as political power, and he harbored an ambition to receive the
command of Continental troops in his state. When the only Continental brigadiership for Georgia was bestowed upon Lachlan McIntosh,
Gwinnett was furious. An obsession was thus created that carried
Gwinnett to a premature grave. Georgia was rife with claims and
counterclaims of Toryism, and the Gwinnett faction seized upon an
accusation that George McIntosh, brother of the general and a council member in his own right, was trading with Tories. Gwinnett had
George McIntosh arrested and jailed, but the council member's support in the government was such that he was released on parole.[17]
    Robert Howe clashed with Button Gwinnett almost from the mo-
ment of their first meeting. Howe, and Lee before him, had high
regard for Lachlan McIntosh and his performance as a Continental officer. On 11 December 1776 Howe described his fellow officer
as "an active, vigilant, and spirited officer."[18] Upon hearing of the
Tory charges against George McIntosh, Howe quickly inquired as
to whether any hint of Toryism had been associated with the general. Naturally, there was none, but Governor Gwinnett—then as
always—placed Lachlan McIntosh in the worst light possible. At
this time Gwinnett was pressuring Howe to cooperate with him on
an ill-planned expedition to East Florida. Gwinnett claimed rank

over the Continental commander and intimated that Howe and the Continental forces should be subordinate to his authority during the campaign. Howe quickly broke off discussions with the governor and returned to South Carolina after curtly informing Gwinnett that he had no intention of invading East Florida.[19]

Although Howe did not participate in an expedition to the southward in 1777, Continental forces under the command of Col. Samuel Elbert did. The irreconcilable differences between Gwinnett and Lachlan McIntosh had precluded the possibility of the state's two highest ranking officials, civil and military, working together. They thus yielded to the advice of cooler heads that Elbert be placed in sole command of the expedition. Elbert, with four hundred Georgia Continentals, embarked from Sunbury on 1 May and proceeded by water toward the St. Johns River. Simultaneously, Col. John Baker led almost two hundred mounted Georgia militia overland for a rendezvous with Elbert. The British at St. Augustine were alert to the American presence and dispatched Tory colonel Thomas Brown with his Rangers and Maj. Mark Prevost with a detachment of British Regulars. The waterborne Continentals were delayed en route, and when Baker arrived at Sawpit Bluff south of the Nassau River Elbert's forces were nowhere to be found. After several encounters between Baker and detachments of Rangers and Indians, Baker moved his camp inland in an effort to avoid the enemy. After bivouac on 17 May, his small army was attacked at Thomas Creek by a vastly superior force composed of Rangers, British Regulars, and Indians. The Americans quickly withdrew from the battlefield, but not before suffering three killed, nine wounded, and thirty-one taken prisoner. Many of the wounded and prisoners died at the hands of the enemy. By the time the remnants of Baker's forces joined up with Elbert's Continentals, the prospects for success in Florida were nonexistent. The British knew the Continentals' every move and food supplies were low; therefore, Elbert called an end to the campaign and ordered his men back into Georgia.[20]

While Colonel Elbert was finding frustration in Florida, relations between Gwinnett and General McIntosh had deteriorated to the point of physical confrontation. Gwinnett demanded satisfaction on the grounds that the general had called him a scoundrel in public.

Both men were wounded in the encounter, but the luckless Gwin-

nett failed to survive. McIntosh was accused of murder, and petitions from pro-Gwinnett Georgians flooded Congress describing
McIntosh as a worthless officer. After the duel Howe—among others
—recommended that McIntosh be transferred to the Northern Department, where his career would not be damaged further by proximity to hostile factions in his native state.[21]

From the early days of his command, Howe was concerned about
the defensive capabilities of the district, particularly as regarded the
ports of Charleston and Savannah, where an attack would be most
likely to occur. As early as October 1776, he addressed the South
Carolina Legislative Council with proposals for means of strengthening the city and its defense. After outlining means of reinforc-
ing works at Fort Johnson, Sullivan's Island, Haddrell's Point, and
Charleston proper, he recommended obstructions for the river channel and the construction of row galleys. Howe urged the joint establishment of provision magazines between North Carolina, South
Carolina, and Georgia; the procurement of blankets, boats, and wagons for public use; and the establishment of minute-battalions pat-
terned after Virginia's troop buildup of the previous fall. The general
further urged the state to strip all livestock and even inhabitants from
the coastal islands, and finally he begged for cooperation with neighboring states to maximize defensive capabilities wherever an invasion
occurred. The legislature, after some debate, agreed to almost every
major point of the Howe recommendations, but relatively few of the
measures were actually implemented.[22]

Several factors contributed to the difficulties of maintaining a high
defensive posture in the area. Once the threat of British invasion had
passed, the South Carolinians were unconvinced that a return of the
enemy would occur. The entire focus of the war during 1777 and 1778
was keyed to the Northern theater, resulting in a stripping of Southern forces and support. When Gen. James Moore was ordered north
in February 1777, he proceeded to remove North Carolina troops to
accompany him. Howe, who was in Savannah at the time, attempted
to delay their departure until he could bolster the South Carolina
forces. The available resources in officers and men were so meager
that Howe agonized over the resignation of officers and the expira-
tion of enlistments. In cajoling them to remain in uniform, Howe

reminded them that they were "actors upon that glorious stage where every incident is to become an historical fact."[23] Howe contended that seven thousand to eight thousand troops were needed to adequately defend South Carolina, and, with only local troops available, the undertaking was beyond the realm of possibility.[24]

Frequently during 1777 Howe appealed to the Continental Congress for support for his district. He pointed to the commerce of South Carolina and to the importance of Charleston as a port. He assured John Hancock that the port was more valuable to the country than any that existed in Maryland or Virginia, and he pleaded for troops and armament to defend the state and pointed to the unreliability of the militia. His appeals included detailed plans—drawn up by French engineers Maj. Jean Baptiste Joseph de Laumoy and Capt. Chevalier de Villefranche—all of which required men, equipment, and funding not available in the Southern Department. "This Town . . . with everything to make it valuable to the Common Cause, everything to make it an object to the Enemy, is in a state so deplorably weak that it seems to invite an attack."[25]

The Southern commander took pride in the importance of Charleston to the nation and, when the Marquis de Lafayette arrived in Charleston in June 1777 to begin his American adventure, joined with other dignitaries in welcoming this personification of America's friendship with France. A party consisting of Howe, Moultrie, Gadsden, and Governor Rutledge provided a tour of the defensive works around the city as well as of the Sullivan's Island battery that Moultrie defended against the British a year earlier. In a five-hour dinner in Lafayette's honor, the American and French officers drank toasts and conversed in broken English. When the anniversary of the Charleston victory arrived on 28 June, the city observed a day of "festivity and rejoicing," complete with ringing bells, a "suitable discourse" at St. Michael's Church, the firing of guns, a military parade, and an evening of entertainment. Only a week later, the festivities were resumed as Charleston celebrated the first anniversary of American independence. The guns of the forts were fired seventy-six times and the day was spent in "elegant entertainment."[26]

During the fall of 1777, concern over the naval defenses of South Carolina prompted state president Rutledge to request 150 Continental troops to serve as marines aboard a small fleet of ships operating in coastal waters under the command of Nicholas Biddle. Howe,

who was in Georgia at the time, ordered Moultrie to call a council of war to consider the propriety of Marine duty for Continental forces and how many troops could be spared for such a naval expedition. When the council of war determined that troops could not be spared for Marine service, Howe ordered the council to reconsider the question since he was anxious to protect commerce and cooperate with the state government. Although the council remained firm, Moultrie was swayed by Rutledge to agree with the commanding general's assessment. Early in the morning of 15 January, a major fire swept through Charleston, destroying some 250 dwellings and about twice that number of stores and outbuildings, including the public library. The suspicion quickly developed that the conflagration had been caused by arsonists from British ships on the coast. The detachment of marines was promptly ordered aboard Captain Biddle's ships in an effort to rid the coastal waters of the enemy menace. At sea the American frigate *Randolph*, with fifty of the marines aboard, engaged a much larger British ship and was blown up, killing all fifty soldiers and most of the crew. This unfortunate incident left Howe and his command helpless to protect the South Carolina and Georgia trade from the continuing naval threat of the enemy.[27]

As concerned as Howe was with the defense of South Carolina and its capital, he gave much energy and attention to the border state of Georgia, despite a recurring claim by Georgia officials that he was negligent and indifferent to their needs. During visits to Savannah and Sunbury in 1776, Howe attempted to gain some grasp of the situation in the state and the best means of countering the threat of Indian hostility on the frontier, Tory raiders from East Florida, and British Regulars from across the sea. He urged Georgia officials to remove all cattle and other livestock from the Sea Islands and strip those coastal areas of all stores that would be attractive to the enemy. Tories from St. Augustine found an abundance of cattle and rice in what constituted a vast storehouse of provisions that was ripe for the gathering. "The idea of defending the islands upon the Sea Board is too absurd for anybody but a mad man to entertain. . . . To suffer the cattle to remain is in my opinion no better than to establish magazines of provisions for the Enemy."[28] Although the Georgia Convention adopted portions of Howe's defensive plans during 1777, the Department commander repeatedly found to his distress that no action was taken to put the plans into effect.[29]

By September 1777 there were substantial indications that individuals were attempting to draw Georgia into a general war with the Creek Indians and their allies. The Georgia Assembly undertook to debate the possibility of an offensive against the Indians, and Howe appealed to them to use reason and to see through the scheme. He warned that the state had neither the manpower nor the finances to undertake such an unnecessary venture and that, if they did pursue an Indian war, support from neighboring states would be doubtful. The Carolinas had been striving at great expense to maintain peace with the frontier tribes. In a strongly worded appeal to the Georgia Assembly, Howe underscored his feelings on the subject. He warned that their energy and resources should be devoted to defensive measures, not hostility toward the Indian population. "Georgia remains almost as unfortified as ever. Language leaves me no new mode of expressing my solicitude upon this Occasion—let me however discharge my duty by reiterating & begging in the name of God, that you would Erect those works recommended and agreed upon & so essential to your Safety, as fast as possible, without which your country if attacked must infallibly be lost."[30]

Time and again, during 1777 and 1778, the Continental commander and the Georgia civil government clashed over the needed defenses for the state. On 28 January 1778 the Georgia Assembly passed a resolution calling on Howe to undertake an immediate expedition into East Florida to "annoy" the enemy. Howe that same day addressed a letter to the governor, in which he detailed the defensive needs of the state. It was his contention that the discontent and pro-Tory feelings of Georgia residents were based on economic considerations rather than on political philosophy. "The common people seldom speculate or refine upon any subject and therefore embrace Political opinions as matters of faith rather than as matters of Judgement."[31] According to Howe, the survival of Georgia was dependent upon trade. Trade would create credit and a basis for currency exchange, in addition to an abundance of consumer goods needed for sustaining life. Howe proposed that the state create an insurance office to protect shippers against loss, at the same time fortifying Savannah and Sunbury in order to provide safe harbors for com-

merce. Forts were recommended on Tybee and Cockspur islands to
protect Savannah and on St. Catherines and Cedar Hammock islands to safeguard Sunbury. The forts should be strongly garrisoned, con- tinuously provisioned, and substantially built. Although expensive, these plans would provide for the defense of Georgia's major cities while permitting commerce to flourish. The proposal described other locations that were in need of fortification and appealed for the manning of galleys to better protect the rivers. The heart of the defense of Georgia rested in the protection of Savannah and Sunbury, along with a series of fortifications on the frontier between the St. Johns and the St. Marys rivers. The overall safety of the state, however, required the development of a sound currency and a contented population made supportive through trade and commerce.[32]

Subsequent letters from the general addressed the various military needs of the state and underscored the fact that only the state government had the power and the resources to successfully defend itself. It was a basic tenet of the revolutionary movement that each state should provide logistical support for its own Continental forces. In other states, the civil authorities provided hospitals, medical treatment, clothing, food, barracks, and a variety of other benefits necessary for the Continental troops. Georgia had addressed none of these problems. Howe contended that good treatment for the men was necessary if they were to remain in service, and bounties and the promise of land were necessary inducements to reenlistment. Effective minute-battalions, which were so important at the time of invasion, were also lacking in Georgia. Minutemen there were paid on a continuous basis, even when not in service; they lacked any training or discipline; and they were free to decide when and where they would serve since they were not subject to military justice.[33]

The Georgia Assembly immediately took offense at Howe's letters as "containing things which belong only to the civil authority & which are without his line of military duty."[34] Efforts were made to establish the recommended insurance office and to institute other of the needed reforms, but state leaders resented the outsider's involvement in their affairs. They were determined not to be "dictated to" by the Continental commander, but they were equally anxious to know what he planned to do about their desire for an invasion of East Florida.

In deference to the Georgia request, Howe called a council of war of his Continental officers to discuss the feasibility of an East Florida invasion. The officers were of the opinion that, short of the capture of St. Augustine, there was no military object in East Florida that would make an expedition worthwhile and that the army and the state lacked the men, equipment, and provisions necessary for the reduction of the "Castle." Their alternate recommendation echoed Howe's earlier contention that strong fortifications should be built at Satilla Bluff, south of the Altamaha River, and that a full battalion of men should be permanently stationed there to raid along the border.

The Assembly promptly attacked the council of war decision as merely a reflection of Howe's views rather than an open forum of Continental officers. They demanded that a new council of war be called, at which the governor should be a full voting member. Howe refused the request as an absolutely unprecedented move by a civil official. The debate degenerated into a contest of accusations and counteraccusations that eventually was appealed to Congress.[35]

Howe, who was ill during much of the spring of 1778 with a "contagious sore throat and very dangerous fever," was totally unable to convince the Georgia civil authorities of the badly prepared, weak state of their defenses. The Continental commander was without a war chest to finance defensive measures himself, despite repeated appeals to the Continental Congress for such an appropriation, leaving the state government as the only source of logistical support for everything from entrenching tools to shoes for the troops. The internal divisions within the state were such that appeals for war preparations fell on deaf ears. "They spent a number of weeks in Assembly without one thought of Defence, almost wholly employed upon a Confiscation Act of which . . . the people are now in a state of confusion and dispute. What with an exhausted Treasury, with such arrears of pay due to the Soldiers so that they were almost in a state of mutiny, most of the men so naked that it was indecent to parade them, with not three days provisions for the Army . . . in short tho' destitute of almost every military requisite they were for impelling the Army to undertake an Expedition into and against East Florida."[36]

The situation did not improve as 1778 progressed. The long-demanded expedition against Florida was ultimately forced upon the Southern command by Congress. It occupied the summer months, only to end in the anticipated frustration resulting from a split command and poor logistical support. The Southern Department of the Continental Army was neglected by Congress and harassed by the states that it attempted to serve; yet the army was expected to perform effectively. When it could not do so, the command was held accountable. The frustrations of 1776 and 1777 were only a prelude to what lay ahead in 1778.

CHAPTER 6

WAR ON

THE GEORGIA

FRONTIER

*A*lthough Robert Howe continued to stress the unlike-lihood of the success of an attack on St. Augustine, pressures from Congress made an expedition against East Florida inevitable. On 13 February Congress debated a resolution that would have ordered Howe or Col. Samuel Elbert to undertake an East Florida expedition; and, although the measure was ultimately tabled, the resolution left no doubt that action was expected. During late February and early March of 1778, Howe was making provisions for such an undertaking despite a severe and prolonged illness. The deputy quartermaster general was ordered to procure two flats and six boats for the army's use. All commanding officers were instructed to equip their men with every military requisite, to assure the readi-ness of all arms and accoutrements, and to have men prepared to march at a moment's notice. Iron fetters with locks were to be made for hobbling the horses; tallow from slaughtered cattle and fat from butchered hogs were to be made into candles and soap; cattle fat was to be boiled for oil; horns were to be saved for the use of the army; hides were to be inventoried; and tailors were to report the supply of clothes available. Obviously, the Continental Army was preparing for action.[1]

Raids by Lt. Col. Thomas Brown and his Tory Rangers from East Florida during the spring of 1778 increased the pressure upon Howe to take the offensive. On 12 March Brown, with one hundred Rangers and ten Indians, traveled through swamps and then swam more than one-fourth of a mile across the Altamaha River during the night to attack Fort Howe (formerly Fort Barrington) at the break of day. With the loss of only one man, the Florida raiders seized the fort—killing two, wounding four, and taking twenty-three prisoners.[2]

This and other excursions into the heart of south Georgia provided ample evidence of the menace created by the British presence in East Florida. The state of Georgia won the approval of Congress for an expedition that would carry the war directly to the enemy's doorstep. Governor John Houstoun contended that only five hundred to six hundred men garrisoned the fort at St. Augustine, assisted by perhaps two hundred Tory renegades from Georgia and South Carolina. In Houstoun's view, the conquest of East Florida was not only desirable but also absolutely essential. As a civilian without battle-field experience or military training to balance his zeal, he perceived that victory required little more than a few troops gathered before the fortress of the British.[3]

As the month of April approached, events crowded upon Howe until the necessity of the moment overcame his cautious nature. The demands of Georgia and the pressures of Congress held sway. An expedition toward East Florida would finally get under way. A body of approximately five hundred Tory "Scopholites" from the backcountry of South Carolina and Georgia had begun a march southward to join the British in St. Augustine. They crossed the Savannah River below Augusta, plundering and marauding as they progressed. At the same time, the movement of Tories and Indians from West Florida was reported, as was an expedition of Regular and Tory forces northward from St. Augustine. Howe realized the danger posed by a juncture of the Scopholites with the East Floridians, and on 6 April he dispatched Colonel Elbert to march with all possible speed to intercept the insurgents. Howe's orders to Elbert directed him to undertake as his first objective the prevention of the joining of the Loyalists with the British forces in East Florida. He was to consider them as enemies and use whatever force necessary, consistent with the rules of war. If other enemy forces presented themselves, Elbert was free to undertake attacks upon them as well—if there was a probability of success.[4]

The problem of fighting a war against Tory raiding parties was reflected once again in this effort to intercept the Scopholites. Howe had to depend almost entirely on foot soldiers to counteract an enemy that was frequently mounted. Despite Howe's repeated appeals to Congress for a substantial body of horse to operate in South Georgia, his pleas had been ignored. As had occurred so frequently in the past, the Scopholites outdistanced Colonel Elbert's troops and passed untouched into East Florida. Howe obviously was correct in lamenting that "they laugh at foot soldiers with scorn. Only cavalry troops can stop them."[5]

All was not bleak, despite the inability of the Americans to stop the threat from East Florida. On 18 April Colonel Elbert and a detachment of three hundred Georgia Continentals aboard the galleys *Lee, Washington,* and *Bulloch* approached Frederica, on St. Simons Island, where the British brigantine *Hinchinbrook*, the sloop *Rebecca*, and a prize brig were moored. After securing the town and taking five prisoners who were onshore from the *Hinchinbrook*, the American band aboard the galleys attacked their prey on the morning of 19 April. Capt. Alexander Ellis of the *Hinchinbrook* was drowned, and Capt. John Mowbray of the *Rebecca* fled, as did the remainder of the enemy crew. Among the spoils found aboard the surrendered *Hinchinbrook* were three hundred uniforms, earlier captured off Charleston by the British, that had been destined originally for Col. Charles C. Pinckney's South Carolina Continentals. The *Hinchinbrook* and the *Rebecca* had represented the primary naval support for the British in East Florida at that moment; had the East Florida command entertained serious thoughts of a full-scale invasion of Georgia for the spring of 1778, those hopes were dashed at Frederica on 19 April.[6]

Though there was jubilation in the American camp, the concern about a British invasion of Georgia had not lessened. By early May, Howe had begun his Southern expedition, although he emphasized that the plan was to chase the British back across the St. Johns River and to secure the area between there and the St. Marys River against "the Predatory War." Spies and deserters had reported to the Southern command in Savannah that the East Floridians were establishing posts between the rivers. Their numbers by best reports included one thousand to fourteen hundred Regulars, two hundred manumitted Greeks, four hundred Florida Scouts, four hundred insurgents, and one hundred renegade Indians—all well mounted and well armed.[7] In preparation to meet the threat, Howe had ordered an additional three hundred Continental troops from South Carolina to augment his meager forces. South Carolina called up eleven hundred men and authorized one-half of their Continental troops to march for Georgia. Howe planned to proceed immediately to the southern frontier, where he would form a junction with Colonel Elbert. "As soon as I form a junction with him if the foe does not advance, I shall most probably seek them and endeavor to dislodge them from the Post which they ought not be suffered to possess."[8]

By 9 May, Howe and his army had arrived at Fort Howe, on the north side of the Altamaha River. The Continental Army consisted of a South Carolina brigade of six hundred men under the command of Col. Charles Cotesworth Pinckney and a Georgia brigade of five hundred men commanded by Colonel Elbert. The Continental artillery of the two states had been drawn together into a corps under Maj. Roman de Lisle. It was projected that, to the Continental force of eleven hundred men, one thousand South Carolina militia under Col. Andrew Williamson and thirteen hundred Georgia militia led by Governor Houstoun would combine with the Continentals to form a uniform fighting force of well over three thousand men.[9]

The heat of south Georgia can be excessive during the summer months, and in the humid swamps of this wilderness the effect can be deadly for both men and horses. The Continental command realized that they had made a late beginning and that to linger far into the summer season would be most unwise. The spring of 1778 had been exceedingly dry, and by May, when the men gathered at Fort Howe, the weather had turned extremely sultry. The officers worried over the results of fatigue in such a climate, and Howe warned that sanitation and cleanliness were critical for health purposes. The camp was

ordered kept clean, garbage and filth were to be burned, and "necessaries" were ordered constructed in an effort to ease the danger of
illness.[10]

The daily routine while the army remained at Fort Howe was fairly
uniform. The men arose early and had a breakfast of boiled rice, beef
steaks, and water or coffee. Duty was limited and much of the day
was consumed in lounging about the encampment. The spot was hot
and dirty but the troops built bowers before their tents as a defense
against the heat. Dinner and supper were repetitions of breakfast,
except that catfish, trout, or bream taken from the Altamaha supple-
mented the diet, as did occasional bacon. General Howe provided
rum as a relief from the boredom of inactivity and the unhealthiness
of the Georgia summer.[11]

While the army awaited provisions ordered from South Carolina,
the command deliberated as to the most expeditious and defensible
route south. Elbert and Pinckney spent much of the time on the
twelfth and thirteenth of May across the river reconnoitering locations for the army's move. The engineer, Capt. John Christian Senf,
surveyed the terrain to determine sites for road construction through
the swamps that bordered the southern bank of the Altamaha. After
reconnoitering both Satilla Bluff (three miles upstream from Fort
Howe) and Reid's Bluff (three miles below the fort), Howe selected
the latter as the most advantageous for their advance camp. Engineers had confirmed that it would provide a more direct route to the
Satilla River, that roads through the swamp could be more easily cut
from there, and that roads for retreat would be easier to prepare.
Therefore, Reid's Bluff was selected over the more pleasant upriver
location.[12]

Though the expedition was barely under way, desertion became a
factor with which to be reckoned. It could not be taken lightly, as
successful desertions soon lead to a general sapping of the forces and
potential disaster for the army. Four men, two of whom were French,
were court-martialed on 16 May and ordered to run the gauntlet
through the brigades. French officers on the expedition were highly
offended over the disgrace associated with such punishment, and they
insisted that their two countrymen would prefer to be hanged or shot.
"The offenders however did not possess such a delicate sensibility,

& preferred Life & the disgrace to the choice their countrymen had
pointed out for them." [13]

Two days later, Sgt. John Tyrrell and a private were convicted of
desertion and ordered shot. Tyrrell had been charged with mutiny
and attempting to persuade a party under the command of Lieutenant Frazer to join him in deserting. Howe upheld the sentence and
the guilty were executed on 21 May. The general issued a proclamation detailing the heinous nature of desertion, which he called "the
greatest of all crimes." The fate of Sergeant Tyrrell and his partner
obviously was not sufficient to deter others. On 22 May eight men
were tried for desertion and ordered executed. Apparently, they had
deserted previously from Gen. John Burgoyne's British army and, as
Continental recruits, had been formed into a unit and sent south from
Pennsylvania. The deserters found themselves in a barren wilderness,
and their capture by a party of Indians and soldiers resulted in only
one death from the unfriendly environment and one scalping. Ultimately, the instigator (James Lister) was hanged and five of his party
were shot. The American command was unyielding in its belief that
such behavior must serve as an example to the troops if the army were
to survive. These executions provided "specticles" of a "Melancholic
Nature" for the little army encamped in south Georgia.[14]

It was not until 27 May that the Continental Army was able to
cross the Altamaha and take up camp at Reid's Bluff. The delays were
occasioned by the failure of a South Carolina galley and a provision
boat bearing ammunition and provisions to arrive on the Altamaha
in a timely fashion. Colonel Pinckney reported that "the reasonable
and candid gentry of this state are throwing a thousand reflections
on the general and the army, for not marching to attack the enemy,
and storm lines, without Provisions and without ammunition." [15]

During the days and weeks that the Continental Army lingered on
the Altamaha, they occupied themselves with preparations for the
march ahead. Howe had requested that three hundred slave "pioneers" be sent from Georgia plantations to help cut a road through
the dense terrain south of the river. Rather than the three hundred
expected, the state Assembly voted him two hundred hands, of which
only fifty-six arrived on schedule. These were divided into two companies to be assigned to the brigades. These pioneers were utilized

not only for clearing roads but also for digging wells and latrines and constructing fortifications. Wells were sunk at Reid's Bluff to provide drinking water, as the command was always concerned about the health dangers associated with drinking surface water. Despite precautions, the heat, oppressive humidity, and swampy terrain soon began to take their toll. A shortage of tents, canteens, and camp kettles added to the health problems as well as the discomfort; and the inability to procure adequate medicine to treat the ill further compounded the danger.[16]

The lack of cooperation or concern displayed by Governor Houstoun and his Georgia government contributed to the frustrations and failures surrounding the expedition. Georgia had failed to equip its Continental regiments with the needed tents and camp equipment, and the militia appeared to be in competition with the Continental forces for the very support necessary to sustain the campaign. On 24 May the Governor ordered two hundred barrels of rice belonging to the Continental forces to be delivered to his own Georgia militia and directed that the galleys accompanying the provision boats proceed forty miles above Fort Howe on the Altamaha. This not only left the remaining Continental provisions unprotected but also forced the galleys to attempt to enter an area far too shallow for them to navigate safely. At the same time, the militia under Houstoun's directions was claiming all boats, horses, and wagons; and early in June the Continental Army went without meat for three days because the militia had seized part of their cattle and monopolized more than they could possibly eat. On one occasion, fifteen Continental horses were impressed by the state, leaving Howe's deputy quartermaster general unable to deliver a supply of clothing and stores. Still later, the militia pulled a Continental wagon from the river where it had sunk and claimed it as plunder of war, refusing to return it to the frustrated Continentals until they paid a ransom of £60 sterling. As William Moultrie commented from Charleston, "The governor seems to be taking the bread out of your mouths. I heartily wish you all success, and a great many laurels; though you have but a barren field to gather them from."[17]

The days continued to slip by and the stifling and increasingly rainy summer season arrived, but still Howe's little army remained stationary on the Altamaha. Williamson's forces from South Carolina had

not yet entered Georgia, and the Georgia militia had not material-
ized. Hostile Indians hovered around the encampment, preying upon
lone travelers from the army. Thomas Pinckney reported on 4 June
that "a flying Party of 16 or 20 Indians has been seen within a mile of
this Post; 3 Days ago they scalped an Armorer belonging to the Georgia Brigade as he was riding along the Road between this place and
Fort Howe which is only distant about 3 miles." By 7 June the general
was fully frustrated by efforts to provision his forces and keep them
healthy while waiting to unify his command. "Puzzled, perplexed,
disappointed, and the devil and all. . . . I have but advanced to this
post having been for several weeks waiting the arrival of the militia, who I have impatiently expected. . . . Had I been seconded as I
wished, something capital might have been expected." [18]

Howe had dispatched Colonel Elbert and his Georgia brigade on
7 June, with the expectation of moving Charles C. Pinckney's brigade
and the remainder of the army in a few days. Shortages of horses and
wagons continued to delay that departure, and by the time Colonel
Elbert had proceeded to the Satilla River, fifty miles away, Howe was
anxious to move forward—despite a lack of knowledge of Houstoun's plans or even the location and number of men constituting the
militia forces. The army finally marched on 14 June and proceeded
some five miles before camping at Spring Branch for the first night.
At that time the governor was just leaving Sunbury, but a messenger
from Houstoun arrived on the following day, requesting that Howe
return to Reid's Bluff for a conference. The result of the meeting on
the sixteenth was Houstoun's promise that the militia would march
in three or four days to meet up with the Continental troops.[19]

The Continental Army proceeded south slowly, covering eight
miles daily on the sixteenth and seventeenth, and camped the second night on a branch of the Little Satilla River. As the army pushed
toward the Satilla, a scouting party—consisting of light infantry
under Lt. Col. Francis Henry Harris and mounted volunteers under
Col. James Habersham—faced a detachment of Florida Rangers.
In the skirmish that followed, the Americans carried the day. The
Rangers lost one man taken prisoner, eight horses, five saddles and
bridles, and their blankets. On 18 June the general called reveille
at 4:00 A.M., and by noon the troops had traveled twelve additional miles under an exceedingly sultry sun that brought on showers

throughout the afternoon. By the nineteenth the main army formed a junction with Colonel Elbert's brigade at Cowford on the Great Satilla River. Here, within striking distance of the British Fort Tonyn on the St. Marys, Howe's forces held up to await the arrival of the long-expected militia. Comm. Oliver Bowen had arrived at Wright's Landing on the St. Marys, and direct communication between him and Howe settled upon strategy for facing the enemy. On 22 June the Georgia militia was still concentrated near Sunbury, and Colonel Williamson's South Carolina militia was only nine miles below Savannah. General Moultrie, writing from Charleston, commented on the inability of the American forces to coordinate their expedition. "If this be the case, for God's sake! when will you all join: if you still continue moving from each other nothing but Augustine Castle can bring you up."[20]

It was on 23 June that the main body of the Continental forces crossed the Great Satilla and encamped in an old field at Cantey's place. They had ferried across the Great Satilla using rafts, fifty feet wide and fourteen feet broad, made of dead pine trees tied with cowhide and laid over with a flooring of fence rails. The rafts were conducted over the river with a rope that stretched from shore to shore. Early the following day, the troops broke camp for the final twelve-mile march to the St. Marys. Morning orders prior to departure instructed every man to have his horn filled with powder and his cartouche box well furnished, and to carry thirty rounds of loose ball and two spare flints per man. Also, each man was to receive four days' ration of rice. The corps of artillery was to carry three brass fieldpieces; two iron two-pounders; two swivel cohorns; three-hundredweights of gunpowder in casks; all the fixed ammunition filled to the calibers of each piece; one hundred rounds of round, canister, and grapeshot for each fieldpiece; and port fires, match, and every necessary apparatus. The American army was ready for battle.[21]

Not until 28 June did Governor Houstoun and the militia arrive and make camp within a few miles of the Continentals. The previous day, the governor had refused to dispatch Maj. John Baker's Light Horse to assist the Continentals and had arrested his own Major Wilder for marching from the Altamaha to the Satilla without orders. With the final arrival of Houstoun and his forces on the American front, a conference ensued between the two commanders.

In this meeting, Houstoun refused to place his militia forces under the command of the Continental officer. By this determination not to relinquish command, Houstoun dashed all hopes that a unified army would face the British. It is apparent that tempers flared as an "altercation arose respecting the sole command." [22]

After neither commander was willing to yield to the other, Howe demanded that the governor make a choice as to whether he wished to march his militia against Fort Tonyn or to attack the British major Mark Prevost, who was posted some fifteen or twenty miles away, astraddle the road to St. Augustine. Houstoun chose the latter and the conference ended. As a final shot, the governor ordered the Continental Army's guides, who were Georgia residents, to leave the Continental camp immediately and report to his headquarters.

On 29 June Howe's forces pushed on to Fort Tonyn, where they found an abandoned and burned installation. The East Floridians had retreated in such haste that they had been forced to bury, burn, and hide provisions in an effort to keep them out of the hands of the Americans. Howe ordered his engineers to examine the remains of the fort to determine whether it could be easily restored. In the meantime, Thomas Brown's Tory Rangers took up camp in nearby Cabbage Swamp in an effort to harass the American forces. Realizing the inferiority of his forces, Brown set out to join Major Prevost at Alligator Creek Bridge, where more action awaited the Tories.

In keeping with the dual command concept required by Governor Houstoun, he dispatched a force of Georgia militia under Brig. Gen. James Screven to reconnoiter Major Prevost's position at Alligator Creek. As the militia approached, they initially were mistaken for Rangers and thus were able to attack the pickets at the bridge before their identity was discovered. During the encounter, Col. Elijah Clarke was severely wounded in the thigh while leading an attack on the British flank. As Brown's Rangers closed on the American flank, the Georgia militia began a withdrawal. The Americans had thirteen killed and several wounded, while the enemy counted one killed and several wounded. Although the militia managed to retrieve most of their casualties, the bodies of an ensign and a black patriot were found on the field by the enemy. It is noteworthy that black Americans apparently were serving in a combat capacity during the expedition. [23]

Early in the morning of 1 July, Governor Houstoun appealed to

Howe to advance against the enemy, assuring the Continental commander that he would march without delay to cooperate with him. When Howe agreed to the scheme, contingent on the governor providing a quantity of rice to subsist his men until the supply ship arrived, Houstoun immediately decided that the Georgia militia would be unable to participate because their supplies not only were insufficient to assist the Continentals but also were inadequate for his own army. This response caused great consternation among the Continentals, since only five days earlier Houstoun had boasted of his ample supply of provisions.[24]

It was not until 8 July that Colonel Williamson and his South Carolina militia arrived on the scene to bring into perspective the fourth and final segment of the American forces. A conference was called in which Howe, Houstoun, Williamson, and Bowen debated the future of the expedition. As Continental commander for the South, Howe was adamant that he should have general command of all American forces. Governor Houstoun once again refused to relinquish control of his Georgia militia; Colonel Williamson asserted that his South Carolina militia would be unwilling to take orders from anyone other than himself; and Commodore Bowen announced that in all naval matters he must remain supreme. Amidst "this Chaos of Command," Howe lamented that, "if I am ever again to depend upon operations I have no right to guide, and men I have no right to command, I shall deem it then, as now I do, one of the most unfortunate accidents of my life."[25]

The American expedition against East Florida had finally lumbered to an inglorious halt. The weeks of exposure to the extreme heat and insects of south Georgia's swamps had taken their toll on the Continental Army. Less than four hundred troops were fit for service. Houstoun's Georgia militia, although relatively free of the illnesses that plagued the field-weary Continentals, had no more than 550 men—rather than the 1,300 he had projected. Along with the unhealthiness of the Continental forces, a continuing problem existed due to the lack of horses and pioneers to help move the army. The horses, which were necessary for pulling wagons as well as for scouting and light-horse duty, had died in numbers during the march. The heat and inadequate provisions had affected men and beasts alike. As to the pioneers, who were largely slaves provided by the state of

Georgia to clear roadways for the movement of the army through the wilderness, only a token number had ever been supplied to the Continentals. One disgusted officer commented that "we have now with great toil and difficulty thro' parching Lands and uncultivated wilds, frequently in the Meridian heat, Marched near 300 Miles to this Place, and the rewards of our trouble has been [*sic*] to find an half demolished Stockade Fort, a few devils Cloaths, Blankets, and trifling Necessaries."[26]

Not only was there no agreement as to command and culpability, but also the separate commanders could reach no agreement as to the ultimate goal of the expedition. Governor Houstoun demanded that the three armies cross the St. Johns and proceed independently against the British fort at St. Augustine; Colonel Williamson advised that the expedition continue as far as the St. Johns in an effort to engage the British, without crossing the river; and General Howe contended that the expedition had accomplished all that was feasible during the summer season and should withdraw.[27]

Continental scouts had reconnoitered the British front and discovered that the enemy had withdrawn from their breastworks at Alligator Creek and obviously were retreating to the St. Johns. Based on observations of the British movements, it was apparent that the British had no intentions of facing the Americans north of the St. Johns.

It was the feeling of the Continentals that an American crossing of the St. Johns could not be executed safely unless the naval force could first take command of the river. Commodore Bowen strongly opposed this proposal, as his galleys would be required to go into the ocean to enter the mouth of the St. Johns. They were not designed for sea duty and would fall easy prey to the enemy. This hurdle notwithstanding, Bowen felt that his little force would be unable to gain command of the St. Johns, even if he could bring the flotilla safely into the river, due to the superior firepower of the British force there.[28]

With Continental and militia forces camping nearby without recourse to a central command, friction and open hostility invariably resulted. On one occasion, two Continental officers were given command of a scouting party made up of ten or twelve privates handpicked from the South Carolina militia. Once out of camp, the privates refused to obey commands or even recommendations made by the Continental officers, with the result that the detachment was surprised by an enemy detachment and lost their horses in the confusion. On another occasion, Houstoun sent a file of men with fixed bayonets into the Continental camp to arrest an officer; and to further exacerbate the situation, the governor attempted to claim for state use a boat that the Continentals had loaded with sick troops for evacuation to a healthier location. This crisis was resolved only after the Continentals offered to provide another boat for the state to use for hauling rice.[29] To add insult to injury, the militia took delight in baiting the Continentals, making great sport of their concern for military procedures: "They declare us to be all Cowards for we get up an hour before day & stand to our arms, that we dare not fight without breast-works (meaning the fleches, which the Engineer has thrown up, for the security and defence of our Camp)[,] that we marched from St. Illas without beating a drum for the Ordinary Duties of the Camp[,] that we put out our fires & take the bells from our Horses at night & that we do not beat the Tattoo every night & that whenever an alarm happens we turn out without beating to arms."[30]

Finally, on 11 July, the Continental command held a council of war, presided over by General Howe, at Fort Tonyn. At this meeting, which included all of the Continental officers above the rank of captain, the officers voted unanimously that they had accomplished their primary goal of chasing the British and Tory raiders out of Georgia and forcing them to give up Fort Tonyn to seek safety south of the St. Johns. They also agreed unanimously that the prospects of success in proceeding further without a unified command were not good, and that, considering the unhealthiness of the men, it was wise to move northward without delay.[31]

The maneuvering among the commanders of the three armies reflects the absolute unwillingness of either officer to recognize a superior command. Howe felt that the superiority of the Continental command must be established without question, in keeping with instructions of the Continental Congress.[32] Colonel Williamson declined to enter the Continental camp for a meeting with Howe, as previously promised; but Howe, in a rare display of firmness, dispatched Captain Drayton to inform Williamson to be in Howe's encampment before returning to his own headquarters. Williamson complied and had breakfast with the Continental commander, but Williamson and Governor Houstoun refused to come to the Continental command post for a conference. After Howe declined to hold

the conference in Williamson's tent, a meeting was scheduled at the head of a branch located between the Continental and Georgia militia camps. After a detailed discussion of the issues, Howe and Williamson withdrew a short distance from the meeting place to discuss the issues with their respective officers. Houstoun, rather than awaiting their return, promptly departed for his own tent and subsequently sent an aide to request Howe's determination of what the Continental Army planned to do. Howe, once again feeling the necessity of giving credence to Continental Army authority, refused to report to the governor until Houstoun had first provided the Continental command with an accounting of his own plans.

After a day passed with no response from Houstoun, Howe forwarded to the governor a copy of the minutes of the Continental council of war of 11 July. The Continentals were undertaking final preparations for departure, and Howe felt that nothing would be accomplished by further silence between the two camps. After leveling and burning the fleches and fort, the Continentals began their withdrawal on 14 July. One hundred twenty men were ordered to return by land with the wagons, while Colonels Elbert and Pinckney marched their forces to Wright's Landing for water transportation back to Savannah. Howe himself chose to travel by land, proceeding almost directly to Charleston. By 26 July he was "hourly expected in town," and the 30 July issue of the *South Carolina & American General Gazette* reported that Howe, Col. Nicholas Everleigh, Maj. Thomas Pinckney, Capt. Roger P. Sanders, Capt. Drayton, and other officers had returned there.[33]

The Florida expedition of 1778 has been described as another disastrous undertaking for Howe. Whether the expedition was a failure—and who was to blame—is open to debate. From the very beginning, Howe characterized his goal for the mission not as an effort to capture the fort at St. Augustine, but as an attempt to stop the Tory raids into Georgia. It was feared that a major invasion by the British and Tories was imminent, and the neutralization of south Georgia as a staging area was seen as a most important goal. These things were accomplished, albeit at a high cost in men. Howe's greatest failure, once again, was his inability to unify the elements of the army under the Continental command. With a unified command responding energetically, the prospects for a major victory in East Florida were relatively bright. The prolonged delays, while the militia forces remained around Savannah, resulted in widespread sickness among the wilderness-encamped Continentals. This, coupled with the reality of four independent commands operating at cross-purposes, reduced the army to impotency. Howe's lack of success in forcing the militia to serve as a necessary adjunct to the Continental forces is reflective of the overriding issue of authority during the early stages of the Revolution.

CHAPTER 7

DEBACLE AT

SAVANNAH

A number of considerations forced Great Britain to re-assess her options early in 1778. The fact that Washington's army remained reasonably intact in the Philadelphia area, the spectacular American victory at Saratoga late in 1777, and—perhaps most importantly—the French entry into the war as a full American ally played heavily upon British war strategy. Lord Germain, British colonial secretary, in March of 1778 drew up a plan to attack the Carolinas and Georgia. These areas were reported to contain large numbers of Loyalists and therefore were believed to be more readily returnable to Royal control. Germain took the position that, once the Carolinas and Georgia were overrun, "all America to the south of the Susquehana [*sic*] would return to their allegiance and . . . the northern provinces might be left to their own feelings and distress to bring them back to their duty." [1]

The raids from East Florida during the spring of 1778 were only a prelude for efforts to forge a British victory in the South. By the summer, the British high command had formulated plans for a Southern invasion, and rumors of an impending British attack were rampant within the American army. General Howe realized that, with the new focus on the South, Congress would be forced to provide troops, armament, and authority to wage a real war. Attention would shift to the South. Howe envisioned himself in command of an army of sufficient scope to actually invade East Florida. [2]

As the rumors swirled, Howe found himself hard-pressed to counter the criticism exacted against him by civil authorities in both South Carolina and Georgia. It was at this point, on 13 August, that Howe and Christopher Gadsden engaged in their highly publicized duel. During the same time, Howe and John Houstoun were busily providing Congress with their respective and highly contradictory versions of the East Florida expedition. The Georgia governor expressed "great surprise" that the Continental forces had resolved to retreat after finding Fort Tonyn in ashes and the British withdrawn. "The particular reason which induced this measure I am unacquainted with. . . . I am happy in being able to say that a more unpopular manuaver [*sic*] never was attempted than this was among all ranks and orders of the militia who were present and saw for themselves."[3] Houstoun further contended that the militia contained more than two thousand "hearty determined" men who were ready to sweep the British and Tory forces from before them and even seize the Castle at St. Augustine. He could not imagine why the Continentals had sickened in the summer heat. He disagreed vehemently with Comm. Oliver Bowen's appraisal of the difficulty of sending the Continental galleys into the St. Johns River and proposed that Congress pass laws putting Continental naval commanders under the control of the state in which they were serving. Finally, he boasted of ample provisions that his forces were required to bring with them back to Savannah. Included were seven hundred steers, four hundred barrels of rice, and a "great plenty" of rum. "It is evident our retreat did not arise from a deficiency of either men, provision or necessities, and with me I assure you not from inclination."[4]

The discord between Georgia and the Continental Army went well beyond the personal animosity of the principal characters. The regimental officers frequently complained that the state authorities undercut their ability to recruit and maintain an army, due to policies detrimental to the service. Georgia currency had deteriorated to the point that it was valueless. After numerous appeals by Howe and his staff, Congress dispatched Continental currency to pay the salaries of Georgia Continental troops. The money was delivered to state officials, who promptly replaced it with Georgia currency and paid the soldiers with the state's own devalued bills. Many of the troops had been recruited in Virginia with promises of pay in Continental currency. In the expedition against East Florida, troops of the South Carolina regiments purchased rum from a sutler for fifty shillings Continental currency while troops serving in Georgia regiments were required to pay £6 for the same or inferior rum. Such inequities made it difficult for Georgia Continental officers to recruit and retain an army, much less increase its numbers.[5]

As a further embarrassment to the Southern commander, he seemed unable to convince the Continental Congress that he had no authority over militia forces during the Florida expedition. Congress had clearly ruled in his favor on the question of Continental control of militia, but Houstoun and Andrew Williamson had refused to comply. When an evaluation of the expedition was undertaken by Congress, they persisted in crediting the militia, consisting of more than sixteen hundred men, to the forces under Howe's command.[6]

On 25 September Congress issued orders that devastated Howe, although it is difficult to believe that the thrust of their action was totally unexpected. Virginia and North Carolina were instructed to send troops for the defense of South Carolina and Georgia. Virginia was to provide one thousand men while North Carolina was responsible for providing three thousand. At the same time, Maj. Gen. Robert Howe was directed to repair immediately to General Washington's headquarters, and Maj. Gen. Benjamin Lincoln was ordered to take command of the Southern Department.[7]

It was not until 9 October that Howe learned of his removal, and his reaction was one of great anguish. "Have I not sacrificed my Fortune & Peace to the service of my Country! have I not by the most unwearied diligence & with a Zeal which at least has some merit attended to the duties of my station & by my every effort endeavored to do my Duty! and shall I, after being kept against my wish from the Scene of immediate Action, be recalled at that moment when this Country is likely to become the Scene of it—How Sir have I deserved this disgrace?"[8] According to North Carolina congressman Cornelius Harnett, the removal of his former neighbor and friend had resulted from an encounter between Howe and a female in Charleston. Harnett contended that the incident caused the South Carolina and Georgia delegates to be greatly incensed against Howe, to the point of demanding his recall.[9]

Lincoln was to learn all too soon that the Southern command

offered few opportunities for laurels; and, although he accepted the challenge offered, he privately assured General Washington that he was not pleased with the assignment. Many of the same problems that proved the undoing of Howe faced Lincoln. Although Lincoln had been promised an army of seven thousand men, he was hard-pressed to count fourteen hundred troops under his command in January 1779. Rather than the abundance of supplies assured by Congress, he found that the Southern army possessed few fieldpieces, arms, tents, camp utensils, lead, or entrenching tools; and without a war chest he had no means to obtain these necessities. Along with these problems, Lincoln complained that Col. Andrew Williamson ignored orders to bring his militia under Continental command, President Rawlins Lowndes of South Carolina initially refused to provision North Carolina militia marching to Charleston, and militia in general refused to accept regular army discipline. Within six months Lincoln had offered to resign his command, and by June public criticism in Charleston was so strong that it was only with great difficulty that Governor John Rutledge, Gen. William Moultrie, and the South Carolina Council convinced Lincoln to remain in his post as Southern commander. To his credit, Lincoln avoided the quagmire of political entanglements that had overwhelmed Howe and thus managed to gain a measure of support from the South Carolina government.[10]

After Howe received official notification in October of his removal, he pleaded with his good friend Henry Laurens, president of the Continental Congress, to use his influence to have the orders rescinded. With a renewal of concern for the defense of the South, Howe was convinced that the command at last offered the prospects for the glory and fame that he sought. True to his wishes, Howe did participate once again in the defense of the South, but he found humiliation—not glory—awaiting him in Savannah.

As early as mid-October, Sir Henry Clinton was busily coordinating his planned invasion with British and Tory forces in Florida. Gen. Augustine Prevost was ordered to the St. Marys to cooperate with Lt. Col. Archibald Campbell, who was scheduled to lead the invasion force. In order to provide ample provisions for the invading army, General Prevost dispatched Maj. Mark Prevost into Georgia to collect cattle in the Newport and Midway settlements. At the same time, a force under Col. Lewis V. Fuser was to pass through the inland waterway and attack Sunbury. The force, consisting of some four hundred Regulars, Rangers, and Indians, was in the area north of the Altamaha by mid-November.

Since the crisis in Georgia developed before Lincoln could arrive in Charleston to assume command, Howe saw no alternative but to proceed to Georgia without delay. Inventories of cartridges, ammunition chests, medical chests, and other equipment under Continental control were ordered, and officers were exhorted to exert themselves "to the utmost." The general hurriedly informed Congress that he was taking what troops were available and hoped that Congress would agree with his action.[11] On the evening of 18 November, the Continental command rode south out of Charleston, hoping to intimidate the enemy into retreating once more into Florida. Three days later, Howe received a letter reporting on the devastation resulting from the attacks. They "destroy everything they meet in their way. They have burnt all the houses on the other side of Newport Ferry, within 4 miles of Sunbury. Our present stand is at Midway Meeting house."[12]

By the morning of 27 November, the small band of Continentals had reached Zubly's Ferry on the Savannah River. Frantically, Howe wrote back to Moultrie in Charleston, informing him of the "dreadful situation" in Georgia and urging Moultrie "to exert yourself to the utmost to hasten up the troops under the command of Col. Huger . . . baggage at this time is not to be considered . . . let the men force on."[13] Howe ordered additional troops to follow Col. Isaac Huger and authorized that the deputy quartermaster general should request from the South Carolina president (the governor) the power to impress wagons and horses. About fifty-five hundred pounds of gunpowder were to be sent, some by land and some by water, as well as five thousand pounds of lead, a surgeon, and all requisite medical supplies.[14]

Before the Continentals under Howe's command could reach Midway Meeting House, Maj. Mark Prevost's forces had turned again southward and were once more out of range. Prevost failed to join up with Colonel Fuser's troops at Sunbury, due to head-wind delays for the water-bound force. Fuser did not arrive in the area until 1 December. Fuser then occupied the town of Sunbury without firing a shot and issued a surrender order to Lt. Col. John McIntosh, whose small Continental and militia army occupied nearby Fort Morris. McIntosh invited the British to "come and take it"; but due to the fact that Prevost's army was well on its way back to Florida, Colonel Fuser refrained from attacking the mud fort. Fuser's forces departed for St. Augustine, but they posted a detachment of Regulars on St. Simons Island to repair the fortification there.[15]

With the immediate threat past, Howe and his small army settled in to devise means for fortifying Sunbury and the Georgia coast. Detachments were ordered to advanced positions of strategic importance along the coast, where they could provide an early alarm of the enemy's advance. The Southern commander detached one galley to take post at Warsaw and another at Tybee, in order to guard the river entrances and provide advance notice of the British entry into the Savannah River. Signals were devised between the galleys and the Continental Army in order to provide immediate communication during an invasion. The general was not insensitive to the plight of Georgia citizens, however; he ordered detachments into the Midway Meeting House community to stand guard while the local residents attempted to salvage belongings not already stolen by the enemy. Not only were the soldiers ordered to scout and patrol for the enemy, but also they were specifically instructed to "take every measure in your power to aid and assist the inhabitants of this state" and to "prevent wicked and designing men from Marauding [*sic*] the Inhabitants & encreasing their distress."[16]

Howe continued to face frustration over the ill-prepared nature of the Georgia defensive structure. The few cannon belonging to the state were unserviceable, and, despite earlier offers by Howe to put them in proper working order, Georgia officials had declined the assistance. As the British closed in on their prey, the cannon remained largely unusable. A deserter from the British transport *Neptune* reported to the Americans on 6 December that a fleet had sailed from Sandy Hook, New York, carrying some five thousand troops for an invasion of Georgia. When the Georgia government heard of the threat, they ignored Howe's presence in the area by dispatching a delegation to Charleston to appeal to General Lincoln, who had just arrived there from the north. Howe concentrated his efforts in the coastal Sunbury area, where he found absolute confusion. He reported that the town was not defensible; and, despite his appeals to the Georgia government for Negro workers and tools, they were not provided. Howe accurately predicted that without immediate assistance "this state will probably be lost."[17]

As days passed and the British fleet did not appear, Georgians resumed an attitude of indifference to the threat of invasion. Howe warned that Savannah was "not defensible for half an hour, should it be attacked the least formidably." These prophetic arguments stirred little concern in the Georgia capital. South Carolina troops, who had rushed south at Howe's call, were dismissed by officials in Savannah and instructed to return home. Georgia did not even have its own militia under arms as the state awaited its fateful hour.[18]

The British fleet began to arrive off Tybee Island on 23 December: Howe reported twenty-six sail at anchor at Cockspur, fourteen miles below Savannah. Howe had at his disposal only approximately six hundred South Carolina and Georgia Continentals commanded by Gen. Isaac Huger and Col. Samuel Elbert, respectively. He ordered these to take up positions in and around Savannah until the movement of the enemy could be more accurately assessed. Very few Georgia militia had been called into service, and on the night of 24 December, with the state obviously doomed, Governor Houstoun agreed to place those few (apparently only slightly over one hundred in number) under Continental command. The state troops were welcomed into the defensive force, and Continental troops were reminded to treat the militia with "Consideration and Respect." Col. George Walton, as militia commander, was to be "respected and obeyed," and contrary conduct was "absolutely forbidden." Even with British troops in the Savannah River, Howe took a brief moment to have his adjutant general issue words of encouragement to the people of Sunbury, promising to rush to their aid at the earliest possible moment if the enemy threat should move in their direction rather than against Savannah.[19]

As the British fleet positioned itself in the Savannah River, Howe repeatedly visited debarkation sites along the river, attempting to determine where the strike would come and where a defense would be possible. He also called a council of war, composed of field officers, to advise him on the course of action to be followed. Despite a four-to-one troop advantage for the British, the council voted to defend Savannah to the last rather than to leave the city to the enemy. As there were a dozen landing places above and below Savannah suit-

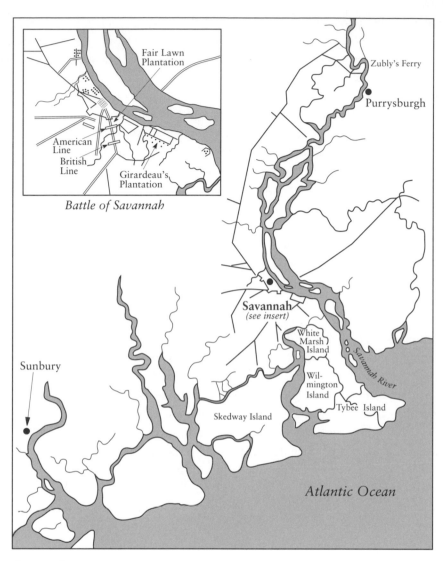

Battle of Savannah

Fair Lawn
Plantation

American
Line

British
Line

Girardeau's
Plantation

Zubly's Ferry

Purrysburgh

Savannah
(see insert)

White
Marsh
Island

Wil-
mington
Island

Savannah River

Tybee Island

Sunbury

Skedway Island

Atlantic Ocean

Savannah, Georgia, Area with Battle of Savannah Insert

able for debarking troops, the Continentals were uncertain of when

or where the landing would take place. Small parties of militia were
posted at each potential landing, with fifty Continentals at Girardeau's Bluff, two miles below the city, as the most probable place
of debarkation. Few concrete measures, however, were possible until
the British made their move.[20]

The British forces were commanded by the talented Lt. Col. Archibald Campbell of the Seventy-first Regiment of Highlander Infantry
and included two battalions of the Seventy-first, Courtland Skinner's
Jersey Volunteers, Oliver DeLancey's New York Provincials, two
battalions of the Wollworth and Wissenbach regiments of Hessian
troops, and a detachment of Royal Artillery. This formidable army
was well trained, experienced, properly equipped, and led by splen-
did officers. Since the British lacked intelligence of the strength and
disposition of the American forces in Savannah, they put ashore on
Wilmington Island on the night of 27 December a company of Highlanders under Sir James Baird. The party was instructed to seize
inhabitants of the area who might provide information that was
needed respecting rebel defenses. Two persons were apprehended
and questioned by Colonel Campbell, who gained "the most satisfactory intelligence concerning the state of matters at Savannah." The
prisoners apparently related the weak plight of the Americans, for
Campbell resolved to land his entire force the next evening at Girardeau's Landing, instead of awaiting Gen. Augustine Prevost's arrival
from Florida.[21]

Girardeau's Landing appeared to be the most logical debarkation
point—and one that offered innumerable problems for the small
band of defenders. The plantation was situated on a forty-foot bluff
two miles below Savannah and approximately three-fourths of a mile
from the river. A long, narrow causeway stretched through broad rice
fields to the riverside landing. From Girardeau's house, a road leading to Savannah passed through Fair Lawn Plantation; and, although
the approach to Fair Lawn appeared at a distance to be wide and
smooth, in fact a rivulet and swamp crossed the road, providing difficult marching for an advancing army. The road toward Savannah
bordered swamps on the left and the river on the right, thus providing
a good natural defensive location at Fair Lawn. Howe, in repeated
visits to the river landing, had found that due to little rain the rice

fields were so hard that troops could move directly across them. Also, the gates were so neglected that it would be impossible to flood the fields; and even if the gates had functioned properly, the prevailing wind was blowing water into the river rather than the fields. Howe felt that if he were to take up a position near the landing his forces could be flanked from both sides, and a position within range of the British warships would be equally foolish. The best prospect, it seemed, was to take position on the high land at Fair Lawn and let the British come to him.[22]

At noon on 28 December, the British fleet began its passage up the Savannah River, but the maneuver came to an abrupt halt at about 4:00 P.M., when several of the transports ran aground, necessitating a postponement of the landing until the next day. At daybreak of 29 December, the river dam in front of the Girardeau Plantation became alive with the scarlet and white uniforms of British troops as Colonel Campbell put ashore his First Division, consisting of all the light-infantry, the Loyalist battalion of New York Volunteers, and the First Battalion of the Seventy-first.[23] The light-infantry moved off immediately down the narrow causeway that led from the landing to the Girardeau house on the bluff. Here a small American picket of some fifty South Carolinians under Capt. J. O. Smith opened a brisk fire on the advancing Highlanders, killing one officer and two men and wounding five others before a swift bayonet charge by the Scots drove the Americans from the house.[24] The action then paused while the British completed the landing of their forces.

General Howe, with a scant force of little more than seven hundred men, took up a position at Fair Lawn Plantation, about one-half of a mile southeast of Savannah. Savannah stood on a sandy bluff on the southern bank of the river. Howe's left flank extended almost to the river and was composed of the Georgia brigade under Colonel Elbert; his center, where he himself commanded, was astride the road that led from Girardeau's Landing to Savannah; his right, composed of the South Carolina regiments under the command of Colonel Huger and Col. William Thompson, extended to a wooded swamp guarded by a small body of Georgia militiamen under Colonel Walton. Howe was deeply concerned over rumors of paths through the swamp and had ordered Walton and other officers to maintain careful surveillance of the swamp. The French engineer Jean Baptiste Ternant, serving as inspector general of the Southern Department, was one of those

dispatched to search for the pass, but he and Georgia militia officers found no trail that would be practical for troops to negotiate. Col. Leonard Marbury later testified that, at Howe's request, he on two occasions reconnoitered the swamp and tried unsuccessfully to find a path that allegedly flanked the American lines. After three failed attempts, his guides declared the area impassable, and the party returned to Fair Lawn after assigning a small detachment of militia to guard the swamp.[25]

The American position—on high ground, with one flank protected by a river and the other by a supposedly impassable swamp—seemed to be a strong one. A council of war convened at about 10:00 A.M. and decided that this position should be held if possible, but that, if the enemy pressed too hard, the troops should retreat through a pass to the east of Savannah. Detailed orders were issued implementing the defensive strategy and providing for the order of retreat if they should be overwhelmed. The reasoning behind this decision seems sound. The exact strength of the British was uncertain but appeared to be about three thousand men. The Americans could muster little more than one-fourth that number to oppose the invaders. Appeals had been dispatched to General Lincoln for reinforcements, and efforts had been made to increase the militia. Howe attempted to encourage the defenders by assuring them that a major relief army from Charleston would arrive within three days. Actually, it was uncertain when Benjamin Lincoln's forces would arrive on the scene or how many troops he could muster.[26] In view of the undetermined intentions of the enemy and the somewhat unlikely prospect of relief, the Americans decided to stand firm in their present position and await developments.

As the debarkation of redcoats progressed at Girardeau's Landing, Colonel Campbell utilized the opportunity to reconnoiter the American lines. Finding them drawn up in position and supported only by a few fieldpieces, he decided upon an immediate advance, thinking "it expedient, having the day before me, to go in quest of the enemy, rather than give them an opportunity of retiring unmolested."[27] Thereupon, leaving a battalion of the Seventy-first and the First Battalion of DeLancey's Provincials to cover the landing place, Colonel Campbell moved his force toward Savannah.

The British advanced down the road toward the center of the American line, with the light-infantry leading, followed by the New York Provincials and the First Battalion of the Seventy-first; the two battalions of Hessians were bringing up the rear.[28] When they reached a point about 1,000 yards in front of the American line, the column halted: the Americans had thrown up an obstacle in the form of a trench approximately 100 yards in front of their own position, while 100 yards in front of the trench a marshy rivulet ran almost parallel to the entire American line. There had been a bridge over this creek, but the rebels had destroyed it. Colonel Campbell, seeing the difficulty posed by the terrain, took advantage of a most fortunate stroke of luck. A local slave had deserted to the British lines and offered to show the attackers the unused and concealed pass that led through the swamp on the British left and opened into the rear of the American right flank. The British commander therefore decided to feint against the American left while sending a flanking force through this pass. The maneuver, if successfully executed, would permit him to strike the Americans at two points simultaneously.[29]

With squealing bagpipes and rolling drums, the First Battalion of the Seventy-first moved forward, and the light-infantry angled off to the right, as if to threaten the American left. When this body reached a point where it was concealed from the American view, it quickly marched to the rear and advanced undetected toward the swamp path, followed by the New York Tories under Colonel Trumbull as support.[30] On Trumbull's left, Colonel Campbell moved his artillery into a concealed position, whence it could be recalled at the opportune time. The Americans replied to these maneuvers with sporadic firing from their field guns but otherwise stood fast. The British light-infantry, under Sir James Baird, rapidly made its way through the pass that had eluded American search parties and burst forth upon the terrified Georgia militia of Colonel Walton. The militia quickly fled in utter panic. This was the signal Colonel Campbell had awaited; out rolled the field guns from their hidden position, as the entire British line moved forward at a trot. General Howe, realizing that his forces were caught in front and flank, immediately ordered a withdrawal.[31] The Americans began an orderly retreat by column toward the pass around Savannah, in accordance with Howe's explicit orders. The center and right of the line moved out first, with the Georgians under Elbert following. Colonel Elbert was concerned

that pressure from the British advance would prevent his troops from reaching the pass, so he ordered his regiment to change from a column formation as ordered by Howe to a file formation, which he felt would provide more protection from bombardment. With the formation change, the Georgia troops were thrown into confusion. Fired on from the rear by the main British column and by the light-infantry, which had begun to press in from the right, the brigade broke and fled through the town. Col. Owen Roberts, with a few field guns, held the advancing forces at bay for General Howe and the South Carolinians to gain the pass as planned, and thus they escaped the jaws of the British pincers. When it was realized, however, that the Georgia regiment was not following as ordered, Roberts proceeded to remove his own forces to safety.[32]

Elbert's Georgia brigade retreated frantically through the streets of Savannah, pausing briefly at the courthouse in their search for safety. When a passerby advised them that they could escape via a foot log across Musgrove Creek, Elbert himself led them toward the mouth of the waterway. Much to their frustration, the log was nowhere to be found; and, although Elbert swam to safety, most of his men who could not swim were trapped. They had no choice but to surrender to the advancing British army.[33]

A South Carolina officer, after successfully retreating from Savannah, penned from Ebenezer, Georgia, a brief note to his father, in which he reported that "we effected a retreat thro' a very heavy fire of the Enemy for near a mile but I believe we have lost but few men kill'd[.] I assure you it is wonderful how so many escaped as the Enemy were six times more than our number. We have been compelled to retreat to this place & are still proceeding towards Augusta the river being so high that we cannot cross over at Zubly's ferry & we being so exceedingly weakened that it is impossible to withstand them should they approach."[34]

Realizing the potential disaster of further contact with the enemy without major reinforcements, Howe led his little band across the Savannah River in search of General Lincoln. In so doing, he in effect was abandoning Georgia to the British.

The total British losses at Savannah were but 2 officers and 5 men killed, 1 officer and 18 men wounded: Campbell reported that 100

Americans were killed. He claimed that 38 American officers, 415 men, 1 stand of colors, 48 cannon, 23 mortars, 94 barrels of powder, a fort with all its stores, the shipping in the harbor, and the capital of Georgia were in his hands by sundown of 29 December 1778.[35]

As the retreat from Savannah was in progress, Howe dispatched orders to Continental forces at Sunbury and at Augusta, ordering the immediate evacuation of both installations. Joseph Lane, who commanded at Sunbury, refused to obey Howe's order and remained to defend the fort in a futile gesture that cost the American army additional troops.[36] Gen. Augustine Prevost captured that American garrison on 6 January 1779. Then he pressed on to Savannah, effected his junction with Colonel Campbell, and assumed command of the united British army. Campbell was dispatched to Augusta to seize that settlement, which he did with little difficulty. Leaving a garrison at Augusta, Campbell established posts at various points in western Georgia. Within six weeks from the time they had landed, the conquest of Georgia was complete and the royal governor was requested to return from England and resume his government.[37]

Robert Howe's place in history is associated primarily with the events of 29 December 1778. Georgians through the centuries have delighted in placing on his shoulders the total responsibility for the loss of Savannah and the "abandonment" of Georgia to the British. Conversely, observers such as William Moultrie subsequently have criticized their fellow officer for attempting to stand against such overwhelming odds. "It is absurd to suppose that 6 or 700 men . . . could stand against 2 or 3000 as good troops as any the British had. . . . Gen. Howe should have retreated." Light Horse Harry Lee, on the other hand, crucified Howe in his memoir for "his negligence betrayed by his Ignorance of the avenues leading to his camp."[38]

It appears likely that Howe, thirsting for victory, succumbed for a variety of reasons to Georgia's demands for a defense of their city. Howe was convinced that Benjamin Lincoln, with a relief expedition, was somewhere south of Charleston. A day or even a few hours could result in the arrival of an army capable of withstanding the invasion. Secondly, the wharf of Savannah was laden with public and private stores, and Georgia residents were frantically removing their possessions to the safety of South Carolina. Howe had issued orders for his quartermaster to remove all public stores, but the unavail-

ability of vessels to transport the goods had complicated the effort.
Every hour of delay before the British arrival was precious.

The defensive position chosen by the Americans was as strong as any available under the circumstances. A location within range of British warships was untenable. If, as Howe later contended, the rice fields at Girardeau's Plantation could not be flooded, the bluff of that plantation was severely flawed as a site to risk his meager force. At Fair Lawn, the American position held defensive promise, especially if the swamp was indeed impassable to an unguided foe. If Colonel Walton's Georgia militia had energetically patrolled the sector during the battle, the British even then could have been caught in a narrow path. The potential for withdrawing successfully from Fair Lawn was good, and, had Georgia's General Elbert followed Howe's orders for moving his regiment by column in quick order behind the South Carolina troops, the retreat may have succeeded with little loss of manpower. Robert Howe was a cautious man when it came to exposing his army, and his contingency plans could have preserved the little army intact with any good fortune at all. Luck, however, was not a commodity available to the North Carolinian.

If, indeed, Howe should bear the blame for the loss of Georgia, that burden should be based primarily on his unwillingness to subvert civil authority to military control. Only by forcing Georgia into a defensive mode through military intimidation could he have prepared the state for an invasion. Instead, he subsequently boasted that he had "warred to preserve civil rights, and pride myself in the thought that I have never violated them."[39] Regardless, Howe's career was now flawed, and the onus of defeat in his only genuine opportunity for glory has remained with him forever.

CHAPTER 8

A NETWORK

OF SPIES

*I*t was at Purrysburgh, South Carolina, on 3 January 1779, that Robert Howe finally met with Benjamin Lincoln and surrendered command of the Southern Department to his long-awaited replacement. Howe proceeded to provide a complete account of his own recent misfortunes, as the two American generals pondered the situation that now faced the Southern states.

Although Howe had been ordered to report to General Washington's headquarters without delay, it would appear that he was in no hurry to depart from Charleston. By early February he was promising to leave "immediately," after having remained behind to give full intelligence to General Lincoln of all he knew. Another month passed without any movement, although he confided to Thomas Sumter that he had suffered from "an inconvenient tho' not very painful disorder in stomach and bowels." By 17 March Howe had signed a power-of-attorney empowering Dr. William Keith, William Bull, Jr., and Alexander Rose to collect all debts due him in Charleston; and on the eighteenth he, along with his military "family," headed north in search of a new command.[1]

Once on the road, the travelers moved rapidly through the Carolinas, despite a series of flooded rivers that delayed their progress. Within seven days, Howe had traveled 155 miles and by 5 April was resting in Halifax, North Carolina. At this stop he found a friend in Brig. Gen. David Mason of Virginia, who was en route south

to join Lincoln's forces. Proceeding northward, he passed through
Baltimore on 23 April and arrived in Philadelphia late in the evening
of the twenty-sixth. Howe had delayed in providing Congress with
a full account of the defeat at Savannah until he could do so personally; therefore, he settled in to recount for Congress the misfortunes
of his Southern command. He hastened to inform General Washington, who had wintered with his army in the vicinity of Middlebrook,
New Jersey, that he would repair to camp as soon as permitted by
Congress, "with whom I have business." [2]

Although the British army had taken possession of Georgia and
obviously was making plans for an attack on Charleston, there were
no indications that the war in the Northern theater had lost any importance for either side. On 30 May 1779 Sir Henry Clinton, with
some six thousand troops, began to move up the Hudson River from
New York City. The target of the British thrust was the strategically
vital Kings Ferry area located between Haverstraw and Peekskill.
The Americans had established fortifications at Stony Point on the
west bank of the Hudson and Verplanck's Point on the east bank in
an effort to protect this key communication link between New England and the Middle states, but the tiny forts were incomplete on
31 May, when the British attacked. After taking possession of the
works, the British proceeded immediately to expand and strengthen
the fortifications. The energy of the British in garrisoning the two
captured forts served notice to the American command that their
enemy planned to remain in control of the lower Hudson valley and
the forts that dominated the Hudson from Manhattan to the Tappan
Zee.[3]

With the British implanted on the Hudson, General Washington
pulled his forces into the Highlands area around West Point, setting up headquarters at New Windsor on the west bank of the river.
Gen. William Heath was ordered out of Boston to join the main
army; and, immediately upon his arrival at New Windsor on 21 June,
Heath and Washington toured the unfinished defenses at West Point
with a view toward strengthening the works there against a possible
British attack. On the twenty-third, Heath was given command of all
American forces to the east of the Hudson.

While the pace of activity along the Hudson had quickened mark-

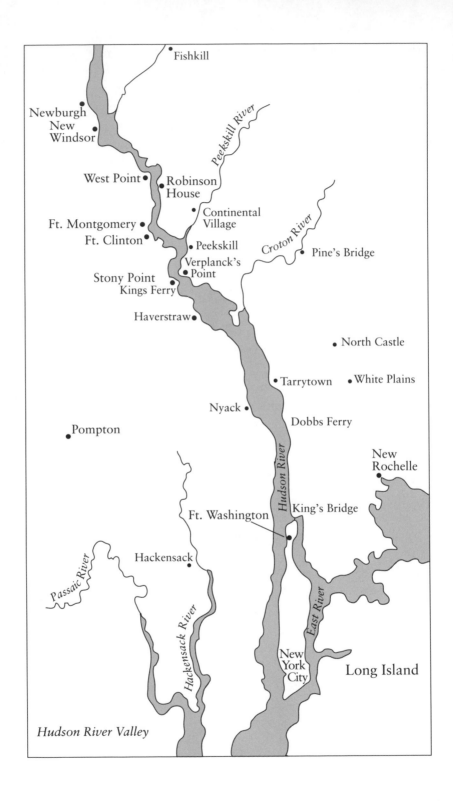

Fishkill

Newburgh
New
Windsor

Peekskill River

West Point • Robinson
House

• Continental
Village

Ft. Montgomery •
Ft. Clinton •

Croton River

• Peekskill

• Pine's Bridge

Verplanck's
Point

Stony Point
Kings Ferry

Haverstraw•

• North Castle

• Tarrytown • White Plains

Nyack •

Dobbs Ferry

Pompton •

Hudson River

New
Rochelle

Ft. Washington

King's Bridge

Passaic River

Hackensack •

Hackensack River

East River

New
York
City

Long Island

Hudson River Valley

edly during May and June, Robert Howe found himself helplessly

sidelined due to a painful accident that left him "maimed, Bruised, wounded, hurt and in torture." [4] Washington left the ailing general behind in Middlebrook when he broke camp, and there he remained for the entire month of June. By 2 July Howe had replaced his crutches with two sticks, with which he was able to "hobble about." Despite his reduced maneuverability, he was appointed to the command of troops defending the western Connecticut border area and headquartered in Ridgefield, Connecticut. This area was vulnerable to enemy raiding parties from Long Island as well as to direct attacks from British forces along the lower Hudson. For the next two weeks, Howe undertook to make contacts within the state governments of Connecticut and New York, as well as with the shadowy network of private sources that would provide him with intelligence on British strengths and movements around New York City. [5]

The expansion of the Kings Ferry fortifications posed a serious threat to American defenses along the river. For weeks General Washington and his officers monitored the British progress from nearby hills, where their spyglasses provided a clear view of the work. Enemy control of this vital waterway could sever New England from the Middle states and thus bring a disastrous end to the quest for independence. Clinton returned to New York, leaving a garrison at the forts that appeared vulnerable to attack. After wrestling with the possibility of attacking both forts simultaneously, Washington decided upon a surprise night assault on the weaker west-bank installation. He ordered the impetuous Gen. Anthony Wayne to command an expedition against Stony Point. A corps of twelve hundred light-infantry were secretly assembled and trained in hand-to-hand combat. On the night of 15 July, the detachment, armed with unloaded muskets and fixed bayonets, was led to the bank of the river, where concealed boats and muffled oars lay waiting for their adventure. Not until the morning of the sixteenth did word arrive at Washington's headquarters that the fort and garrison had been taken. The British were unaware of the American presence until they stormed the works at bayonet point. [6]

With Stony Point under American control, Washington quickly ordered two brigades, commanded by Brigadier Generals John Nixon and John Paterson, to march immediately from West Point toward the

Continental Village. Since General Heath was on a reconnaissance mission into Connecticut, Robert Howe was ordered to proceed without delay to take command of the American army as it marched south. Once he intercepted the troops at the Continental Village, he was to move the forces through Peekskill and take up positions above Verplanck's Point. The British fortification was to be thoroughly reconnoitered, and, if possible, batteries were to be erected that would threaten the enemy. Howe was instructed to spread alarm among the enemy in anticipation that they might abandon the post and retreat downriver. However, he was cautioned against endangering his forces, and Heath with his army was recalled from Connecticut to form a junction with Howe's forces as quickly as possible.[7]

General Howe soon discovered that fortune smiled no brighter at Verplanck's Point than at Savannah. Upon assuming command late on 16 July, he discovered that Maj. Gen. Alexander McDougall at West Point had failed to dispatch cannon or ammunition for bombardment, entrenching tools for erecting batteries, provisions for subsisting the men, or horsemen for communications. Howe hastily prepared an order that the missing fieldpieces be rushed forward from Fishkill and that the necessary ammunition for the artillery be ferried across the river from West Point without delay. He then appealed to Heath for horsemen and to Washington for the logistical support that was lacking. Verplanck's Point appeared to be well-constructed and capable of considerable defense. The British gave no indication that they intended to retreat or surrender as a result of the bombardment that Howe's forces finally were able to muster. As the American army proceeded with their attack, intelligence reached Howe that Sir Henry Clinton and a substantial British force were advancing up the Hudson to relieve the fort. With land and water troops threatening to sever the American route of escape, Howe at 4:00 P.M. on the eighteenth finally ordered a hurried withdrawal back toward the Highlands. He was joined by General Heath at Peekskill, and the army proceeded to move into the Highlands. Washington feared a British advance on the strategically critical positions around West Point and favored a defensive position there rather than at Peekskill. With Verplanck's Point still in British possession and the enemy approaching, Wayne was required to strip Stony Point and abandon it to the British.[8]

Although some contemporaries placed the blame with Howe for "finding many supposed obstructions," it is apparent that he acted judiciously and as effectively as the circumstances would permit. General Heath, reporting to Washington, commented that "Major General Howe was very fortunate in making his retreat at the instant he did, had he remained I think that he would have been Burgoyned, His Intelligence being good he escaped." Washington, in his report to Congress on 21 July, commented that the failure to take Verplanck's Point was due to several of his own dispatches going astray and to accidental delays that prevented the artillery and entrenching tools from reaching their destination. Whatever the cause of the American failure at Verplanck's Point, it did not dilute General Washington's confidence in the North Carolinian. As historian Douglas Southall Freeman pointed out, Howe "had and doubtlessly deserved the full confidence of Washington."[9]

With the American army positioned in the gorge and Highlands surrounding West Point, the British army decided against an attack on the vital Highlands position and on 20 July began to return down the Hudson to Dobbs Ferry. The fortifications at Stony Point and Verplanck's Point were left adequately garrisoned to discourage another American strike, but for now the Highlands appeared to be safe.

During July, while attention was riveted on the Hudson River defenses, Clinton systematically ravaged the countryside north of Long Island into Connecticut, utilizing Governor William Tryon's Tory forces and British troops under Brig. Gen. George Garth. New Haven was plundered; and Fairfield, Green's Farm, and Norwalk were put to the torch. These raids, and the incessant rumors of enemy action in the border areas between the American army and the British stronghold in New York City, required a high measure of vigilance on the part of the revolutionaries. In an effort to improve organizational structure, General Washington on 20 July divided his army into a Right Wing—to consist of divisions from Virginia, Maryland, and Pennsylvania under the command of Gen. Israel Putnam—and a Left Wing—to be commanded by General Heath. The Left Wing was to consist of two Connecticut brigades, Massachusetts brigades under Generals John Nixon and John Glover, cavalry regiments under Colonels Stephen Moylan and Elisha Sheldon, and an independent corps commanded by Marquis de LaRouerie Tuffin (Colonel

Armand). Robert Howe was appointed as division commander for Nixon's and Glover's brigades, along with the cavalry and the independent corps; and Gen. Alexander McDougall was assigned to command the garrison at West Point. Howe was ordered by Washington to establish his headquarters at Ridgefield, Connecticut, so he could "cover the country and prevent as far as possible the depredations of the enemy." Washington, however, cautioned Howe against risking the corps under his command. "Great vigilance and care will be necessary on your part . . . you should use every precaution to have timely notice." [10]

Upon arrival at Ridgefield early on 31 July 1779, Robert Howe tackled the new challenge without a moment's hesitation. After breakfast, he set out to examine advance posts along Long Island Sound in an effort to better acquaint himself with the countryside and to improve his perspective of the current situation. The primary object of the American presence in the district was to gather intelligence concerning British movements, to guard against raids such as the Connecticut coast raid during July, and to harass the enemy at every opportunity. Howe pledged "to impress the enemy with that alarm and terror they so delight to spread," [11] and indications are that there was no delay in pursuing this course of action.

The network of spies operating along Long Island Sound provided Howe and the American army with an abundance of information on British strengths, movements, internal crises, and possible intentions. Naturally, the American command was wary of their contacts and thus relied on a preponderance of intelligence from varied sources that would confirm each other. Rarely did the Americans act on information furnished by any one of the faceless and often nameless individuals with whom they dealt; instead they pitted one against another before acting upon a report. Both Howe and Washington depended upon the counterspy Elijah Hunter, whom neither of them trusted. Washington feared that any man who was in the pay of both armies would be swayed to favor the one who could produce the richest reward, and there was no question but that the British could provide the greater remuneration. Washington was careful to furnish Hunter with inflated troop-return figures and cautioned Howe on numerous occasions to provide to the notorious double agent and his cast of informants only information that could not compromise the

American positions. Hunter and other informants made it possible

for the American armies hovering around the British stronghold in New York to check efforts of the enemy to project its control far into the countryside or to inflict a deadly blow upon the rebel forces.[12]

The secrecy required for the covert operations of Washington, Howe, and the other general officers left the uninformed coastal guards convinced that widespread smuggling was taking place with the sanctions of the high command. One such Connecticut militia officer reported that "there is [*sic*] Boats passing & repassing to & from Long Island. . . . There is Capt. John Conkling a Refugee from the Island he has got a pass from General Howe to go to Long Island when he pleases & he carries who he pleases in his Boat & leaves them on the Island at one time & fetches them off the next & sometimes they come off one way & some another." General Samuel Parsons subsequently took the officer to task for intimating that boats under his and Howe's control were involved in illicit trade, despite the officer's charge that "their transactions are so secret that no man could find them out." [13]

A war of harassment commanded the scene during the summer and fall of 1779. While the Americans cautiously observed their enemy across Long Island Sound and along the Hudson, both sides sought to strike minor blows through raids, ambuscades, and other surreptitious enterprises. Operating out of Ridgefield, Lower Salem, Bedford, and other communities along the lower Connecticut–New York border, Howe assigned detachments of horse troops to constantly patrol the enemy frontier north of the sound. On 6 August troops of Howe's division under the direct command of Lt. Col. Anthony W. White conducted a raid within enemy lines beyond Delaney Mill near Morrissania. The successful raiders brought off fifteen prisoners, three Negroes, thirty horses, and a quantity of arms and accoutrements.[14] Shortly thereafter, General Parsons sought and received permission from General Washington to attack the enemy post at Lloyd's Neck on Long Island. Howe was instructed to advise Parsons on the enterprise and to provide assistance and expertise if he considered the project worthwhile. After several days, the ever-cautious commander in chief recalled a detachment scheduled to assist in the affair, and on 15 August he instructed Howe to lay the enterprise aside entirely if it had not been undertaken at that point.

It was not until the following month, on 5 September, that the raid on Lloyd's Neck was finally undertaken. Maj. Benjamin Tallmadge, commanding 150 dismounted dragoons of Howe's division, slipped across the sound from Shippan Point, Connecticut, and surprised 500 Tories. Not a single man was lost in the undertaking.[15]

An enterprise of Howe's that never came to fruition held his attention for several weeks during August and early September. A garrison of British troops occupied and guarded King's Bridge, across Spuyten Duyvil Creek, which separated Manhattan Island from the Bronx. The bridge was strategically important, and a raid against the troops there would provide another in a series of "insults and injuries" to the British outposts. Detachments from Howe's command observed enemy movements around King's Bridge with great interest, and, when the enemy withdrew forces from north of the bridge in mid-August, Howe began to ease his forces closer to the prey. Howe desired to drift closer to the bridge on the pretext of foraging, but Washington suggested double-mounting troops on horses, if sufficient horses were available, and using a night march to improve the element of surprise. By 28 August Howe still had not undertaken the enterprise, and the arrival in New York of the British admiral Marriot Arbuthnot—with several thousand men—brought an end to the prospective adventure.[16]

The uncertainty of British intentions, and the anticipated arrival of Count d'Estaing and his French fleet, resulted in widespread speculative strategic planning during September and October. The arrival of the British fleet presumably provided Clinton with the military might to confront Washington on the Hudson or to assault American divisions that were vulnerable to attack. Throughout the summer, the British had suffered repeated insults from American raids, including an attack on Paulus Hook in New Jersey by Maj. Henry Lee; and it was feared that the British reinforcements would allow revenge for the British. Washington was particularly concerned about the proximity of Howe to the enemy, and he cautioned his division commander that "the enemy will feel themselves much hurt, at the repeated instances of disgrace their arms have lately met with, and will most assuredly attempt to bury it in some stroke of retaliation, on such parts of the army as is [*sic*] most accessible, Than which, none is more so, than that under your command, because every preparation for it can be concealed, and the Troops are on the spot, ready to operate at a moments warning."[17] In anticipation of a British thrust, Washington began to recall various regiments to rejoin the main army in the Highlands around West Point. Although he could not spare Howe's division from the lower reaches of the state, he ordered him to end the King's Bridge scheme and "to incline a little this way," where he would be more accessible in the event of a major attack.

In early September, rumors began to circulate that Count d'Estaing was en route to New York and would arrive at Sandy Hook at any moment. General Washington envisioned a great French-American campaign in which the British would be trapped in New York, the French would be in control of the harbor and the river, and the American army would command the mainland. After preparing a communication to the French ally, Washington began to position the various elements of his command in order to take advantage of the situation. Concluding that in the event of a French attack the British would be forced to abandon the Kings Ferry fortifications and retreat by land toward New York City, he ordered Howe into a strategic location at Pine's Bridge on the Croton River, where he could intercept the two thousand troops in their flight.

Howe's division arrived at Pine's Bridge about noon on 10 September, as ordered by the commander in chief; but for logistical reasons he moved his troops to a site at nearby North Castle Church, where he awaited the arrival of General Nixon's brigade. The scheme as perceived by Washington required Howe's division to station itself near Pine's Bridge until the British were forced to evacuate Kings Ferry. Howe would then move swiftly to gain the new bridge at the mouth of Croton and thus intercept the British retreat. By 18 September Washington realized that the rumors were without substance and that the joint attack would not materialize. He therefore instructed Howe that the French fleet was not coming and that he could return with his men to Lower Salem to resume the tactics of the past several months.[18]

The whereabouts of Count d'Estaing and the French fleet was a matter of considerable interest not only to Washington but also to the Continental Congress and the British command in New York City. While the French, with General Lincoln, were actually coordinating an attack on Savannah, Georgia, the British were faced with a serious dilemma. The French threat to the British island of Jamaica had led Clinton to order Lord Charles Cornwallis and several thousand men to prepare an expedition to relieve that island. News of d'Estaing's presence off the American coast, however, caused a delay in these plans while the British attempted to ascertain the greatest danger. The fear of a French attack also forced Clinton to call in troops from outlying posts in Rhode Island and the Hudson River valley, and the prospect of a British withdrawal from Stony Point and Verplanck's Point tantalized the American command no end. The fear of the French fleet spread through New York, spurring both panic among the Tories and frantic defensive measures by the British. According to one of Howe's spies, "Confusion & distress . . . prevails in N. York, the Tories exclaim they are going to be deserted, one Fourth of the Troops are Sick. The arrival of the French fleet is publickly talked of, momentarily expected, & very much dreaded. Fortifications are Building on Long Island, & on other places."[19] As the Americans watched eagerly from nearby observation sites, the British made what appeared to be plans to remove from the Kings Ferry fortifications. General Howe, who was operating in the Bedford area during late September and early October, received regular reports on the situation, but it was not until 21 October that the forts were actually abandoned by the enemy.

Although Washington by 18 September had dismissed the d'Estaing visit as mere fantasy, the Continental Congress was unwilling to despair of hope. Even after it was established that the French were attacking Savannah, Congress envisioned them moving up the coast after a successful assault in Georgia; in keeping with this scenario, they ordered Washington in October to prepare for a joint attack upon New York. On 4 October the commander in chief began once again to reposition the elements of his army as they had been in early September. Howe was instructed to return to Pine's Bridge with his division in anticipation of intercepting the Kings Ferry garrison if they were forced into a ground retreat. In actuality, the French were unsuccessful at Savannah, whereupon they returned to the West Indies rather than sailing north to New York. General Washington and his command waited for an ally that never came, and when the British did evacuate Kings Ferry on 21 October, it was by water rather than through the forced march desired by the Americans.[20]

Even with the British clear of Kings Ferry, their intentions and the danger they posed to the American army represented a major concern. The transports carrying the enemy garrison dropped anchor off the mouth of Croton River, and speculation spread that they yet planned an offensive action against the American front. Howe's division, in position at Pine's Bridge, constituted the front line of defense; and General Heath hurriedly dispatched a detachment of five hundred men to reinforce Howe's flank. The North Carolinian appeared anxious for a fight. He confided to his colleague, "They may still make me a visit; should they do so, may Heaven Enable me to give a good account of them." [21] About noon of the following day, however, the enemy transports came to sail with the ebb of the tide and beat down the river against the wind. They soon disappeared from view, and the threat for 1779 had come to an end.

On 27 October Howe was ordered to move his forces to Peekskill to form a junction with General Heath's Connecticut division. Fatigue parties were assigned to begin work on the repair of the Verplanck's Point and Stony Point installations, as the Americans began to make plans for a winter encampment. By mid-November the results of the Savannah siege were well known at Washington's headquarters, and the reality of d'Estaing's failure to appear was official. Howe's Massachusetts brigades were assigned to winter quarters in the Highlands, and Washington stretched his army from Monmouth, New Jersey, to Danbury, Connecticut. Provisions had been almost nonexistent for some weeks; and in anticipation of a meager winter all cattle, horses, and wagons not absolutely necessary to the post were ordered sent to the quartermaster general, Udny Hay, at Fishkill. Once the troops actually moved into their winter huts, all tents likewise were to be packed and forwarded to Hay, where they could be stored for the winter.[22]

Although 1779 was not a year of noteworthy engagements, it was a period of watchfulness. The year was typified by small encounters and the promise of potentially great events. The regular exchanges between Washington and Howe reflect the cautious nature of both men: they sought victory without the risk of crippling defeat. Washington repeatedly reminded his division commander to avoid making his forces vulnerable to attack and at the same time assured him that he had every confidence that his warnings were unnecessary. Howe revealed his own philosophy when he wrote: "I am from nature devoted to enterprise, but rashness is my utter aversion, all conformable to the first I shall do, all dictated by the latter renounce." [23]

The friendly banter between the general officers as they performed their respective duties is revealing of their dispositions, and their personal humanity is refreshing. On 3 August 1779 Howe wrote to General Heath, reporting on his fatigue from recruiting efforts in which he had been involved. "Had I not had a backside of brass or rather buff leather, I should have had half of it off with half the exercise," he joked to Heath. He closed by admonishing his friend to "keep yourself chaste if possible as I do." Since Howe was continentally celebrated as the most notorious womanizer imaginable, it shows Heath's humor when he thanked Howe for his kind advice and assured him that he would endeavor to do it. Several days later, Heath lamented his inability to be near to Howe, "that I might enjoy the Sociability of your Company, and with you partake of those good things with which I know you are surrounded." [24]

Even more entertaining is an exchange between the two during late September, while Heath was ill with a prolonged disorder. Howe wrote to recommend "a very smart application of Port wine & if you have it not of your own that you quarter yourself upon the general [Washington] & cost him at least two Bottle per Diem. I have known this wine course pursued by others (especially sober fellows like you) with great success, who by a small degree of tipsyness have lost the Maidenhead of their sobriety, and their Ague together; don't apply this to me, for my Virginity in the wine way has long since been gone, & I never had the Ague in my life." Howe added a postscript to the letter: "Were you an Arch Bishop instead of a Deacon I would reiterate the same application for to be Drunk is better than to be Sick." [25]

As the troops settled into their winter encampment, one major responsibility that Robert Howe found neither pleasant nor easily avoidable rested on his shoulders. During the early spring of 1779, repeated petitions were thrust upon Congress and General Washington demanding an investigation of Maj. Gen. Benedict Arnold's conduct as military commander of Philadelphia between June 1778 and March 1779. By May Washington had organized a general court-martial to hear the charges and chose Howe as president of the proceedings, "for particular reasons." Although Washington did not

explain his reasoning, it is logical that Howe's problems with civilian
politicians in South Carolina and Georgia would have equipped him
to understand Arnold's problems in Philadelphia. Also, the fact that
the North Carolinian was a newcomer to the area would minimize
his emotional involvement in the issues in question.[26]

The initial session convened at Howe's headquarters in Middleton,
Connecticut, on 1 June. Due to Howe's injuries at the time, the proceedings had been moved from the court-martial room. It was at this
juncture that Sir Henry Clinton invaded the Hudson River, capturing
Stony Point and Verplanck's Point and forcing an adjournment of the
court-martial trial until a more propitious time. The uncertainties of
the summer campaign left no time for courtroom deliberation; therefore, despite Arnold's repeated protests, December arrived without a
resolution of the issue. It would appear that Howe was less than en-
thusiastic over his role in the events: he cautioned Washington that he
was needed in command of his troops on the Hudson. Washington instructed Howe that the court-martial would resume at Morristown,
New Jersey, on 20 December and that Howe, as president, "will not
fail to attend." Even with orders as precise as these, Howe harbored
a hope that the commander in chief would countermand the order
and thus leave him free to observe British movements in New York.[27]

The court that finally convened at Norris's Tavern in Morristown
on 23 December was drastically different from the June assem-
blage. Of the original jury, only Howe, Brig. Gen. Henry Knox, and
Col. David Hall remained. Brigadier Generals William Smallwood,
William Woodford, and William Irvine; Colonels James Wood,
Charles Harrison, Stephen Moylan, and Richard Butler; and Lieutenant Colonels John Popkin, Charles Simms, and Josiah Harmar had
been replaced by Brigadier Generals William Maxwell and Mordecai
Gist and Colonels Elias Dayton, Philip Burr Bradley, Philip Van Cort-
landt, Henry Sherburne, Henry Jackson, and Oliver Spencer. The
charges against Arnold fell into four primary categories: that Arnold
had allowed vessels that had sailed from an enemy port to enter
Philadelphia; that he had ordered all shops and stores in Philadelphia
closed immediately upon his arrival in the city yet had proceeded to
make purchases while the shops were closed; that he had ordered
menial offices upon the son of a freeman of the state (i.e., a mili-

tia sergeant); and that he had ordered wagons under contract to the government to haul private cargo for his own personal gain.[28]

The testimony droned on during the final week of December, and by 4 January it appeared that all available evidence had been heard. During the proceedings, Howe continued to receive communiqués from his spies concerning British movements in New York, and he therefore promptly informed Washington of the pending embarkation of Lord Cornwallis and his troops for Georgia and South Carolina—where an attack on Charleston was being planned. The court did not meet between the fourth and nineteenth of January, thus prompting Washington to order a resumption of the proceedings. Arnold thereupon continued to argue his case effectively, in the absence of concrete evidence from the prosecution. By 22 January all arguments had been heard and the court adjourned to consider the evidence. On 26 January Howe and his colleagues rendered their decision. In allowing a vessel from an enemy port into a U.S. port, Arnold had breached the articles of war; he was acquitted on the second and third charges; and on the fourth charge it was the opinion of the court that Arnold had intended to pay for the private use of the wagons used to move goods out of the enemy's path, but his action was "imprudent and improper." Much to Arnold's chagrin, the court sentenced him to receive a formal reprimand from the commander in chief.[29]

Washington considered Arnold among his finest officers, and, although he complied with the sentence, a milder reprimand is difficult to imagine. It was very carefully couched not to give offense and was coupled with the promise of choice commands in the future.

> Our profession is the chastest of all. Even the shadow of a fault tarnishes the lustre of our finest achievements. The least inadvertence may rob us of the publick favor, so hard to be acquired. I reprimand you for having forgotten, that, in proportion as you have rendered yourself formidable to our enemies, you should have been guarded and temperate in your deportment towards your fellow citizens: exhibit anew those noble qualities which have placed you on the list of our most valued commanders. I will, myself furnish you as far as it may be in my power, with opportunities of regaining the esteem of your country.[30]

CHAPTER 9

THE HIGHLANDS

COMMAND

*A*lthough the unfortunate winter that General Washington and his forces faced at Valley Forge, Pennsylvania, in 1777–78 is ordinarily remembered by historians as the zenith of sacrifice and privation suffered by the revolutionary army, there is little doubt that the suffering experienced in the Hudson River cantonment in 1780 was comparable. By late November 1779, as the troops were moved to winter quarters, numerous soldiers marched barefoot over hard, frozen ground, and predictions of food shortages proved well founded. As early as mid-December, troops in the Highlands had done without bread for up to ten days. The frozen ground of November and December gave way to record-breaking snows; a three-day storm commenced on Sunday, 2 January, dropped four to six feet in New Jersey, and accumulated to a depth along the Hudson never previously known. The river froze solid all the way to the ocean, and subzero temperatures and howling winds paralyzed the American cantonment. "No man could endure its violence many minutes without danger to his life . . . and some of the soldiers were actually covered while in their tents and buried like sheep under the snow."[1] The intense cold continued through the month, resulting in numerous cases of frostbite and at least one fatality from freezing.

To compound the miseries of inadequate food and clothing, a four-foot snowfall, and a frozen Hudson River, fire struck the fortifications repeatedly between 9 January and 1 February. The first conflagration was discovered under the rampart of the north redoubt and threatened the entire structure. The timbers of the rampart were so strongly dovetailed and strapped that firefighters appeared to work in vain to reach the fire. Fatigue detachments from West Point joined the redoubt garrison and worked frantically through the night to remove ammunition and one hundred barrels of salted provisions while attempting to extinguish the blaze. A second fire on 26 January destroyed the quartermaster's barrack on the West Point plain, with the loss of 6 marquees, 26 horseman's tents, 80 common tents, 900 knapsacks, 250 narrow axes, and a variety of other articles. Six days later, fire broke out once again in the north redoubt and spread among the joints of the large timbers, where it raged for two days. Only unflagging effort prevented the complete destruction of the redoubt. It was severely damaged, however, thus weakening the Hudson defenses and leaving West Point obviously vulnerable to enemy attack.[2]

Gen. William Heath, then in command of the Hudson River defenses, anxiously awaited the return of his comrade-in-arms, Robert Howe, who was presiding over the Arnold court-martial in Morristown. Heath, who complained that his health was damaged by a recent illness, was to be replaced by Howe as soon as the latter could report for duty. Heath hoped to depart for Boston by 1 February, assuming that the North Carolinian could arrive in the Highlands by that date.

It was not until 21 February, however, that General Howe actually assumed command of the Highlands defenses. He moved into the Beverly Robinson house, which served as headquarters for the West Point command, and began to plan for work necessary to overcome the weakened condition of the installation. Before departing, Heath informed Howe of the limited supply of provisions and the unfinished condition of the works. The north redoubt, severely damaged by the recent fires, required substantial rebuilding, and the defensive works at Stony Point and Verplanck's Point awaited improved weather before work could resume. Howe immediately requested teams of horses from New York governor George Clinton so that work on the Highlands forts could commence, but the lack of provisions for the animals further compounded the immediate problem.[3]

The challenge faced by Howe in this command was multifaceted

*Beverly Robinson House, headquarters for commanders of West Point
(Courtesy of the New-York Historical Society)*

and virtually overwhelming. West Point constituted the most critical fortress in the American defensive structure. General Washington considered it to be "the key which locks the communication between the Eastern and Southern states; and of all the posts in the United States, this is the most important."[4] West Point must be made strong and defended above all other considerations. By 1 March Howe had ordered workers to begin at West Point; and in the weeks that followed he scheduled crews daily for the north redoubt, West Point, and the Kings Ferry defenses. Throughout April he continued to push for completion of the works, urging Gen. John Paterson to utilize every available man on the project. All public boats, most of which had not been secured during the winter due to inclement weather, were counted and repaired; and ships' carpenters, boat builders, and caulkers were drawn from each brigade to proceed with the work.[5]

An important aspect of the Highlands defenses rested with the maintenance of a giant chain that the Americans stretched from West Point across the river to block passage by British ships. During March, fatigue crews under the supervision of Col. Thaddeus Kosciuszko labored to repair the chain and to float it at the river's surface. As early as 1776, the use of a great chain had been recommended, and by the spring of 1777 one was floated on log booms into position between Fort Montgomery and Anthony's Nose. When the British successfully attacked forts Clinton and Montgomery in October, the chain was severed and British ships were once more free to sail into the Highlands' gorges. Once West Point was selected as the cornerstone of the Hudson River defenses, it was agreed that a chain should be forged to span the river from the fort to Constitution Island. It was this chain, first contracted for in 1778 and stored during the winters when the river froze, that Howe's forces labored to repair and refloat during the spring of 1780. After one attempt failed, the chain was finally floated on 5 April, and the Americans breathed a sigh of relief for the defense of their fortress.[6]

Discipline apparently had been lax during the previous command, causing Howe to take a stern and unyielding stand on enforcement. Anyone found carrying fire in a careless manner in or near the works, barracks, or other buildings was to be immediately confined; and anyone found guilty of arson was assured of an "instant death." Although Howe was fond of wine himself, he warned that drunkenness within the command would not be tolerated. General Washington expressed support for Howe's strong disciplinary stand, agreeing that it was too often overlooked by the commanders. Howe was aided in the training and discipline of the West Point troops by the Prussian general Baron Frederick William von Steuben, appointed by Washington to assist the North Carolinian in an unofficial capacity. Steuben initiated a training regimen that relieved recruits from guard and fatigue duty so that they could concentrate on military exercises. The troops were required to participate in training exercises for one-and-a-half hours each morning at reveille and for an equal time in the evening at sunset. For the first six days, recruits concentrated on proper military posture, dress, and march, after which they were trained in the use of weapons. Howe apparently accepted and appreciated Steuben's talents, for he subsequently wrote to the Prussian that "your children for so I call our army . . . universally think and speak of you with love, pleasure, gratitude and applause."[7]

Even more threatening to the army's existence was the ever-present problem of desertion and treason. Howe had never displayed the slightest compassion for soldiers guilty of what he termed "the greatest crime a soldier can be guilty of," and on more than one occasion

during 1780 he upheld the sentence of death in such cases. After
watching one such public execution on 26 April, he warned that in committing desertion "every moral sanction, is violated. The cause of freedom, the darling rights and privileges . . . are basely relinquished and betrayed." Howe further called on the troops "to avoid a crime so detestable in its nature and so fatal in its consequences." [8]

Human emotion and the personal rancor of desperation were played out among the personnel stationed in the Highlands fortress. An affair of honor between Nathaniel Stone and Capt. Luke Hitchcock, which took place at West Point early in 1780, undoubtedly reminded General Howe of earlier personal confrontations in which he had been directly involved. There had been bad relations between Stone and Hitchcock, but the problem supposedly was resolved prior to Hitchcock's departure southward. Upon his return to West Point, however, he demanded to know if Stone, whom he called a "scondrel," had been talking about him. Such an aspersion forced Stone to demand satisfaction, and Hitchcock was killed in the ensuing duel. Stone was indicted for murder by the state of New York. A petition signed by more than 255 officers was addressed to the state legislature, begging for Stone's pardon. Not only is Robert Howe's signature first among the petitioners, but the wording sounds typically like his. Other general officers signing the petition included Rufus Putnam, Edward Hand, Horatio Gates, and Henry Knox.[9]

As the men labored to complete the defenses in the Highlands, Howe recognized a potential labor force that was going completely untouched. Throughout the area, there was a sizeable group of men who would not participate in the militia yet would undoubtedly befriend the British if they should gain the upper hand. Howe proposed to Governor Clinton that these "vermin" be turned out by the militia and forced to work on the fortifications that so desperately needed manpower. The governor was sympathetic, but he assured the general that state law prohibited that they be called out except as part of the regular militia.[10]

It would appear that the greatest threat to the American army during the spring of 1780 came not from the British army but from the fiscal crisis that virtually enveloped the civil and military structure. The Continental Congress had no power of taxation and therefore depended upon revenue from the states to maintain the framework of government and the machinery of war. Congress, from its very inception, had resorted to the printing of paper currency. In theory, the states were expected to levy taxes that would bring revenue into the Continental government, which in turn would allow redemption of the currency after a period of circulation. In reality, this theory was unworkable, and the excessive paper triggered a spiraling inflation that threatened to wreck the infant country and bring an end to the revolutionary effort.[11]

Overwhelmed by a worthless currency and a public that grew weary of accepting unsupported paper, Congress grappled frantically for a solution. Ultimately, Congress was forced to return responsibility to the individual states for feeding, clothing, and paying their own regiments. In the meantime, by spring 1780 farmers, victualers, and teamsters all refused to accept the Continental indebtedness in payment for goods and services. The army was left without food, due not to a shortage of food products but to the lack of acceptable money to make the purchases. In a letter of 28 April, General Washington assured Howe that the Highlands army was not unique in its suffering. "It is lamentable that we should be obliged to experience such distresses as we do every where. Those we feel here are not inferior to yours, we are constantly on the point of starving for want of provisions and forage. A deficiency of Money is the cause. . . . We are at a most delicate crisis. I dread with you the consequences."[12]

Between April and July, the Highlands forces were almost void of supplies, and Robert Howe, as commander of the department, resorted to every device to secure provisions for his troops. He repeatedly dispatched impassioned appeals and personal emissaries to Governor Clinton of New York and Governor Jonathan Trumbull of Connecticut, while using General Heath as his contact in Massachusetts. He reminded Governor Trumbull of the importance of West Point to his state—and to the survival of the nation—and warned that it would fall without relief. Howe's commissaries even had the audacity to waylay a herd of cattle that was en route to General Washington's headquarters in Morristown, an action that brought a quick and stern reaction from the commander in chief.[13] The need for rum for the troops was recognized as an integral part of both diet and morale, and when funds were not available to purchase the needed "draught" Howe requested permission from Governor Clin-

ton to allow him to seize the liquor. "Experience has taught me, &
you cannot but know it also, that when men have been stinted in
the Rations they have a just claim to, the only quieting Draught was
the serving out to them of a small Portion of Rum." When Clinton
informed Howe that no legal way existed to seize the rum ("It must
be purchased"), Howe ordered his deputy quartermaster, Udny Hay,
to seize it anyway. Some 6,933 gallons were involved, and as late as
October Howe was still appealing to Congress to pay for the supply.[14]

The crisis was such that the purchasing department informed
Howe that they had no money and that they were unable to make
contracts or send forward the stock of supplies previously purchased.
Howe in turn ordered his quartermaster agents to contract for supplies for hard money to be paid by 1 October; and, if specie were
not available by then, the government would pay in paper at the
exchange rate for gold and silver at the time of payment. Hay was
even instructed to use government property as security against payment. Some supplies were procured in this fashion, which created
additional problems for Howe in the fall, when the notes began to
come due.[15]

Despite the efforts of all concerned, the supply of rations continued
to diminish at the Highlands post. By 17 May West Point was reduced to a six-day supply of provisions and could "not expect more
until they receive cash." Even when the Connecticut Assembly in late
May approved an expenditure of £2,500 to transport salted provisions from that state to West Point, it was learned that the teamsters
would not move the food for less than £5,000. As the situation deteriorated, Howe was forced to use the reserve food supply stored in
the redoubts in case of enemy attack. At the joint urging of Howe
and General Washington, a committee of Congress appealed to the
Connecticut governor for relief. It took the immediate threat of an
enemy attack to loosen the purse strings of the states and to convince the various governors of the threat to their provincial safety.
As Howe intoned on 24 June: "Repeated Information . . . confirm[s]
the likelihood of an attack in force here. . . . The hastening up the
Supplies is of the most capital Consequence—every thing depends
upon it—For God's Sake exert yourself. Move Earth & air to effect
it. . . . No time is to be lost." [16]

A second ramification of the money shortage was reflected in the difficulty of maintaining a standing army. Spring was normally the season of recruiting new troops and planning the return of those on winter furlough. The absence of acceptable Continental currency for paying and feeding the army caused a sharp drop in reenlistments. States experienced a variety of difficulties in attracting recruits, forcing more officers to take to the countryside in search of prospective enlistees. In early March, General Heath reported to General Washington from Roxbury, Massachusetts, that, "as many of them came home almost naked . . . a principal inducement to their enlisting is the expectation of being immediately clothed." A few days later, he continued in a similar vein: "There are at present two impediments in the way of successful recruiting; one is the want of money for the Continental bounty, the other is clothing for the recruits." [17]

John Paterson, commander of the Massachusetts Line serving under Howe, painted an even bleaker picture when he described "the shattered remains of the once respectable line for the state of the Massachusetts Bay. . . . What remain are mostly composed of nine months' abortions, sent here with bounties which ten times exceed those given for the war, naked, lifeless, and dead, who never saw action, are now counting days, hours, and minutes they have to tarry in service. Recruiting is now intirely [sic] at an end." [18]

The Connecticut forces also were severely depleted, and Howe dispatched recruiting officers from West Point into Connecticut and Massachusetts to rally prospective troops. As the threat of a British attack on the Highlands worsened during the spring, Howe was forced to request the commander in chief to order Gen. Enoch Poor and his brigade down to augment Howe's army. As late as June, when Benedict Arnold called on Howe at West Point, Arnold was struck by the lack of men garrisoning the works. Only fifteen hundred soldiers, "which will not half man the works," were available to the command.[19] The obvious weakness of the fort was not lost on Arnold and may have been a factor in his determination to gain command of the installation and offer it to the British.

The cadre of general officers could not avoid a feeling of "infinite mortification" and helplessness at the chaotic monetary situation facing the army and the republic. Meeting at Preakness, New Jersey, on 11 July, sixteen American generals—including Nathanael Greene, Lord Stirling, Arthur St. Clair, Henry Knox, Anthony Wayne, Alexander McDougall, Baron von Steuben, and Robert Howe, supported

by the Marquis de Lafayette—prepared a formal memorial of grievances to be submitted to Congress. They highlighted depreciation of
the money and lack of rations as their most "intollerable" complaints.
Requesting "justice," the officers demanded that depreciation of pay
should be immediately settled and paid off, that military widows and
orphans should be provided for, and that general officers should be
more equitably provided with rations and allowances. The petition
closed with a reminder of the magnitude of the army's distress, along
with a veiled threat that the world would judge who was responsible
if the army should quit the service. Congress appointed a committee on 3 August to consider the complaints and responded nine days
later, urging that the states compensate their troops for the depreciation in pay. Congress promised that the army would henceforth
receive pay in new nondepreciated bills, that officers would be given
extra monthly allowances according to rank, and that generals would
receive land grants for their service.[20]

The fiscal chaos facing the American command obviously complicated the military strategy for 1780. A full-scale offensive campaign
by the enemy was anticipated. While the Continentals awaited in
July the arrival of their French ally—the Comte de Rochambeau—
at Newport, Rhode Island, they closely watched other international
developments for indications of British weakness. The American officers anxiously devoured newspaper accounts of rebellions against
the British that would divert their attention elsewhere, and these accounts were circulated with glee. In their eyes, uprisings in Scotland
and Ireland encouraged speculation that England would give up in
America in order to concentrate on problems closer to home.[21]

The war in the Northern theater during 1780, as during the previous year, was one of watchful waiting. The British repeatedly probed
the American positions for signs of major vulnerability. Howe longed
to return to the Southern Department, where certain action awaited
and the prospect of glory appeared possible, but his repeated requests
for reassignment fell on deaf ears. Regardless of the desire for adventure, the enemy on Manhattan Island was not willing to oblige.
Supreme caution was the rule of the day along the Hudson; and,
without guarantees that the American lines were severely flawed, the
British in New York were unwilling to risk a confrontation.

By early April General Washington was concerned that a British attack up the Hudson was imminent, and he agreed that General Poor's brigade should be drawn down to reinforce his own troops and that ample provisions must be obtained for the garrison. Every effort already was being made to locate supplies, but on this occasion Howe was not in agreement with the supreme commander with regard to British intentions. For the past month, there had been activity in New York, and reports from the city warned of an attack on Washington in Morristown or on the Highlands fort. Howe's spy network provided him with sufficient intelligence to discount an April invasion. Howe felt that the British would await reinforcements that were expected in July before advancing up the Hudson.[22]

The anticipated British attack did not materialize, and as May progressed some of Howe's forces went adventuring on their own. A detachment commanded by Lt. Col. James Millan undertook a raid that succeeded in bringing off a number of prisoners, much to the chagrin of the enemy. Naturally, retaliatory measures were expected, thus prompting Howe to urge vigilance at all points.[23]

As May progressed, the vigilance that Howe demanded paid off in another fashion. Howe prided himself on the vast spy network that provided extensive intelligence of British movements, strengths, and intentions. The British learned, much to their consternation, that numerous spies that they had dispatched to observe the Highlands defenses were actually double agents working for Howe. Nevertheless, during May, the West Point command became alarmed that a number of British spies were operating around the fortification. The general issued orders to increase security and to prevent unknown civilians from crossing the ferry at West Point. "No persons but those properly known to be deserving of confidence, are to be suffered to visit the works at West Point—Commanding officers everywhere, will scrutinously examine all suspicious characters, and act by them, as circumstances shall point out."[24]

Regardless of the reliability of the intelligence moving from New York up the Hudson, details of British intentions could not be anticipated when the British themselves appeared to lack direction or form. Incursions into Connecticut during May resembled the tactics practiced the previous year by both sides. Then, on 7 June, Baron Wilhelm von Knyphausen, who was in command of New York City

during Sir Henry Clinton's absence in South Carolina, made his move
against Washington's army in New Jersey. He landed some five thousand troops near Elizabethtown and marched to Morristown. American forces blocked Knyphausen at Springfield Bridge; and, much to the Hessian officer's surprise, local residents did not flock to join his command. As the enemy withdrew to De Hart's Point and dug in, Washington was convinced that they were preparing for a strike up the Hudson in the direction of West Point. He promptly warned Howe of the imminent danger, and during this period the commander in chief, Howe, and New York governor George Clinton were in constant communication concerning British movements.

By 20 June six British warships had sailed up the Hudson toward Kings Ferry, forcing Washington to redeploy forces to defend against the anticipated attack on West Point. Connecticut dispatched two thousand men to West Point "for the defense of that post." As Washington's forces reached Pompton, where they could assist in the defense of the Highlands fortifications and the Jersey plains, Knyphausen—reenforced by Sir Henry Clinton's forces, who were just returning from the capture of Charleston, South Carolina—once more attacked Springfield. Although they set the town to the torch, their efforts against the American forces of Nathanael Greene and William Maxwell were unsuccessful.

By late in the day of 23 June, the enemy had withdrawn the ships that had started up the Hudson, but they still appeared to be readying for some form of offensive action. They had loaded heavy cannon and mortars, ready-framed platforms, and such siege tools as spades and pickaxes. Both Howe and Washington held their respective armies in readiness for the attack that never came. By the twenty-seventh, British forces had withdrawn from New Jersey, but their intentions were still in doubt. By 28 June the threat had subsided, and Howe decided that the British simply "intended to perplex, confuse & harass."[25] In actuality, it is questionable whether West Point had been a target in the June raids. It appears that Knyphausen had received faulty intelligence indicating that the people of New Jersey were pro-British and that a show of force on the Jersey plains would result in a popular uprising as well as a mutiny against the American commander. When Sir Henry Clinton returned in the midst of the enterprise, he had heard of the anticipated French arrival at Newport, Rhode

Island. His movement of ships up the Hudson was intended to prevent Washington from crossing the Hudson to join the French forces and to test the American commander's reaction to a possible threat to the Highlands.[26]

It was not until 10 July that the French army of the Comte de Rochambeau, along with a small French fleet commanded by Adm. Chevalier de Ternay, arrived off Newport. Washington had anticipated the French arrival as the long-awaited opportunity to gain naval as well as ground superiority over the enemy and thus permit a destructive blow to the British in New York. Much to his frustration, Adm. Thomas Graves, with thirteen powerful ships of the line, arrived off Sandy Hook three days later, allowing the British to maintain the upper hand. Despite his inferior force (Washington's army consisted of only three thousand men at the time), the American commander pressed Rochambeau to set a date for their joint attack on New York. Admiral Ternay informed Washington that he had no intention of risking his ten ships in New York harbor.

Sir Henry Clinton, aware of his own advantage, decided on an attack upon the recently arrived French as an offensive blow to the allies. Adm. Marriot Arbuthnot's fleet proceeded to blockade Ternay's small fleet in Newport harbor, while a sizeable British force was transported to Rhode Island to attack Rochambeau. Washington, realizing that Clinton would have to strip the New York defenses in order to attack the French, left his own camp at Preakness on 29 July. His forces crossed the Hudson on the thirty-first, where they formed a junction with Robert Howe's division. Washington had decided to take advantage of Clinton's absence; and, if the attack on the French was actually undertaken, he—with Howe's support—would attack the British headquarters. With a hostile army approaching New York, Clinton hurriedly relinquished his designs on Rhode Island and rushed back to his headquarters. Washington, having forced the British to abandon their project, recrossed the Hudson on 4 August and resumed his original plans for the summer campaign.[27]

The summer campaign of 1780 was influenced to a great measure by the shadow of Benedict Arnold and the treason that brought him legendary infamy. Arnold had offered his services to the British while he was a military commander in Philadelphia the previous year and had provided Sir Henry Clinton with intelligence concerning American strengths and movements since that time. Fortunately, Arnold

had been in no position to be of substantial benefit to the enemy—
until he settled upon West Point as a strategic entity within his grasp,
whose possession would ingratiate him with the British command.
In mid-June he visited Robert Howe at West Point and toured the
fortress for the first time. He was overwhelmed by the congressional
neglect of so important a post, as reflected by the lack of troops
available to Howe and the inadequate provisions provided for their
sustenance. He felt that the works were "wretchedly planned" but
that they appeared to be "well executed." Arnold was particularly
interested in those locations that could be taken with relative ease.
This struck Howe as strange, although he had no suspicion of the
reason for Arnold's inquisitive behavior.[28]

The scheming Arnold appealed to Robert Livingston and Philip
Schuyler, both powerful New York politicians, to assist him in gaining command of West Point. Livingston, admitting that he did not
know Howe personally, nonetheless feared that he was not enter-
prising enough to command this critical post and urged Arnold's
appointment. Howe had previously requested to be relieved at West
Point so that he could return to a field command, and Washington
had promised to comply when he organized the army for the summer
campaign. Washington admitted to Livingston that he did not know
Howe's military capabilities well enough to judge his performance,
but he was confident West Point was safe. Both Baron von Steuben
and Maj. Gen. Alexander McDougall were with Howe, and there
was no immediate threat of enemy attack. Although Washington did
assure Livingston that he would appoint Arnold to the West Point
command, the commander in chief had better plans for Arnold—
whom he considered one of his most competent generals. Instead of
leaving Arnold garrisoned at West Point, Washington assigned him
to the highest post he had to offer: commander of the Left Wing
of the army. Serving as division commanders under Arnold's command would be Robert Howe, Alexander McDougall, and Baron
von Steuben. When Arnold learned of his assignment, he was furious.
Rather than appreciating the confidence Washington had placed in
him, Arnold emphatically informed the commander in chief that he
was physically unable to serve in the field. Claiming that his old leg
wound from Saratoga was causing him great pain, Arnold limped

about Washington's headquarters to demonstrate the difficulty with which he maneuvered. Reversing his order of 1 August, Washington two days later awarded the garrison command to Arnold and assigned Lord Stirling to succeed to the Left Wing post.[29]

An army command is no stronger than the intelligence network that serves it; and, when that command is committed to treason, the level of concern for spies and spying is substantially heightened. Before taking command at West Point, General Arnold appealed to Howe to make known to him the identity of those shadowy individuals who were in his service. Arnold argued that he was in desperate need of adequate intelligence on enemy movements and plans and that those sources that served Howe could likewise serve Arnold. Howe refused to divulge his agents without their authorization; and, when the spies refused to approve the request, Howe stood firm in preserving the integrity of his sources. One can only speculate whether these men suspected more than they could confirm; on a previous occasion, one had reported to Howe that an officer high in the American command was on the British payroll, but they had been unable to identify the culprit.[30]

One common acquaintance of both Howe and Arnold was the controversial Joshua Hett Smith, who lived near Haverstraw on the Hudson. Howe had first met Smith in Charleston, South Carolina, and, upon renewing his acquaintance after arriving in New York, Howe utilized Smith as an intermediary for transmitting intelligence along the river.[31] Smith was from a well-known Tory family, but Howe and other highly placed officers considered him an invaluable Whig ally. Smith was to become the fateful link in the most celebrated case of espionage and treason in the annals of the United States.

When British adjutant Maj. John André rowed ashore from the *Vulture* at Haverstraw on the night of 21 September, Arnold and Smith led the British officer to Smith's house for their treasonous rendezvous. Smith later contended that he knew the visitor only as "John Anderson" and, since he was not party to the conversation between the two officers, assumed that "Anderson" was delivering information vital to the American cause. When André was subsequently captured two days later, disguised as a civilian and carrying plans of West Point in his boot, Arnold fled to safety in New York. Both André and Smith were tried for their role in the plot, and Robert

Howe was involved in each case. He was one of the fourteen general officers who served on the board that convicted André of spying and ordered him to be hanged. In the case of Joshua Hett Smith, Howe testified in his behalf that the defendant had provided intelligence for him on numerous occasions and that he had no reason to doubt Smith's attachment to the American cause. Smith was acquitted but remained confined to jail under the threat of double jeopardy, until in desperation he finally escaped to the British lines.[32]

After the Arnold plot was discovered and André executed, the British attempted to incriminate other high-ranking American officers. Sir Henry Clinton leaked the rumor that Robert Howe was in British pay, but General Washington dismissed the story as pure fabrication, intended to sow suspicion among the American officers. Historian Douglas Southall Freeman takes the position that the charge against Howe was totally false and "probably was circulated as attempted revenge for General Howe's vigilant efforts to trap spies and to prevent trade between the lines."[33]

CHAPTER 10

CRISES AND

CAMARADERIE

*D*uring the fall of 1780, General Washington, from his headquarters at Preakness, New Jersey, weighed the options for offensive action in the closing weeks of the year. The major generals commanding from his headquarters were Lord Stirling (William Alexander), Arthur St. Clair, the Marquis de Lafayette, and Robert Howe. Along with their brigadiers—Henry Knox, John Glover, John Paterson, Anthony Wayne, Edward Hand, Jedidiah Huntington, and William Irvine—these men constituted Washington's council of war. Since Sir Henry Clinton reportedly had dispatched three thousand additional men to augment Lord Charles Cornwallis's army in the South, Washington debated the wisdom of sending additional reinforcements to that theater. Washington had just appointed one of his favorites, Nathanael Greene, to replace the recently defeated Horatio Gates: one can be sure that Washington was anxious to support Greene in every way possible. The council was overwhelmingly opposed to sending the detachment south, and it must have brought a mixture of emotions to Howe's mind as he voted with the majority, knowing that his own failures in the South may never have happened had a respectable force of troops been available to him.[1]

As the 1780 campaign came to an end, the Americans welcomed a celebrated visitor to their camp—the future Marquis Chevalier de

Chastellux. Although third in command of Rochambeau's French
expeditionary force, Chastellux was widely known in America as a writer and philosopher as well as an experienced military officer. He traveled from Newport to Preakness to visit Lafayette and to meet General Washington, arriving at the American headquarters on 23 November amidst some confusion. By the time he reached Washington's quarters, the commander in chief (along with Knox, Wayne, Howe, Alexander Hamilton, and Tench Tilghman) was finishing dinner. A fresh meal was prepared for the guest and everyone remained to keep him company. Afterward, the party enjoyed a few glasses of claret and Madeira while they visited until 9:00 P.M. The following day, despite a driving rain, the visitor was treated to a review of General Knox's artillery, the Pennsylvania Line, and Lafayette's troops. Upon his return to Washington's headquarters, dinner was served; about twenty guests, including Howe and General St. Clair, were present. As the Frenchman observed, "The repast was in the English fashion, consisting of eight or ten large dishes of butcher's meat, and poultry, with vegetables of several sorts, followed by a second course of pastry, comprised under the two denominations of pies and puddings. After this the cloth was taken off, and apples and a great quantity of nuts were served, which General Washington usually continues eating for two hours, toasting and conversing all the time."[2]

While Chastellux was visiting the American army headquarters, Washington had already begun to order the various elements of his army into winter quarters. The prospects for a cold, hungry, naked winter were no different from past years, so the commander in chief proceeded to separate his tiny army into strategic locations at which provisions could be provided with a minimum of transportation. The New York brigade was sent to Albany; the Pennsylvania Line was stationed at Morristown; the New Jersey brigade was placed further north, at Pompton, New Jersey; and the New England brigades were clustered around West Point. Washington moved his headquarters to New Windsor, on the Hudson above West Point, and Howe was instructed to move his Connecticut Line up the east side of the river and the Massachusetts Line up the west side, to West Point. Gen. William Heath, who was once more overall commander in the Highlands, would designate precisely where the divisions would locate.[3]

The early winter of 1780–81 lacked the intense cold of previous years, but in all other respects there was little difference. The Revolutionary War had become a continuous exercise in hunger, privation, and frustration. Everything necessary for sustaining an army was in short supply; and intense suffering from inadequate food, clothing, shoes, and even firewood was commonplace throughout the ranks. Salaries were usually months in arrears; and, due to the inability of the Continental government to control the inflationary spiral, soldiers found that their pay was of no value upon receipt. Ultimate victory undoubtedly appeared unattainable to officers and men alike. Writing a few months earlier, Howe reflected the depression that permeated the structure of the army. "The prospects before us in this Department are gloomy indeed. You know me too well to suppose that I see any thing thro' a Disagreeable medium when I can behold it thro any other, but much as I am that 'Hardly a loop remains to hang a hope upon.' My exertions however shall not be wanting whenever and whereever [*sic*] I find them necessary, and tho' I may not obtain success I will endeaver to deserve it."[4]

On 1 January 1781, the long-dreaded but generally unspoken ultimate stepping-stone to disaster struck. The Pennsylvania Line committed mutiny. Some twenty-four hundred Pennsylvania soldiers, along with their noncommissioned officers, quit their quarters, seized arms, fired upon their officers, and marched off toward Philadelphia. Brig. Gen. Anthony Wayne and the officers of the Line followed after the insurgents, attempting to reason with them. When General Washington was informed of the situation on 3 January, his first reaction was to hurry toward Philadelphia; but after a conference with his generals he decided to remain at New Windsor, where he could exercise control over the army in that quarter. The consensus among the general officers was that the mutiny could very easily spread throughout the army. One misstep and the entire army could turn on its leaders. Washington was deeply concerned that the British would sway the mutineers to their side—to say nothing of the dangerous precedent of officers negotiating with the troops over whom they are required to have complete authority. Despite these reservations, Washington cautioned Wayne against using force.[5]

Although negotiations were under way between Pennsylvania authorities and the mutinied Line of that state, Washington decided that an able detachment must be in readiness to confront the mutineers if

negotiations failed. Robert Howe requested command of the detachment, and Washington—although admitting that "of right he ought to have it"—felt that "in point of policy, it might be better to give it to either General Parsons or General Glover."[6] Since Samuel Parsons was from Connecticut and Glover from Massachusetts, Washington undoubtedly reasoned that the troops of those states, which were to make up the backbone of the detachment, would be more likely to obey orders from one of their own. Despite Washington's reservations, however, Howe did receive the appointment to command a detachment of two Massachusetts battalions (500 men), one Connecticut battalion (250 men), one New Hampshire battalion (200 men), and one battalion (200 men) to be taken equally from Col. Moses Hazen's regiment and Lt. Col. William Hull's regiment. The detachment consisted of the best-clothed and best-fed men available; and, along with their equipment, they were placed on alert for immediate departure.[7]

It was fortunate for the American cause that a confrontation with so formidable a force as the rebellious Pennsylvanians did not materialize. Twenty-four hundred armed veterans represented a sizeable army, and no one was certain whether regular troops would indeed fire upon their fellow Americans rather than join them in their protest. Although a negotiated settlement was successful, the toll was extremely high, and General Washington fretted over the precedent that had been established. More than one-half of the Pennsylvania Line were discharged from service, and the remaining troops were furloughed until 15 March. In reality, the entire Line was disbanded for a period of two months.

It was only a matter of days before the inevitable happened, but insurrection this time proved fortuitous for the American cause. On 20 January, approximately two hundred troops of the New Jersey Line marched from their camp at Pompton and headed for Chatham, where the remainder of the brigade was camped. When Washington received word of the mutiny, he immediately forbade any negotiations with the mutineers and ordered General Heath to prepare a detachment of six hundred good troops to march from West Point without delay. Once more, Robert Howe was placed in command, with specific instructions for handling the mutiny. "The object of

your detachment is to compel the mutineers to unconditional submission, and I am to desire you will grant no terms while they are
with arms in their hands in a state of resistance. The manner of executing this I leave in your discretion according to circumstances. If
you succeed in compelling the revolted troops to a surrender, you
will instantly execute a few of the most active and most incendiary
leaders." [8]

As General Howe and his detachment prepared to depart West
Point, gray, foreboding clouds hung low over the Highlands. During
the evening of 22 January, a blinding snow began to fill the moun-
tainous terrain. By morning, some twenty inches of snow covered
the detachment as it slowly moved southward. The severe weather
hampered communications between New Jersey and army headquarters at New Windsor. When Washington had heard nothing further
concerning the mutiny by the twenty-fifth, he decided to set out for
New Jersey in order to "act as circumstances may require." Much to
the commander in chief's frustration, he found that his horses had
not been fed in three days and were so weak that they could hardly
stand. He thereupon demanded a two-horse team and sleigh from
the quartermaster and at 8:00 A.M. on the twenty-sixth set out over
the snow for Ringwood, New Jersey.[9]

Robert Howe's detachment arrived at Ringwood on 25 January to
discover that, contrary to General Washington's orders, New Jersey
officers had negotiated with the troops. Col. Elias Dayton had offered
pardon, which the mutineers ostensibly accepted. They had returned
to their huts at Pompton. They had continued, however, to make demands, and they refused to give up their arms or accept orders from
most of their officers. Howe decided that the insurgents had merely
returned to their huts to seek shelter from the weather and that they
were still in a state of rebellion.[10]

After midnight on 26 January, Howe's detachment moved toward
Pompton. Lt. Col. Ebenezer Sprout's party, with a piece of artillery,
took post to the left of the encampment; Lt. Col. Miller, with another
party and two fieldpieces, was stationed on the mutineers' right;
Maj. Robert Oliver, with his men, formed a line across the front; and
Maj. Benjamin Throop's forces took a position to their rear. Howe
stationed the New Hampshire detachment along the Charlottenburg
Road, thus closing every avenue of escape. As the first streaks of

morning light shimmered off the blanket of snow, the peacefully sleeping mutineers were jolted to reality by the realization that they were completely surrounded. Col. Francis Barber of the New Jersey Line was sent forward with orders for them to parade immediately without arms. Some of the mutineers demanded conditions, exclaiming, "If we are to die, it is as well to die where we are as any where else." Howe ordered Colonel Sprout to advance, and a deadline of five minutes was allowed for the insurgents' complete compliance. The ultimatum had its effect, and the huts immediately emptied of their occupants. From a list of ringleaders provided by the Jersey officers, one man was selected from each of the three Jersey regiments. A field court-martial was convened on the spot, and the three men were convicted and sentenced to death. A firing squad was selected from among leading mutineers, and two of the men were executed as the others looked on. Due to an intercession by the Jersey officers, however, the third condemned man was pardoned and allowed to rejoin his regiment. Thus the mutiny in the Jersey Line was brought to a swift and forceful conclusion.[11]

The commander in chief was delighted with the results of the Howe expedition. The crushing of the Jersey mutiny had served notice to all troops that orders must be obeyed. It was Washington's feeling that it would "completely extinguish the Spirit of Mutiny"; but he cautioned that, unless the grievances were corrected, it was inevitable that the same violence would break out again. For Howe and his detachment, Washington had great praise. The supreme commander reported to Congress that "all his measures were taken with decision and propriety," and to Nathanael Greene he noted that "indeed the detachment under General Howe deserves infinite credit."[12]

With the "Spirit of Mutiny" extinguished, Howe was at last free to spend a long-promised leave in Boston. It was at this point, however, that General Washington decided to undertake a hasty trip to confer with Rochambeau at the French headquarters in Newport, Rhode Island. Washington had for some time urged the French commander to send his fleet to the Chesapeake Bay in an effort to capture Benedict Arnold and his British forces, who were preying on the Virginia countryside from their base at Portsmouth. After some hesitation, Rochambeau informed Washington that the fleet would sail to Virginia, but there was objection to sending transports up the Chesapeake Bay to pick up Lafayette and his army, which Washington had sent scurrying overland from the Highlands to Virginia. Washington felt that he could resolve the problem through a conference with the Frenchman, and General Howe was requested to join the supreme commander in the trip to Rhode Island to meet with Rochambeau.[13]

Whether the North Carolinian actually participated in the Newport conference is uncertain, but the commander in chief was quite perturbed that the French delayed sailing for the Chesapeake Bay for several days while they wined and dined him. Once the fleet departed, Washington felt a necessity to return to his headquarters at New Windsor rather than to inspect military installations in the eastern states, as he had originally planned.

Howe remained in Rhode Island, Massachusetts, and New Hampshire during much of the spring, spending substantial time in Portsmouth and Boston. By early May General Washington was trying frantically to locate him, writing to Rochambeau and to Governor John Hancock of Massachusetts and requesting that they forward a letter to Howe if they knew his whereabouts. Washington was anxious for Howe to return "as speedily as possible," to assume command of West Point. It was urgent that General Heath be dispatched to the eastern states; and with Heath's departure Washington was left without a suitable general to take command of the Highlands defense.[14]

The crisis that faced the American army in May 1781 was no different from the refrain repeated so often since 1776. The army was out of food. Fort Schuyler, on the western frontier of New York, was on the verge of collapse, and Washington had been forced to strip the reserve barrels of beef from West Point to send, via Albany, to the starving soldiers on the frontier. Heath, who had great popularity not only in Massachusetts but also throughout New England, was the individual most effective in pleading for support throughout the area. Washington was convinced that without a supply of food not only would Fort Schuyler and all of western New York fall to the enemy, but also West Point and the entire army probably would collapse.[15]

General Howe had returned to West Point by early June and was hard at work inventorying provisions and water at the various redoubts, training troops, and attempting to strengthen defenses. The

general was frustrated to find that not only were flour, meat, and
other provisions in short supply, but also that there were no nails for construction and no paper on which to write. Discipline obviously had deteriorated during Howe's absence, resulting in filthy living quarters and waste-littered grounds. Howe was appalled over the "noisome offensive & unwholesome" conditions and ordered fatigue parties to be at work by 5:00 A.M. the next morning—cleaning, raking, burning, and burying the filth. Due to a persistent problem of men relieving themselves near their barracks and throwing pot liquor, meat bones, and filth close by, they were made to dig latrine vaults that were to be filled and moved weekly. Within two weeks, however, the long barracks again had relaxed into "nastiness," and Howe was threatening to arrest and court-martial anyone who ignored his orders on cleanliness.[16]

The lack of concern for military security was equally evident among the troops assigned to duty stations at West Point, and the North Carolina general expressed disappointment at the laxness during his absence. Doors to redoubts were left open, and Howe found he could approach the positions without being challenged. Prompt action was taken against the offending soldiers, and the officers who allowed it were appropriately reprimanded. Howe naturally felt frustrated that men and officers alike failed to understand that an undisciplined army, without pride in their military bearing and cleanliness, would be equally ineffective in battle.[17]

On 12 June, the commander in chief called for a board of general officers to meet at his headquarters at New Windsor. Major generals present included Howe, Lord Stirling, Parsons, and McDougall and brigadier generals Knox, Paterson, Hand, Huntington, and Louis le Béque DuPortail. Washington reported on a recent conference with Rochambeau at Wethersfield, Connecticut, and on the allied options for an attack on the British. The central theme centered on an attack against New York City. Rochambeau presumably had agreed to a joint venture against the British stronghold, and the French army was to march from Newport to participate in the enterprise.[18]

In keeping with the scheme, Washington organized his army for the summer campaign. Recruiting had been very poor and the ranks were thin. Washington hoped that troops returning from extended winter leave would arrive in time and in numbers to provide a respectable fighting force. The Right Wing was commanded by General Heath, with Lord Stirling, Howe, and Benjamin Lincoln as division commanders. This wing was ordered to move on 18 June from West Point to Peekskill and then to Dobbs Ferry. With headquarters at Dobbs Ferry, Washington proceeded to plan excursions that would at least harass and perplex Sir Henry Clinton and his army, and with any luck an all-out attack on the city might materialize.[19]

During much of July, the American and French armies lurked above New York City, probing its outposts and attempting raids along the Harlem River and on the north end of York Island. On 15 July a small flotilla of British vessels passed the American positions at Dobbs Ferry and attempted to seize three or four river vessels that had docked at Tarrytown. Howe, commanding a detachment of American and French troops, marched with great rapidity to Tarrytown, where he opened fire upon the British ships. The enemy vessels were forced to withdraw, but not before setting torch to the boats loaded with ordnance. Several of Howe's officers distinguished themselves by extinguishing the flames of the burning riverboats and rescuing the entire shipment of ordnance and stores from destruction. The enemy remained on the river for several more days before fleeing back to New York. In attempting to pass the American position at Dobbs Ferry, they were heavily damaged by the batteries thrown up at that location.[20]

Although Washington's desire to attack New York was thwarted by the general wariness of the French to attempt action in New York harbor, the positioning and reconnoitering undertaken at this point played an important role in the success of the Allied army at Yorktown. While this army hovered just across the Harlem River, the indecisive Clinton was unlikely to weaken his forces significantly in order to augment those of Lord Cornwallis in Virginia. Washington had deliberately publicized his intention of attacking the British stronghold, and a major departure of British troops for the Chesapeake would have provided ample imbalance in comparable forces to have made such an attack feasible.[21]

By mid-August the die was cast. Dispatches from the French notified Washington that the Comte de Grasse had departed from Cape François in the West Indies, en route to the Chesapeake, with thirty-two hundred land troops. Lafayette, Frederick William von Steuben,

and Anthony Wayne—with some two thousand Continentals and
a large body of militia—had been in Virginia for months, harass-
ing the enemy and monitoring Cornwallis's movements. Without the
prospect of French cooperation for an assault on New York, the
commander in chief agreed to a Virginia campaign. Rochambeau,
with his French army, Washington, and a detachment of twenty-five
hundred men from the American army, would race to Maryland to
be transported down the Chesapeake to the York River.

Major General Lincoln was selected as field commander of American forces for the expedition. Howe, who remained behind with his
division on the Hudson, was distraught. The North Carolinian had
long dreamed of returning triumphantly to the South; and on an
earlier occasion he had exacted a promise from General Washington
that, if the commander in chief undertook a Southern campaign, he
would be "happy" to have Howe with him. Washington attempted
to soothe his officer's ruffled feelings by explaining that his failure
to be included was not a matter of design, as "the matter turned up
merely from the common routine of duty." Only one major general
(in addition to those already in Virginia) was required for the expedition. Washington had simply selected the senior officer who was
willing and physically able to undertake the campaign, and Lincoln
was above Howe in seniority.[22] The ultimate victory at Yorktown,
with the surrender of Cornwallis on 18 October, was a cause of great
jubilation within the American army.

Although the substantive fighting ended with Yorktown, almost
two additional years of readiness and military discipline would be
required before the American soldier could sheath his sword and return to his own fireside. This, naturally, was a difficult period for
officers and troops alike; they grew increasingly impatient with the
necessity to remain in uniform until a treaty was formally signed.

As all eyes turned toward the York River in the fall of 1781, more
personal events were demanding the attention of Maj. Gen. Robert
Howe. After a delay of almost three years, congressional delegates
from Georgia had demanded an inquiry into Howe's conduct during
the battle of Savannah in December 1778. George Walton, who had
been wounded and captured by the British at Savannah, served briefly
as Georgia's governor (November 1779–January 1780) before being
elected to Congress. In both capacities, he led an active campaign to

strip Robert Howe of rank and command. The Continental Congress on 5 September acquiesced to Walton's demands and ordered Washington to appoint a court-martial to hear the charges. Howe appealed to his general to postpone the trial until after the 1781 campaign was completed, so that he "may have an opportunity . . . to exert myself in the service of my country," if the department should become the scene of action as he anticipated. Washington and Heath, who was handling administrative matters of the army during the commander in chief's absence in Virginia, were at a loss to understand who the state of Georgia planned to use to support the charges or what papers existed that would "illucidate [*sic*] the matter."[23]

By early October, Howe had removed to Philadelphia, where he attempted to prepare his defense. He was handicapped by the passage of time, the death or dispersal of numerous witnesses who could bear testimony to his conduct, and the loss or destruction of papers pertinent to the Georgia invasion. He requested of General Heath and the Congress that they proceed without delay in scheduling the trial and that it be scheduled to meet in Philadelphia, since the Georgia delegates and most of the evidence would be more convenient to that location than anywhere else.[24]

The general court-martial of Maj. Gen. Robert Howe was formally ordered to convene at 10:00 A.M. on 7 December at the City Tavern in Philadelphia. Maj. Gen. Baron von Steuben was president of the trial, who with Brig. Gen. Henry Knox, Colonels Walter Stewart, John Lamb, Stephen Moylan, and Richard Humpton, and Majors Sebastian Bauman, Matthew Clarkson, Robert Burnett, James Moore, William McPherson, William Galvan, and John Bernard Gauthier de Murnans constituted the court. Initially, Capt. Benjamin Walker was appointed as judge advocate, but by 15 December he had been replaced by Capt. Nicholas White. Due to illnesses and conflicting duty assignments as the trial progressed, Moore, Humpton, and Burnett were replaced by Col. Lewis Nicola, Maj. John Singer Dexter, and Maj. Jeremiah Olney. The Georgians brought two charges before the court: first, that Howe sacrificed by his conduct the capital of the state of Georgia and the troops of that state on 29 December 1778; and, second, that he crossed the Savannah River on the day following 29 December with troops that escaped from Savannah and ordered the abandonment of posts at Sunbury and Augusta, thus leaving the state at the mercy of the enemy without any Continental troops.[25]

The charges had been instigated primarily by George Walton, and it was Howe's contention that the former militia-officer-turned-politician was attempting to use the fall of Savannah in 1778 as a subterfuge to divert public attention from his own political failures. In Walton's scenario, Robert Howe became the culprit responsible for the disaster that had befallen that state. Walton and Col. Samuel Elbert were the leading witnesses for the prosecution. Their testimony was designed to lay blame squarely at the feet of the Continental commander. Under cross-examination, however, the testimony largely confirmed Howe's version of the events of that fateful Christmas, and the accusers reflected their own culpability in events leading to the fiasco.[26]

The trial droned on, with intermittent breaks, until 23 January 1782. The prosecution was weak and sometimes contradictory. Howe handled much of the defense questioning himself. He portrayed himself as working against overwhelming odds, with very little cooperation from a recalcitrant state government. He argued that the charges, coming as they did three years after the fact, were simply intended to prop up an incompetent governor searching for a scapegoat, which would in turn propel Walton once more into the role of a state hero. Howe, long celebrated for his eloquence as a speaker, used his talents to their fullest. His defense must have been quite effective, because the verdict rendered on 23 January acquitted him, with "highest honors," of all charges. The ordeal past, Howe then demanded to have the proceedings published by Congress as a public vindication of his conduct.[27]

Although the trial had concluded with Howe's exoneration, he found himself unable to resume command in a timely manner. During his three-month stay in Philadelphia, the general had developed a substantial debt for living expenses. Much to his embarrassment, he was unable to cover the debt and thus could not depart Philadelphia until the bills were paid. It was not until 10 February that he was able to leave for the Highlands, and then only after borrowing much of the expense money under an agreement to pay $100 for every $60 borrowed, with 6 percent interest due on the total. After the experiences in Philadelphia, the general surely looked forward to returning to his division and the routine of camp life.[28]

Since offensive measures by the British were not expected, the primary concern was to keep an army together, alert, and occupied until an official termination of hostilities. After defending himself for some six weeks before a military tribunal, it is doubtful that Howe looked with any pleasure at orders that emanated from headquarters at Newburgh on 7 April. Assistant Adj. Gen. John Carlisle ordered Howe to serve as president of a general court-martial then convened at West Point to try Maj. Gen. Alexander McDougall. The charges had developed as a result of differences between McDougall and Maj. Gen. William Heath, his superior in command. McDougall had a very low opinion of Heath's military ability, and on several occasions the two men had issued contradictory orders. As a result, Heath brought eight charges, primarily involving insubordination, against the officer. Heath's case hinged primarily on McDougall's attempts to counter the commands of the senior general. Howe undoubtedly found himself in the uncomfortable position of being friends of both men. The court met irregularly between April and August, and during this period Howe maintained his official residence across the Hudson at the Beverly Robinson house. In the verdict on the eight charges, McDougall was convicted only of telling other officers the details of a council of war held in 1776 and of calling Heath, because of his views at the council of war meeting, a "knave." On this charge, he was ordered reprimanded by the commander in chief, but on the other charges he was acquitted. In the opinion of the court, it was felt that several of the charges against McDougall were "vexatious."[29]

The results of these proceedings surely represented an embarrassment and an affront to Heath, and one can only wonder if the friendship between Heath and Howe was not irreparably damaged. Evidence of this is to be found in an incident that occurred two months later, as the army was being moved from Verplanck's Point to winter quarters at New Windsor. In a report directed to General Washington on 28 October, Heath charged that Major General Howe had not been with his division during the march on the twenty-seventh and twenty-eighth and had been absent without leave: he had not communicated his reason for absence to Heath. The commander in chief curtly demanded of Howe an explanation for his absence. The North Carolinian immediately responded by explaining that he had been with his division all day on the twenty-sixth, slogging through a driving rain. That night, he had requested permission of Heath to spend the night at General McDougall's headquarters. The next

Major General William Heath (Courtesy of the Massachusetts Historical Society)

morning, Howe was too ill to join his division right away but did arrive in time to oversee their crossing of the river at West Point. Since he "felt too unwell" to walk with the troops and his horse was too sick for him to ride, Howe decided to proceed by boat up the river to their cantonment at New Windsor. After arriving at their destination on the twenty-eighth, the division commander claimed to have unsuccessfully sought Heath. Due to the continuing rain and his illness, he had not attempted to call on Washington. Howe's closing declaration tells much about the relationship between Heath and Howe:

"Courtesy, politeness as well as tenderness of an officer's reputation, which every feeling mind will extend to all, where service is not injured by it, ought to have induced General Heath to have demanded the reason of my conduct of myself previous to his reporting me to my general."[30]

The closing months of the war did have their lighter side, and it appears that Robert Howe retained a sense of humor, despite years of frustration. On one occasion, while Howe was headquartered at the Robinson house, he went to great trouble to borrow fish from a friend because the commander in chief was dining with him and was "exceedingly fond" of salt fish. Howe solemnly swore to repay, in a very few days, "as good Dam [*sic*] fish as ever you saw."[31] A few months later, while Howe was stationed at Verplanck's Point, General Knox requested the return of a boat that was in Howe's possession. In a long and protracted letter, he responded that surely Knox misunderstood his need for a boat. In Howe's current situation, a boat was absolutely essential: he made all of his movements by boat, and he must be ready at a moment's warning. "Whilst I . . . have the alternatives of walking on the water, which had I not a Broken leg I really want Faith to do."[32]

With the threat of an enemy attack at last remote, the American army was better able by 1782 to enjoy the ceremony and celebration that had been impossible for some years. On 31 May the army in the Highlands celebrated the birthday of the Dauphin of France. An edifice six hundred feet long and thirty feet wide, supported by a grand colonnade of 118 pillars made of tree trunks, was constructed on the plain at West Point. One thousand men labored for ten days to prepare the structure, which was covered by interwoven tree branches, muskets and bayonets, evergreens, and American and French military colors. According to army surgeon James Thacher

> The whole army was paraded on the contiguous hills on both sides of the river, forming a circle of several miles in open view of the public edifice, and at the given signal of firing three cannon, the regimental officers all left their commands, and repaired to the building. . . . At five o'clock, dinner being on the table, his Excellency General Washington and lady and suite, the princi-

pal officers of the army and their ladies, Governor Clinton and his lady, and a number of respectable characters . . . moved . . . through the line . . . to the arbor, where more than five hundred gentlemen and ladies partook of a magnificent festival. A martial band charmed our senses with music, while we feasted our appetites. . . . The cloth being removed, thirteen appropriate toasts were drank, each one being announced by the discharge of thirteen cannon. . . . The arbor was, in the evening, illuminated by a vast number of lights . . . thirteen cannon were fired as a prelude to a general *feu de joie,* which immediately succeeded throughout the whole line of the army on the surrounding hills; and being three times repeated, the mountains resounded and echoed like tremendous peals of thunder. . . . At half-past eleven o'clock, the celebration was concluded by the exhibition of fire-works, very ingeniously constructed of various figures. . . . General Washington . . . attended the ball in the evening . . . having Mrs. Knox for his partner, carried down a dance of twenty couples in the arbor on the green grass.[33]

On 14 September the entire army once again paraded under arms in honor of Comte de Rochambeau and his French officers and their return from the south. The American soldiers were in complete uniform as they marched past Washington's headquarters, and they performed with such discipline that Rochambeau commented to Washington that the Americans seemed to have formed an alliance with the king of Prussia: "These troops are Prussians." During the next few days, Howe had the pleasure of dining with a number of the French officers, Baron von Steuben, and Dr. Thacher.[34]

During the closing months of the war, as officers and men alike were awaiting the final terms of peace and the dissolution of the army, Howe appealed to the commander in chief for permission to visit Boston on urgent personal business. Washington refused the request on the grounds that Howe and Horatio Gates were the only major generals available at the time and that Howe simply could not be spared from service. A lengthy exchange ensued, in which the North Carolinian pointed out his dedication to duty during the four years of service under Washington's command. He had remained in camp, on duty, without any leaves, except for his four-month sojourn to Philadelphia for court-martial, the trip with his commander to Rhode Island in 1781, and the subsequent reconnoitering expedition to Massachusetts and New Hampshire. Washington finally relented and on 26 February Howe departed for a two-month leave.[35]

During Howe's absence in Boston, officers of the Continental Army headquartered at Newburgh, New York, became involved in what has become known as the Newburgh Conspiracy. With the war drawing to a close, the Continental officers had become increasingly alarmed over their own financial situation. Throughout the war, they had suffered silently as, time after time, they failed to receive proper remuneration for their sacrifices in the cause of American liberty. A group of officers, loyal to Horatio Gates, prepared an address to the Continental Congress, insisting that Congress meet their demands for pay and reimbursement. The demand implied that if Congress did not satisfy their needs they would refuse to disband when the war ended; or, if the war continued, they would withdraw from the states and leave the country unprotected. To the chagrin of the conspirators, Washington unexpectedly appeared at their meeting on 15 March. In an emotional speech, he defused the movement that had the potential for developing into a military coup d'état. Had Howe been present, there can be little doubt that he would have supported the commander in chief and the civil government to which he was unswervingly loyal.[36]

Even though actual hostilities with Britain had ended in April, one last incident required Howe to command troops offensively. During June 1783, a body of Pennsylvania troops, frustrated over the failure of Congress or the state legislature to deal with their concerns, began a march on Philadelphia to seek a redress of grievances. Congress, terrified by the action, fled Philadelphia and reconvened in Princeton. General Washington once more called on Howe to command a detachment to march from the Highlands to Philadelphia to suppress the mutiny. Howe kept his corps light and unencumbered with luggage and, despite the heat, marched them rapidly via Ringwood, Pompton, Morristown, Princeton, and Trenton—and from there by water—to Philadelphia. The general, ever devoted to the supremacy of civil authority, paused briefly in Princeton to write the Pennsylvania governor that "to pay implied submission to the Laws of the State, to hold the rights of citizens inviolate, and to treat with the utmost respect, deference, and attention the Legislative and Executive authorities, shall be the rule of my own conduct and that of those under my command."[37]

As the detachment approached its destination, the resistance collapsed. Congress asked Howe to set up headquarters in Philadelphia and investigate the situation. With the assistance of the judge advocate, Howe instituted an inquiry and, during July and part of August, remained in Philadelphia. Leaders of the insurrection were tried by court-martial and sentenced to death. Congress thereupon reviewed the sentences and extended mercy, pardoning those convicted for their role in the affair. On 13 September Congress passed a resolution praising Howe and thanking him "for the prudence and propriety with which he executed the inquiry into the late mutiny of a part of the Pennsylvania Line."[38]

Robert Howe remained in command of his troops until the army was finally disbanded late in 1783. During this time, he made numerous trips between West Point and Philadelphia, but as long as the army existed he was determined to remain a part of the structure. As late as mid-November, he was issuing orders against marauding by soldiers and taking measures to see that the troops did not rob the civilian population.[39]

It is uncertain where Howe spent the closing days of the war. The British evacuated New York City on 17 November, the same day that Howe issued his order against marauding; and the American army entered Manhattan. After traversing the city, General Washington bid farewell to his officers at Fraunces' Tavern on 4 December. There is no indication that Howe was present at this emotional and historic occasion: the question remains as to his location at this point. General Washington left New York immediately after his farewell and rode to Philadelphia, where he resigned his commission on 22 December. By the new year only seven hundred rank and file were still in uniform, and the Continental Army, for all intents and purposes, ceased to exist.

Before Robert Howe left the Massachusetts and Connecticut regiments that had formed his division almost continuously since 1779, he issued a rather lengthy farewell of his own. Only the final paragraph is necessary to understand the emotion of this man who had been consumed with the war since its earliest beginnings.

> In the course of service sympathies have been excited, affections impressed and friendships established in his mind, which time, absence or accident shall never wipe away. How anxious then to him must be the hour of separation. . . . For as his sensibility upon this occasion is too big for utterance, he will fly if possible from the painful reflection and hasten to do what he shall always take pleasure in: that is, to hope the officers and men of the army in general, and of his command in particular, may be as happy as he wishes them; and they will be very happy indeed.[40]

A TIME OF

MELANCHOLY

*T*he final year of the American Revolution was obviously one of great inner turmoil for North Carolina's only major general. With the end of the war, the military establishment for all intents and purposes would cease to exist. Robert Howe had devoted eight years of his life to a military career and thrived on the discipline, the regimentation, and the honor that was part and parcel of the army life. Whereas other officers longed to return to family and fireside, Howe had little awaiting his attention on the Cape Fear. His home life had been a disaster, he had not set foot in his home state for almost five years, and he had not practiced the art of planting since donning a uniform.

It is difficult to determine exactly what Howe was doing or where he was located during at least some of the closing months of his active duty. He was present at each of the early meetings that led to the formation of the Society of the Cincinnati. This patriotic organization, made up entirely of Continental Line officers, developed out of meetings at the cantonment of the Continental Army at New Windsor on 10 May 1783 and, subsequently, at Verplanck Mansion on 13 May. Robert Howe was the second officer to sign—directly beneath Baron von Steuben, who was president of the organization—the society charter.[1] Unfortunately, there is no further record of his participation in this august body. His lack of involvement in the society may have

been related to the fact that the organization was divided into chap-
ters by state; Howe did not return to North Carolina until shortly
before his death.

It is obvious that Howe was not anxious to return to the civilian
pursuits that appeared so inevitable. Privately, he appealed to Secretary of War Benjamin Lincoln for an appointment, assuring him that
"*anywhere* would be agreeable to me but particularly Eastwardly."[2]
After receiving no assurances from Lincoln, Howe turned to the commander in chief to inquire of a command. Washington expressed
ignorance of congressional plans for the army but assured Howe that
he doubted that any army that remained would need the services of
a major general. He promised that, if the occasion arose, he would
submit Howe's name and desires along with all the others who had
expressed similar interests.[3]

To add to the uncertainty of his future, financial woes were beginning to create serious embarrassment. During October, he was
retained in Philadelphia to settle a debt, "which ought long since
to have been paid by the publick." Howe could avoid a suit only
by pledging to remain in the city until the debt was settled.[4] It does
not appear that Howe was with Washington for his victorious entry
into New York City in December. During much of 1784, however,
he traveled repeatedly between Philadelphia, New York City, Newburgh, and other locations, attempting to settle his financial accounts
with the government. Quartermaster General Timothy Pickering and
his associates personally disliked Howe and appeared to delight in
minimizing his accounts and questioning his figures with great for-
mality. On one occasion, Samuel Hodgdon reported to Pickering that
"I shew'd him the only additional estimate I could consent to make
in his favour, the amount twelve pounds, the trifling sum has piqued
his pride, and erased his poverty."[5]

By March 1785 Howe was reduced to such poverty that he made
an impassioned plea to Congress, in which he pointed out his plight.
Over the past nine years of service to his country, he had served far
from his native state and had drawn pay only on a few rare occasions. Due to the distance from home, he had been unable to visit his
plantation or manage its affairs. It had been overrun by the enemy,
and all of his slaves had been stolen. Other general officers had been
paid by their home states, but since he had not served the state di-

rectly he was neglected by its government. Left without income, he had been forced to borrow money to maintain his household. He had attempted to have his lands sold to satisfy these debts, but advisors in North Carolina had warned him that times were so bad that the lands would bring but a fraction of their value. Due to his pledge not to leave New York without paying his debts, Howe could not return to North Carolina to rebuild his property. If Congress did not intercede, he was surely bound for prison. "It is a melancholy consideration at this *time of day*, to have the world to begin a new, for lands without the means of Occupancy are useless, if not a burden. Born to affluence, I have been bred to no trade, or profession, and it is not now in my power to adopt them. A comparison between my *former*, and my *present circumstance* awakens anxieties [?] too poignant to be borne, were they not alleviated by the reflection that my distresses have occurred from having endeavored to serve my Country."[6] While the negotiations were pending, Howe managed to mortgage his Kendal Plantation for £758 "lawful money of the state of New York." Before the mortgage was even finalized, however, Congress took action on the petition and within the month agreed to advance $7,000 to the "late" general until the accounts could be properly settled.[7]

Howe remained in New York and in late summer Congress notified him that he had been appointed to a commission to negotiate with the western Indians. George Rogers Clark, Richard Butler, and Samuel H. Parsons, all revolutionary officers of some reputation, were appointed with Howe to travel to western Pennsylvania to resolve the question of U.S. sovereignty over Indian lands on the Ohio. As the commission was preparing to depart in late September, Howe informed Congress that he had just received letters from North Carolina that made it absolutely necessary for him to proceed there before going west. He apologized for the situation, assuring Congress that he had prepared to go to the backcountry, to the point that his stores had already departed, when he discovered the necessity of a hasty trip to Carolina. Whether or not Howe actually traveled to North Carolina at this time is uncertain; he appears to have been in New York on 27 October. He was in North Carolina in late December when the General Assembly, meeting at New Bern, passed a joint resolution expressing appreciation for his long and faithful service. The legislature refused to act, however, on Howe's petition for the state to redeem almost £10,000 in interest-bearing certificates awarded him by Congress in payment for his service. His plea for conversion of the Continental paper was simply held over until the next session, which did nothing to resolve his poverty. Howe did not participate in the Indian negotiations, and the three other commissioners concluded the treaty without him on 23 January 1786 at Fort Finney in western Pennsylvania.[8]

When the warrior did return to his home state, Archibald Maclaine Hooper, nephew of William Hooper, participated in the event. Reminiscing many years later, Hooper claimed that Howe and his black servant, Cuffee, traveled from New York to Charleston, South Carolina, by packet boat. After a brief visit in Charleston, he traveled overland to Fayetteville, where he was met by a number of friends and well-wishers. Town commissioners and a company of cavalry escorted him into town after presenting him with an appropriate address from the citizens. The general was guest of honor at a succession of parties that lasted a full week—every prominent family vied for the opportunity to host a dinner in his behalf. During the dinners, the guest of honor enthralled those present by relating military anecdotes. One that stuck with the young Hooper was Howe's description of the trial of Maj. John André, in which Howe told of shedding tears when the British spy addressed the court.

On the trip from Fayetteville to Brunswick County, Howe allegedly stopped one night with Thomas Owen in Bladen County and the next with Gen. Thomas Brown. He parted with his companions at the point where the Brunswick road crossed the Fayetteville-Wilmington road and proceeded toward his Kendal Plantation on the west bank of the Cape Fear.[9]

After resolving his immediate financial embarrassment, the general commenced to make the transition from soldier to planter. He undertook to restore his long-neglected fields, building new canals and floodgates for the once-productive rice fields that bordered the Cape Fear River. He also obtained a land warrant to add to his lands the adjoining Lilliput Plantation, which had been confiscated from former Royal governor William Tryon. In addition to this 492-acre rice plantation, he had bid on some three thousand acres on Allens Creek that had been confiscated from Thomas Hooper. With the new plantation, the general would be prepared for a major farming

venture. Howe also became immersed in local public affairs, joining with such leaders as future governor Benjamin Smith in planning a lighthouse to be built on Bald Head Island at the mouth of the river.[10]

As the summer election campaign got under way in 1786, Robert Howe stood for election to represent Brunswick County in the General Assembly. He "openly avow[ed] the most liberal principles" in a heated race made worse by the sweltering weather of a coastal Carolina July. Howe had taken a stand in support of former Loyalists who were attempting to resume their livelihoods in North Carolina, appealing to the General Assembly in behalf of Dr. Daniel McNeil, whom the superior court justices were attempting to banish from the state. He also railed against the disgraceful performance of the judges, who were involved in a direct confrontation with such prominent Conservative lawyers as Archibald Maclaine, William Hooper, and James Iredell over the issues of confiscation, the treatment of former Loyalists, courtroom decorum, and the very performance of the judiciary.[11]

Howe faced formidable opposition in the election campaign, but he was victorious in his first bid for political office in over a decade. He had energetically canvassed throughout the county, despite record heat and flooding rains. The campaign and the weather took a toll, however: Howe was stricken with a severe case of bilious fever. After a period of recuperation, he began making preparations for the trip to Fayetteville, where the General Assembly was scheduled to convene on 20 November. Although he "looked feeble," he proceeded upriver, stopping off to visit his friend, Brig. Gen. Thomas Clark, at Point Repose Plantation near the mouth of Hood's Creek. There, he suffered a relapse and died after lingering for more than a week.[12]

It is uncertain where his body was buried. Tradition has been that the body was transported by water up the river to Grange Farm, near the mouth of Waymans Creek, in what was to become Columbus County. Howe had owned the property and lived there as a young planter, although the land was once the plantation of his estranged wife's family. Nothing is known of Sarah Howe's whereabouts or activities after her legal separation from the general in 1772, except that she was living in Brunswick County during the 1790s. A more logical scenario for Howe's burial is developed by a contemporary of his who claimed that, after Howe died at Point Repose, his remains were conveyed to Kendal and interred in a family burying ground. Whatever Howe's final resting place, it appears that no slab was placed over the grave, and its location is lost to posterity.[13]

Robert Howe as a person and as a Revolutionary War officer aroused a disparate mixture of admiration, praise, distaste, and ridicule. Though it is difficult at this distance to fairly and accurately judge the man and his accomplishments, some notable qualities as well as faults and blemishes are apparent. In appearance, he was tall and had a scar on his nose and a great mane of auburn hair. As a revolutionary general, he had a striking military bearing that contemporaries compared to Gen. Charles Lee.[14]

As a young man, he was brash, coddled, and insufferably spoiled by a family that possessed wealth and position. He developed a taste for good literature, fine wine, art, music, and an expensive life-style. He had little sense for business and found sociable company more to his liking than the rigors of financial management. Howe, along with his early revolutionary friends William Hooper and Cornelius Harnett, was an active member of St. John's Masonic Lodge in Wilmington. He thrived on rhetoric, speaking with a fervent, impassioned voice; yet, in writing, his talent for words was almost lost in a handwriting that was virtually indecipherable.[15]

As a citizen of the emerging United States, he was an effective and courageous political leader in the cause of American freedom and independence. As a legislator and political leader, he had a special ability in verbalizing and formulating public sentiment in a time when America was defining its purposes and its future. As a military officer, Robert Howe's place in history is somewhat obscure. Several contemporaries labeled him as "competent," "very sensible," and "not without talent," while Joshua Hett Smith concluded that he "was well versed in tactics, a rigid disciplinarian, and was acknowledged to be an engineer of the highest reputation."[16] There is no question that he was devoted to a high degree of military discipline within his command. He also was extremely cautious as a commander, especially after the debacle at Savannah in 1778. Undoubtedly, the loss of Georgia had a permanent impact on the man and his career. The Southern command was the graveyard of American generals, and for a man obsessed with a desire for military glory, the experience was devastating. The American Revolution was a war that

permitted few heroes and fewer opportunities for glory. The overwhelming problems, many of which were beyond the control of most
individual men regardless of their position, compromised the opportunities for victory and created a degree of caution in those who had
previously tasted defeat. At least some of his fellow officers doubted
Howe's general capacity in a serious emergency; and, although General Washington continuously utilized him in field commands along
the Hudson, there was no opportunity for the North Carolinian to
dispel this distrust among his colleagues.[17]

Howe never claimed extraordinary military talent, but he did claim
an exceptional degree of desire and perseverance to succeed in his
chosen profession. At one point early in his career, Howe mused that
"if real attachment to the noble cause . . . and the strictest attention
to . . . duty" could compensate for want of abilities, then he could be
relied upon to serve well. Regardless of the quest for glory and success in arms, he never lost sight of the civilian public that he served.
During eight years of active duty, he continuously yielded to civil
ascendancy and on numerous occasions warned his troops to never
compromise the rights and property of the public.[18]

Howe enjoyed people and pleasure even during wartime, but it
appears that he had difficulty maintaining close friendships on a long
term basis. His passion for honor and fame led some to see in him a
pompous demeanor that alienated rather than attracted friendships.
As the war approached its inevitable end, Howe, realizing that glory
had eluded him and that his career as a general officer was drawing to
an end, faced the necessity of grappling for the monetary remuneration that he had ignored so cavalierly in the past. His frantic efforts to
extricate himself from pauperism undoubtedly repulsed many who
still looked upon him with friendship. His early death, the instability
of his family ties, the absence of a body of personal records to document his career, his service so far from home, and his failure to attain
the military glory he so fervently desired all contributed to obscuring
his memory. Whether he was truly competent as a general we will
never know; that he was unlucky is a certainty. Also a certainty was
the fact that both in political leadership and military command he
labored long and with little reward for American independence and
a government of civil domination. The greatness of that cause and
his dedication to it should give to his memory the touch of glory that
in life he never realized.

NOTES

ABBREVIATIONS

AAS   American Antiquarian Society
DU   Duke University
LC   Library of Congress
MHS   Massachusetts Historical Society
MSA   Massachusetts State Archives
NARA   National Archives
NCSA   North Carolina State Archives
NYHS   New-York Historical Society
NYPL   New York Public Library
NYSA   New York State Archives
SCHS   South Carolina Historical Society
SCL USC South Caroliniana Library, University of South Carolina
SHC UNC Southern Historical Collection, University of North Carolina
WH   Washington Headquarters

CHAPTER I

1. Quincy, "Journal," p. 460.
2. "Letters from John Stewart to William Dunlop," pp. 12–13; Edgar, *Biographical Directory*, 2:335–37; McCrady, *History of South Carolina*, p. 293.
3. J. P. Greene, *Quest for Power*, p. 480; Cheves, "Middleton of South Carolina," pp. 228–30; McCrady, *History of South Carolina*, pp. 376, 453. The family name in England and South Carolina was Howes; the "s" was dropped by the family in North Carolina.
4. "First Governor Moore," pp. 1–23; Edgar, *Biographical Directory*, 2:335–37; Sirmans, *Colonial South Carolina*, pp. 41–46, 70.
5. E. L. Lee, *Lower Cape Fear*, pp. 91–106.
6. Ibid.
7. New Hanover County Deed Books, A and B, pp. 255, 265–66; D, p. 353; *South Carolina Gazette*, no. 16, Sat. 25 Mar.–Sat. 1 Apr. 1732.
8. Thomas Clifford Howe settled near New Bern and was very successful   *157*

as a planter and legislator from Craven County. Arthur had holdings in New Hanover, Bladen, and Chowan counties and, prior to his death in 1775, was a lawyer and clerk of court for Bladen County. Mary was the first wife of Capt. Benjamin Heron and obviously died young. Joseph and Elizabeth apparently died without marrying. When Joseph died in 1767, he left his estate to be divided among Job, Thomas, Arthur, and Mary's children. His brother Robert was left one shilling.

9. Schaw, *Journal of a Lady of Quality*, p. 191; Robert Howe to William Heath, 17 Apr. 1780, Heath Papers, 15:455; Robert Howe to Gov. George Clinton, 14 Mar. 1780, Miscellaneous Manuscripts, Gov. George Clinton, NYHS; Robert Howe to Baron von Steuben, 21 July 1780, Steuben Papers.

10. Iredell, *Life and Correspondence*, 2:262–73; Watson, Lawson, and Lennon, *Harnett, Hooper and Howe*, pp. 71–72.

11. Josiah Martin to Earl of Dartmouth, 24 Dec. 1773, Saunders, *Colonial Records*, 9:798–99; Smyth, *Tour of the United States of America*, chap. LIV, p. 56; Brunswick County Deed Books, B, pp. 94–95; A, pp. 168–69; A, pp. 44–45; A, pp. 90–91; A, p. 125.

12. Robert Howe to Continental Congress, 10 Mar. 1785, Papers of the Continental Congress, m. 247, r. 178, i. 173, pp. 531–37, NARA.

13. Brunswick County Will Books, A, pp. 31–32. The Daughters of the American Revolution application of one direct descendant claims six children (Ann Goodlet, Rachel, Elizabeth, Rebecca, Mary, and Robert), whereas another DAR application on file lists a seventh child, Sarah. Robert, Jr., who served as sheriff of Brunswick County during 1790 and 1791, died without issue. Frances Daniell Hough to author, 11 July 1988.

14. Schaw, *Journal of a Lady of Quality*, p. 167; Iredell, *Life and Correspondence*, 1:194.

15. Schaw, *Journal of a Lady of Quality*, p. 191; Shakespeare, *Complete Works*, pp. 697–98.

16. R. Rankin, "'Mosquetoe' Bites," p. 188; Schaw, *Journal of a Lady of Quality*, p. 167.

CHAPTER 2

1. Saunders, *Colonial Records*, 6:378, 475, 516; Clark, *State Records*, 22:824.

2. Saunders, *Colonial Records*, 6:654–55; Clark, *State Records*, 23:539–41.

3. Saunders, *Colonial Records*, 6:675; Clark, *State Records*, 23:546–47.

4. British Public Record Office, War Office 34/47 (mf. Z.5.189n), NCSA (hereinafter cited as PRO War Office); Stewart, *William Woodford*, 1:523, 571; Treasurers and Comptrollers Papers, Military Papers, 1747–

79, NCSA; Saunders, *Colonial Records*, 7:40. In a letter from Jeffrey Amherst to North Carolina governor Arthur Dobbs, dated 25 January 1763, Amherst promised to find a position in the British army for Lt. Howe, whom Dobbs had dispatched to New York in search of a commission. PRO War Office 34/36 (80.1148.1), NCSA.

5. Other commissioners, in addition to Howe, included William Dry, William Bartram, Hugh Waddell, and Robert Johnson. Clark, *State Records*, 23:522–25; Saunders, *Colonial Records*, 6:1257; New Hanover County Deed Books, E, pp. 238, 240.

6. J. P. Greene, *Quest For Power*, p. 490.

7. Saunders, *Colonial Records*, 7:320, 346–51, 394, 619, 661–62, 681–83, 940.

8. Saunders, *Colonial Records*, 7:xviii–xix, 940; 9:212.

9. Saunders, *Colonial Records*, 7:69, 373, 425, 427, 573–74, 624, 938, 940, 950; 9:164–65, 171, 212, 452, 491, 501, 899; Clark, *State Records*, 23:858–59.

10. Saunders, *Colonial Records*, 6:378, 475, 641, 664, 1259; 7:60, 62, 346, 351, 357, 373, 394–95, 568; 8:309.

11. Saunders, *Colonial Records*, 7:90–91.

12. Saunders, *Colonial Records*, 7:630–31, 950; 7:326, 329, 418; 9:163.

13. Saunders, *Colonial Records*, 8:333.

14. Saunders, *Colonial Records*, 7:40.

15. Saunders, *Colonial Records*, 7:160, 244, 249, 271; Clark, *State Records*, 22:845–46; Treasurers and Comptrollers Papers, Military Papers, 1747–79, NCSA.

16. Saunders, *Colonial Records*, 5:158, 595; 6:1028, 1099, 1183; 7:246; Schaw, *Journal of a Lady of Quality*, p. 142.

17. Powell, Huhta, and Farnham, *Regulators in North Carolina*, pp. 71, 137, 168, 410; Saunders, *Colonial Records*, 7:829, 842, 982; 8:594.

18. Saunders, *Colonial Records*, 9:798–99.

19. Taylor, "Foreign Attachment Law," pp. 20–22; J. P. Greene, *Quest For Power*, pp. 420–24.

20. Josiah Martin Message to House, 4 Dec. 1773, General Assembly Session Records (Legislative Papers), NCSA; J. P. Greene, *Quest For Power*, pp. 420–24.

21. This resolution, dated 21 Dec. 1773, included in the General Assembly Session Records (Legislative Papers), NCSA, is in Robert Howe's very distinctive handwriting.

22. "Committee of Assembly to William Tryon, Gov. of New York," English Records, Dartmouth MSS, pp. 85–88; Saunders, *Colonial Records*, 9:737, 738, 787, 876–77, 902, 798–99.

23. Quincy, "Journal," p. 460. Quincy visited with Howe on 30 Mar. 1773, when he was still commander of Ft. Johnston. It appears that Howe continued to command the fort until July or August. "Subsistence Cer-

tificates for Ft. Johnston," Treasurers and Comptrollers Papers, Military Papers, Box 1, NCSA.

24. Taylor, "Foreign Attachment Law," p. 33.
25. Taylor, "Foreign Attachment Law," pp. 33–36.

CHAPTER 3

1. Saunders, *Colonial Records*, 9:786–87.
2. Quincy, "Journal," pp. 457–60.
3. Saunders, *Colonial Records*, 9:737, 741; Tarter and Scribner, *Revolutionary Virginia*, 2:58–59.
4. H. F. Rankin, *North Carolina Continentals*, p. 7; Saunders, *Colonial Records*, 10:xxxvii–xxxviii; Clark, *State Records*, 11:245–48.
5. Lefler and Powell, *Colonial North Carolina*, p. 261; Saunders, *Colonial Records*, 9:xxix.
6. *Calendar of Virginia State Papers*, 7:58–59.
7. *Calendar of Virginia State Papers*, 8:64–65.
8. Saunders, *Colonial Records*, 9:1029–30.
9. Saunders, *Colonial Records*, 9:1016, 1041–49.
10. Saunders, *Colonial Records*, 10:16–19; McEachern and Williams, *Wilmington-New Hanover Safety Committee Minutes*, pp. 29–30.
11. McEachern and Williams, *Wilmington-New Hanover Safety Committee Minutes*, pp. 29–35.
12. Saunders, *Colonial Records*, 9:1157.
13. Saunders, *Colonial Records*, 10:96.
14. Saunders, *Colonial Records*, 10:149–50.
15. Schaw, *Journal of a Lady of Quality*, pp. 167, 190. The celebrated British general James Wolfe was killed during the French and Indian War as he led troops to victory over the French at Quebec on 13 Sept. 1759.
16. Saunders, *Colonial Records*, 10:97.
17. Saunders, *Colonial Records*, 10:113–14. Among other charges, the committee contended that Collet had "threatened vengeance against magistrates, whose official opinion he chose to disapprove—had set at defiance the high sheriff of the county, in the execution of his office, and treated the King's writs, when served on him for just debts . . . with the shameful contempt of wiping his b__k s_de with them."
18. Saunders, *Colonial Records*, 10:93, 96–98, 100–104, 108–9; Schaw, *Journal of a Lady of Quality*, pp. 187, 187n.
19. McEachern and Williams, *Wilmington-New Hanover Safety Committee Minutes*, pp. 27, 35. Still another plea was sent to Johnston on 13 July by the Wilmington Safety Committee's Committee of Intelligence, stating that they "adjure you by your love to your country to call a provincial convention at an early day" (p. 43).
20. Saunders, *Colonial Records*, 10:171–72, 199.

21. Saunders, *Colonial Records*, 10:186–88, 196–201; H. F. Rankin, *North Carolina Continentals*, pp. 16–21.
22. Saunders, *Colonial Records*, 10:290, 292.
23. H. F. Rankin, *North Carolina Continentals*, pp. 23–24; Saunders, *Colonial Records*, 10:341; Hast, *Loyalism in Revolutionary Virginia*, pp. 20–21.
24. Mays, *Edmund Pendleton*, 2:69–76; Boatner, *Encyclopedia of the American Revolution*, pp. 447–48; "Letters of Col. William Woodford," pp. 106–9.
25. Stewart, *William Woodford*, 1:511, 523, 527, 529, 571.
26. "Letters of Col. William Woodford," pp. 125–49.
27. Saunders, *Colonial Records*, 10:366.
28. Saunders, *Colonial Records*, 10:365, 372.
29. Saunders, *Colonial Records*, 10:365, 366–68; Clark, *State Records*, 11: 264; Stewart, *William Woodford*, 1:523–60, passim; Troop Returns, Morning Report of Col. Howe's Force in Norfolk, Military Collection, NCSA.
30. Clark, *State Records*, 11:262–64.
31. Stewart, *William Woodford*, 1:585–90; Saunders, *Colonial Records*, 10: 379–82; "Letters of Col. William Woodford," pp. 152, 154; Eller, *Chesapeake Bay*, p. 88.
32. Saunders, *Colonial Records*, 10:544; Clark, *State Records*, 11:270.
33. Mays, *Edmund Pendleton*, p. 96; Force, *American Archives*, 4th ser., 4:124, 127, 1488.

CHAPTER 4

1. Ford, *Journals of Continental Congress*, 4:15–16, 132–33, 174–75; Alden, *General Charles Lee*, pp. 108 9.
2. C. Lee, *Lee Papers*, 1:342–43.
3. John Hancock to Charles Lee, and John Hancock to Gen. Andrew Lewis & Gen. Robert Howe in Virginia and Gen. James Moore in North Carolina, 1 Mar. 1776, Papers of the Continental Congress, m. 247, r. 23, i. 12A, pp. 58–59, NARA. In a letter to Daniel Hitchcock, dated 3 Aug. 1776, John Adams defended the action of Congress in appointing a disproportionate number of Southerners as general officers. In speaking of Howe, Moore, Lewis, and Hugh Mercer of Virginia (who was appointed brigadier on 5 June 1776), Adams asserted that they "were not only Men of Fortune and Figure in their countries and in Civil Imployments, but they were all veteran soldiers, and had been Collonells [*sic*] in a former war." Adams rated them equal to several New England generals, except "that the Gentlemen themselves were Superior in Point of Property and Education." P. H. Smith, *Letters of Delegates to Congress*, 4:613–14.
4. Clark, *State Records*, 11:287–88.

5. Charles Lee to Robert Howe, 5 Apr. 1776, C. Lee, *Lee Papers*, 1:375–76.

6. Lefler and Powell, *Colonial North Carolina*, pp. 280–81; Saunders, *Colonial Records*, 10:504, 512.

7. Lefler and Newsome, *North Carolina*, p. 218.

8. Robert Howe to Charles Lee, 10 Apr. 1776, C. Lee, *Lee Papers*, 1:398–400; Lefler and Powell, *Colonial North Carolina*, p. 280; John Armstrong to [?], 23 Apr. 1776, North Carolina Manuscripts. While in Halifax, Howe visited Loyalist general Donald MacDonald, who was imprisoned in the common gaol after his capture at the Battle of Moores Creek Bridge. Howe thought MacDonald's "treatment erroneous and without a precedent" and used his influence with the convention to gain a parole to the limits of Halifax for the prisoner. Petition of Donald Mac-Donald to Congress, 29 May 1776, Papers of the Continental Congress, m. 247, r. 99, i. 78, v. 15, pp. 49–51, NARA.

9. Robert Howe to John Hancock, 8 June 1777, Papers of the Continental Congress, m. 247, r. 178, i. 160, pp. 360–64, NARA.

10. Charles Lee to Robert Howe, 5 Apr. 1776, and Charles Lee to George Washington, 5 Apr. 1776, C. Lee, *Lee Papers*, 1:375–78. In a letter to the president of Congress, dated 19 Apr. 1776, Lee admitted that arms were in such short supply that he was training the men to use spears rather than musket and bayonet. The plan was to arm two companies of each battalion with spears. C. Lee, *Lee Papers*, 1:432–34.

11. James Moore to [?], 14 May 1776, Emmet Collection. Howe further commented that they were prevented by a party of men from doing further mischief. Robert Howe to Charles Lee, 10 Apr. 1776, C. Lee, *Lee Papers*, 1:401–2. In a letter written from Tarboro on 26 May 1776, Howe added the following postscript: "I have the honor to find that I am proscribed, and that my house is burnt." Robert Howe to [?], de Coppet Collection. Apparently this information was erroneous. *The Virginia Gazette* (Williamsburg) of 29 June 1776, reported that the women at Howe's plantation "were treated with great barbarity; one of whom was shot through the hips, another stabbed with a bayonet, and a third knocked down with the butt of a musket." No mention is made in this account of the house being burned.

12. "Letters of Col. William Woodford," pp. 154–55.

13. "Proclamation by Gen. Henry Clinton to the magistrates of the Province of North Carolina," 5 May 1776, Council of Safety Papers, Secretary of State Papers, NCSA; Clark, *State Records*, 11:297–98; "Letters of Col. William Woodford," pp. 156–58; C. Lee, *Lee Papers*, 2:41–42.

14. John Rutledge to Maj. Gen. Charles Lee, 4 June 1776, C. Lee, *Lee Papers*, 2:53–54.

15. John Armstrong to John Hancock, 7 May 1776, Papers of the Continental Congress, m. 247, r. 179, i. 162, pp. 243–44, NARA; John Armstrong to Charles Lee, 8 May 1776, C. Lee, *Lee Papers*, 2:7–8. This situa-

tion is not unlike the experience of Gens. Philip Schuyler and Richard Montgomery at Fort Ticonderoga in New York in October 1775. Connecticut troops refused to obey the Continental generals until their own Connecticut general arrived. In complete frustration, Montgomery commented, "I cannot help observe to how little purpose I am here . . . at the head of Troops whose operations I cannot direct." White, "Standing Armies," pp. 136–37.

16. Henry Laurens to John Laurens, 14 Aug. 1776, C. Lee, *Lee Papers*, 2:220–21; *South Carolina and American General Gazette*, 31 May–2 Aug. 1776; entries for 15 June–20 June 1776, Howe Orderly Book.

17. Alden, *General Charles Lee*, pp. 123–24; Moultrie, *Memoirs*, 1:140–41.

18. Robert Howe to Committee of Safety on Cape Fear, 29 June 1776, Howe Papers, SHC UNC; Alden, *General Charles Lee*, pp. 124–29; Moultrie, *Memoirs*, 1:141–45; *South Carolina and American General Gazette*, 31 May–2 Aug. 1776; Force, *American Archives*, 5th ser., 1:435–39. A deserter reported approximately 180 British killed and wounded in the engagement. The Americans reported 12 killed and 23 wounded.

19. Charles Lee to John Armstrong, 7 July 1776, C. Lee, *Lee Papers*, 2:126. Lee commented that "an Angel from Heaven cou'd not get the better of the indolent & procrastinating spirit of these people." Charles Lee to Pres. John Rutledge, 9 July 1776, C. Lee, *Lee Papers*, 2:130.

20. For a discussion of the Indian problem see Searcy, "Georgia-Florida Campaigns."

21. Coleman, *Colonial Georgia*, pp. 280–88; W. C. Smith, "Mermaids Riding Alligators," pp. 445–46, 456–57.

22. John Armstrong to Charles Lee, July 1776, C. Lee, *Lee Papers*, 2:184–85.

23. Moultrie, *Memoirs*, 1:184; Francis Otway Byrd to William Byrd, 6 May 1776, Byrd Papers; Searcy, "Georgia-Florida Campaigns," pp. 61–62; Saunders, *Colonial Records*, 10:737–38; Charles Lee to John Rutledge, 23 July and 3, 5, and 7 Aug. 1776, Lee Letterbook, pp. 32–33, 58–62.

24. Robert Howe to Charles Lee, 10 Aug. 1776, C. Lee, *Lee Papers*, 2:207–8.

25. Charles Lee to Board of War and Ordnance, 23 Aug. 1776, C. Lee, *Lee Papers*, 2:241–45.

26. Charles Lee to Board of War and Ordnance, 27 Aug. 1776, C. Lee, *Lee Papers*, 2:241–45; Force, *American Archives*, 5th ser., 1:6–8, 435–36, 910–11.

27. Charles Lee's Conference with Georgia Council of Safety, 19 Aug. 1776, and Charles Lee to Pres. John Rutledge, 20 Aug. 1776, C. Lee, *Lee Papers*, 2:233–36.

28. C. Lee, *Lee Papers*, 2:246.

29. John Hancock to Maj. Gen. Charles Lee, 8 Aug. 1776, C. Lee, *Lee Papers*, 2:205–6.

30. Robert Howe to Gen. George Washington, 4 July 1777, Society Collection; entries for 3 Sept.–20 Sept. 1776, Howe Orderly Book; *Historical*

Manuscripts Commission Report, 1:58; Searcy, "Georgia-Florida Campaigns," pp. 61–62.

31. John Armstrong to John Hancock, 7 Oct. 1776, Papers of the Continental Congress, m. 247, r. 179, i. 162, p. 253, NARA; Force, *American Archives*, ser. 5, 3:49–53. In lieu of arms, Howe ordered training exercises using pikes and spears, urging that "the soldiers . . . be attentive in learning what in the course of service may so essentially contribute to their honour and Safety." After Gen. Moore finally arrived in Charleston, Howe made a return expedition to Savannah, where he remained from 29 November to 11 December. Entries for 23 Oct.–23 Dec. 1776, Howe Orderly Book.

32. Entries for 24 Nov.–14 Dec. 1776, Howe Orderly Book.

33. Moultrie, *Memoirs*, 1:189; entry for 21 Feb. 1777, Howe Orderly Book; Jones, *History of Georgia*, 2:263; H. F. Rankin, *Francis Marion*, pp. 24–25.

34. Boatner, *Encyclopedia of the American Revolution*, pp. 730–31; Clark, *State Records*, 10:xiii. According to Samuel Johnston, Moore died of "a fit of Gout in his stomach." Clark, *State Records*, 11:454.

CHAPTER 5

1. Flexner, *George Washington*, p. 135; Rossie, *Politics of Command*, pp. 8, 25–26; Carp, *To Starve the Army*, pp. 9–15.

2. John Armstrong to Charles Lee, 8 May 1776, C. Lee, *Lee Papers*, 2:10; John Armstrong to John Hancock, 7 May 1776, Papers of the Continental Congress, m. 247, r. 179, i. 162, pp. 243–44, NARA; Charles Lee to Board of War and Ordnance, 7 Aug. 1776, C. Lee, *Lee Papers*, 2:203–5.

3. John Armstrong to John Hancock, 6 Aug. 1776, Papers of the Continental Congress, m. 247, r. 179, i. 162, p. 247, NARA.

4. Charles Lee to Board of War and Ordnance, 7 Aug. 1776, C. Lee, *Lee Papers*, 2:203–5; Charles Lee to John Rutledge, 22 and 23 July and 3, 5, and 7 Aug. 1776, Lee Letterbook, pp. 31–33, 58–62.

5. Robert Howe to Henry Laurens, 28 Aug. 1777, Laurens Papers, Letterbook #16, pp. 83–84; Robert Howe to Board of War, 25 Aug. 1777, Papers of the Continental Congress, m. 247, r. 178, i. 160, pp. 372–76, NARA; "Report of Committee to whom were referred the letter from Mr. Prest. [Rawlins] Lowndes & the Letters from Maj. Gen. Howe," 13 Nov. 1778, Papers of the Continental Congress, m. 247, r. 27, i. 19, vol. 3, pp. 203–4, NARA.

6. William Moultrie to Henry Laurens, 20 Apr. 1778, Papers of the Continental Congress, m. 247, r. 177, i. 158, pp. 453–57, NARA; Ford, *Journals of Continental Congress*, 11:551–52.

7. Robert Howe to Continental Congress, 4 Apr. 1778, Papers of the Continental Congress, m. 247, r. 178, i. 160, pp. 434–38, NARA.

8. Grimké, "Campaign to the Southward," pp. 125–33; Jones, *History of Georgia*, 2:289; Clark, *State Records*, 12:68–69; Ford, *Journals of Continental Congress*, 10:163.

9. Gervais, "Letters," 66:21–23.

10. [?] to Gentlemen, 30 Aug. 1777, Miscellaneous Papers, SCL USC; Gervais, "Letters," 66:22; Henry Laurens to John Laurens, 30 Sept. 1777, Laurens, *Papers of Henry Laurens*, 2:540.

11. Robert Howe to Henry Laurens, 28 Aug. 1777, Laurens Papers, Letterbook #16, pp. 83–84.

12. Henry Laurens to Robert Howe, 20 Oct. 1777, Laurens Papers, Letterbook #10, pp. 185–87.

13. Gadsden, *Writings*, p. 139.

14. Gadsden, *Writings*, pp. 151–53.

15. Christopher Gadsden Miscellaneous; Gadsden, *Writings*, pp. 134–44, 146–54; Godbold and Woody, *Christopher Gadsden*, pp. 178–87; *Historical Magazine*, Sept. 1860, 4:265–67.

16. The entire verse is included in Sargent, *Life of Major John André*, pp. 202–3. The "E." in the poem was Col. Bernard Elliott; "P." was Charles Coteworth Pinckney. Most 19th century accounts of the duel report that Howe's shot nicked Gadsden's ear. Since none of the contemporary versions—including Gadsden's and the Charleston newspaper's—report the wound, its authenticity is doubtful.

17. Button Gwinnett to John Hancock, 28 Mar. 1777, Papers of the Continental Congress, m. 247, r. 87, i. 73, pp. 19–26, NARA.

18. 11 Dec. 1776, Howe Orderly Book, p. 35.

19. Mrs. Button Gwinnett to Continental Congress, 1 Aug. 1777, Papers of the Continental Congress, m. 247, r. 87, i. 73, pp. 64–66, NARA. Gwinnett's widow claimed that Howe "feasted with the Tories . , . was at their dancings several evenings & spent his time mostly with them." Button Gwinnett to John Hancock, 28 Mar. 1777, Papers of the Continental Congress, m. 247, r. 87, i. 73, pp. 19–26, NARA.

20. Searcy, *Georgia-Florida Contest*, pp. 192–97.

21. Robert Howe to George Washington, 3 Nov. 1777, Vail Papers; petitions and letters from People of Georgia, Papers of the Continental Congress, m. 247, r. 87, i. 73, pp. 65–100+, NARA.

22. Force, *American Archives*, ser. 5, 3:49–53, 79–81; Hemphill, Wates, and Olsberg, *Journals of the General Assembly*, pp. 126–30.

23. Gibbes, *Documentary History of the American Revolution*, 3:55.

24. Robert Howe to Continental Congress, 26 Feb. 1777, Papers of the Continental Congress, m. 247, r. 178, i. 160, pp. 348–49, NARA.

25. Robert Howe to Continental Congress, 8 June and 15 Aug. 1777, Papers

of the Continental Congress, m. 247, r. 178, i. 160, pp. 360–64, 368, NARA; [Robert Howe] to Continental Congress, [1 June 1777], Continental Congress Miscellaneous, LC.

26. Lafayette, *Lafayette in the Age of the American Revolution*, 1:10, 61, 63; *South Carolina and American General Gazette*, 3 and 10 July 1777.

27. Williams, *A Founding Family*, pp. 112, 114, 116; Moultrie, *Memoirs*, 1:194–98; Hazard, "View of Coastal South Carolina," pp. 182–83.

28. Jenkins, *Button Gwinnett*, pp. 97–98.

29. *South Carolina and American General Gazette*, 13 Mar. 1777; Robert Howe to Continental Congress, 8 May 1777, Papers of the Continental Congress, m. 247, r. 178, i. 160, pp. 352–57, NARA.

30. Robert Howe to Georgia Assembly, 4 Sept. 1777, Papers of the Continental Congress, m. 247, r. 87, i. 73, pp. 7–9, NARA; Robert Howe to Continental Congress, 12 Sept. 1777, Papers of the Continental Congress, m. 247, r. 178, i. 160, pp. 396–99, NARA.

31. Robert Howe to Gov. [John Houstoun] of Georgia, 29 Jan. 1778, Miscellaneous Manuscripts, Robert Howe, NYHS.

32. Robert Howe to Gov. [John Houstoun] of Georgia, 29 Jan. 1778, Papers of the Continental Congress, m. 247, r. 87, i. 73, pp. 161–64, NARA and in Records of Georgia House of Assembly, 2 Feb. 1778, Papers of the Continental Congress, m. 247, r. 178, i. 160, pp. 418–24, NARA.

33. Robert Howe to Gov. [John Houstoun] of Georgia, 3 Feb. 1778, Papers of the Continental Congress, m. 247, r. 87, i. 73, pp. 149–53, NARA.

34. Minutes of Georgia House of Assembly, 10 Feb. 1778, Papers of the Continental Congress, m. 247, r. 87, i. 73, p. 141, NARA.

35. Resolution of Georgia House of Assembly, 10 Feb. 1778, Papers of the Continental Congress, m. 247, r. 87, i. 73, pp. 141–46, NARA; Howe's Response to Act of Georgia Assembly, n.d., Papers of the Continental Congress, m. 247, r. 87, i. 73, pp. 199–205, NARA; Robert Howe to Gov. John Houstoun, 22 Feb. 1778, Papers of the Continental Congress, m. 247, i. 73, pp. 179–80, NARA; Robert Howe to Henry Laurens, 26 Apr. 1778, Laurens Papers, Letterbook #16, p. 93.

36. Robert Howe to Henry Laurens, 25 Apr. 1778, Laurens Papers, Letterbook #16, pp. 92–93.

CHAPTER 6

1. Entries for 24 Feb.–3 Mar. 1778, Howe Orderly Book.

2. Thomas Brown to Gov. [Patrick] Tonyn, 13 Mar. 1778, PRO Colonial Office 5/558/227A–232, LC.

3. John Houstoun to [president of Congress], 20 Mar. 1778, Papers of the Continental Congress, m. 247, r. 87, i. 73, pp. 181–85, NARA.

4. Moultrie, *Memoirs*, 1:202; Robert Howe to Samuel Elbert, 6 Apr. 1778, Laurens Papers, Letterbook #16, pp. 95–96; Rawlins Lowndes to Henry Laurens, 13 Apr. 1778, Papers of the Continental Congress, m. 247, r. 86, i. 72, pp. 445–48, NARA; Robert Howe to Continental Congress, 13 Apr. 1778, Papers of the Continental Congress, m. 247, r. 178, i. 160, pp. 450–54, NARA. The Scopholites (Scoffelites, Scovelites) were followers of a Col. Joseph Scophol (Coffell), who gained a reputation for violence during the Regulator uprisings in the backcountry of South Carolina. The Scopholites were considered "vermin" by Whig observers, and William Moultrie characterized their leader as "an illiterate, stupid, noisy blockhead." Moultrie, *Memoirs*, 1:203.

5. Robert Howe to Continental Congress, 13 Apr. 1778, Papers of the Continental Congress, m. 247, r. 178, i. 160, pp. 444–49, NARA.

6. *South Carolina and American General Gazette*, 23 Apr. 1778; Samuel Elbert to Gen. [?], 19 Apr. 1778, Laurens Papers, Letterbook #16, pp. 94–95.

7. Robert Howe to Henry Laurens, 26 Apr. 1778, Laurens Papers, Letterbook #16, pp. 96–97.

8. Ibid.

9. The Georgia government issued a proclamation inviting all "well-wishers to freedom and Right to come in with the utmost Expedition, and partake of the Laurels and Profits of this Enterprize." Those who were "inclined to adventure" would serve under the command of the governor, provisions and ammunition would be supplied, and plunder was offered as a special inducement. PRO Colonial Office 5/558/317–18, L.C.

10. Entry for 10 May 1778, Howe Orderly Book; Grimké, "Campaign to the Southward," p. 61.

11. Pinckney, "Letters," p. 150.

12. Grimké, "Campaign to the Southward," pp. 61–64, 67; entries for 26 May–28 May 1778, Howe Orderly Book.

13. Grimké, "Campaign to the Southward," p. 63.

14. Entries for 18 and 21 May 1778, Howe Orderly Book; Charles C. Pinckney to William Moultrie, Moultrie, *Memoirs*, 1:213–14; Elbert, *Order Book*, pp. 146–49.

15. Charles C. Pinckney to William Moultrie, 24 May 1778, Moultrie, *Memoirs*, 1:212.

16. Entry for 26 May 1778, Howe Orderly Book; Grimké, "Campaign to the Southward," p. 68.

17. Pinckney, "Letters," p. 154; Grimké, "Campaign to the Southward," pp. 67, 118–20; William Moultrie to Charles C. Pinckney, 5 June 1778, Moultrie, *Memoirs*, 1:220–21.

18. Robert Howe to William Moultrie, 7 June 1778, Moultrie, *Memoirs*, 1:222; Pinckney, "Letters," pp. 152–55.

19. Grimké, "Campaign to the Southward," pp. 126–27.
20. William Moultrie to Robert Howe, 22 June 1778, Moultrie, *Memoirs*, 1:227.
21. Grimké, "Campaign to the Southward," p. 133; Grimké, Journal, 26 June–27 June 1778, Grimké Military Records, SCHS. This page of the original journal was not included in the published version in the *South Carolina Historical and Genealogical Quarterly*.
22. Grimké, "Campaign to the Southward," p. 127; Grimké, Journal, 27 June 1778, Grimké Military Records, SCHS.
23. Searcy, "Georgia-Florida Campaigns," pp. 412–14; Bennett, *Southernmost Battlefields*, pp. 33–37.
24. Grimké, "Campaign to the Southward," pp. 190–91.
25. Robert Howe to William Moultrie, 5 July 1778, Moultrie, *Memoirs*, 1:227–29; Charles C. Pinckney to William Moultrie, 10 July 1778, Moultrie, *Memoirs*, 1:230–32; Pinckney, "Letters," p. 159.
26. Pinckney, "Letters," p. 156.
27. Grimké, "Campaign to the Southward," p. 196.
28. Grimké, "Campaign to the Southward," pp. 198–99.
29. Grimké, "Campaign to the Southward," p. 200.
30. Grimké, "Campaign to the Southward," p. 199. Fleches were small V-shaped earthworks that were open to the rear.
31. Entry for 11 July 1778, Howe Orderly Book; Moultrie, *Memoirs*, 1:232–33.
32. Congress had declared that "as to the propriety of undertaking distant Expeditions and Enterprizes, or other Military operations, and the mode of Conducting them the General or commanding officer must finally judge & determine at his Peril." Ford, *Journals of Continental Congress*, 10:163.
33. William Moultrie to Col. [John] Laurens, 26 July 1778, Moultrie, *Memoirs*, 1:238–39; *South Carolina and American General Gazette*, 30 July 1778.

CHAPTER 7

1. Miller, *Triumph of Freedom*, p. 514; William Cruden to Earl of Dartmouth, 10 Mar. 1778, English Records, Dartmouth MSS, NCSA.
2. Robert Howe to Henry Laurens, 22 Sept. 1778, Laurens Papers, Letterbook #16, pp. 100–194.
3. John Houstoun to Henry Laurens, president of Congress, 20 Aug. 1778, Papers of the Continental Congress, m. 247, r. 87, i. 73, pp. 218–29, NARA; Robert Howe to Continental Congress, 18 Aug. 1778, Papers of the Continental Congress, m. 247, r. 178, i. 160, pp. 465–67, NARA.

4. John Houstoun to Henry Laurens, 20 Aug. 1778, Papers of the Continental Congress, m. 247, r. 87, i. 73, pp. 218–29, NARA.

5. Georgia Second Regiment Officers to Samuel Elbert, 31 Aug. 1778, Papers of the Continental Congress, m. 247, r. 94, i. 78, 8:295–304, NARA.

6. Robert Howe to Henry Laurens, 12 Oct. 1778, Papers of the Continental Congress, m. 247, r. 178, i. 160, pp. 495–99, NARA.

7. Congressional Resolution of 25 Sept. 1778, Emmet Collection.

8. Robert Howe to Henry Laurens, 9 Oct. 1778, Laurens Papers, Letterbook #16, p. 104.

9. Cornelius Harnett to Richard Caswell, 26 Sept. 1778, Clark, *State Records*, 22:982–83.

10. Cavanagh, "American Military Leadership," pp. 102–12; Sparks, *Correspondence of the American Revolution*, 2:21–22. During the British siege of Charleston in 1780, acting Lt. Gov. Christopher Gadsden claimed rank over Lincoln and attempted to force his will on the Continental commander. When Lincoln called a council of Continental officers, Gadsden attended, although he was not entitled to be there. Godbold and Woody, *Christopher Gadsden*, p. 199.

11. Robert Howe to Henry Laurens, 24 Nov. 1778, Papers of the Continental Congress, m. 247, r. 178, i. 160, pp. 499–500, NARA; entries for 9 Oct. 1778, 14 Nov. 1778, Grimké, "Order Book" (Apr. 1912), p. 95, (July 1912), p. 151.

12. John White to Robert Howe, 21 Nov. 1778, Papers of the Continental Congress, m. 247, r. 178, i. 160, pp. 503–4, NARA.

13. Robert Howe to William Moultrie, 27 Nov. 1778, Moultrie, *Memoirs*, 1:243–44; Kapp, *Life of Frederick William von Steuben*, pp. 657–58. In letters to Steuben, the French volunteer and inspector general in the Southern Department, Jean Baptiste Chevalier de Ternant, characterized the American leadership in the South as careless, slothful, and indecisive. He undertook to instruct Howe and, later, Benjamin Lincoln in the proper method of organizing and training the troops under their command.

14. Robert Howe to William Moultrie, 27 Nov. 1778, Moultrie, *Memoirs*, 1:243–44.

15. Gov. Tonyn subsequently reported that many rebels were killed and militia general James Screven was wounded and taken prisoner near Midway Meeting House. The Tories carried off 2,000 head of cattle and 200 Negroes. Gov. Patrick Tonyn to David Taitt and William McIntosh, 20 Dec. 1778, PRO Colonial Office 5/559/113–14, LC.

16. Entries for 1–27 Dec. 1778, Grimké, "Order Book" (Oct. 1912), pp. 210–12, (Jan. 1913), pp. 44–52.

17. Robert Howe to William Moultrie, 8 Dec. 1778, Moultrie, *Memoirs*,

1:247–48; *Gazette of State of North Carolina*, 23 Dec. 1778; Robert Howe to [?], 25 Dec. 1778, Howe Papers, DU.

18. Robert Howe to William Moultrie, 8 Dec. 1778, Jones, *History of Georgia*, 2:312–13; Testimony of Col. George Walton, *Proceedings of a General Court Martial . . . of Major General Howe*, pp. 242–43.

19. Entries for 25–27 Dec. 1778, Grimké, "Order Book," (Jan. 1913) pp. 46–51; *Proceedings of a General Court-Martial . . . of Major General Howe*, p. 281.

20. Robert Howe to [?], 25 Dec. 1778, Howe Papers, DU; *Proceedings of a General Court-Martial . . . of Major General Howe*, p. 281. William Moultrie later termed the decision to defend Savannah as absurd and described it as "the most ill advised, rash opinion that possibly could be given." Moultrie, *Memoirs*, 1:253; entries for 25–26 Dec. 1778, Grimké, "Order Book" (Jan. 1913), pp. 46–50.

21. *Royal Gazette Extraordinary*, 4 Feb. 1779; Dawson, *Battles of the United States*, 1:477.

22. *Proceedings of a General Court-Martial . . . of Major General Howe*, pp. 285–91.

23. Dawson, *Battles of the United States*, 1:477; *Royal Gazette Extraordinary*, 4 Feb. 1779.

24. Dawson, *Battles of the United States*, 1:477; F. V. Greene, *Revolutionary War*, p. 190.

25. Gen. Howe's Order of Battle at Savannah, 29 Dec. 1778, Moultrie, *Memoirs*, 1:252–53; Adams, "Jean Baptiste Ternant," pp. 226–27; *Proceedings of a General Court-Martial . . . of Major General Howe*, pp. 252–57. Maj. Benjamin Porter of the Georgia Line testified in Howe's trial that both he and Maj. Deheyser had been dispatched by Howe to watch the area. Howe also had horse troops patrolling the woods near the swamp. Robert Howe to Benjamin Lincoln, 30 Dec. 1778, Papers of the Continental Congress, m. 247, r. 177, i. 158, pp. 189–92, NARA.

26. Entry for 29 Dec. 1778, Grimké, "Order Book" (Jan. 1913), pp. 54–56. Subsequent testimony revealed that most Georgians who should have served in the militia were frantically trying to remove their personal property from the area during the battle and thus did not serve.

27. *Royal Gazette Extraordinary*, 4 Feb. 1779.

28. Ibid.

29. Ibid; *Proceedings of a General Court-Martial . . . of Major General Howe*, pp. 276–78.

30. *Royal Gazette Extraordinary*, 4 Feb. 1779.

31. Ibid.

32. *Proceedings of a General Court-Martial . . . of Major General Howe*, pp. 268–70.

33. *Proceedings of a General Court-Martial . . . of Major General Howe*, pp. 268–72.

34. Entries for 29–30 Dec. 1778, Grimké, "Order Book" (Jan. 1913), pp. 55–57.
35. *Royal Gazette Extraordinary*, 4 Feb. 1779.
36. Joseph Lane to Robert Howe, 30 Dec. 1778, and Joseph Lane to [?], 22 Feb. 1779, Emmet Collection; *Proceedings of a General Court-Martial . . . of Major General Howe*, p. 235.
37. *Royal Gazette Extraordinary*, 4 Feb. 1779.
38. Moultrie, *Memoirs*, 1:253; Lee, *Memoirs of the War*, p. 120.
39. *Proceedings of a General Court-Martial . . . of Major General Howe*, p. 302.

CHAPTER 8

1. Robert Howe to Continental Congress, 6 Feb. 1779, Papers of the Continental Congress, m. 247, r. 178, i. 160, p. 507, NARA; Moultrie, *Memoirs*, 1:236; Robert Howe to [Thomas Sumter], 2 Mar. 1779, John Rutledge to Delegates of South Carolina in Congress, 18 Mar. 1779, Emmet Collection; Robert Howe Power-of-Attorney, 17 Mar. 1779, Whitwell Autograph Collection. Apparently spies misunderstood Howe's trip north through North Carolina. They reported that the North Carolina general had recruited 500 fresh troops in his native state in early April and had marched to Georgetown, South Carolina, in preparation to reinforce Lincoln. *Revolution in America*, p. 275.
2. Robert Howe to [Benjamin Lincoln], 5 Apr. 1779, Miscellaneous Collection, NYPL; Clark, *State Records*, 14:289, 295; Nathanael Greene to George Washington and Robert Howe to George Washington, 27 Apr. 1779, Washington Papers, ser. 4, LC. Washington's army wintered in a zigzag line for some seventy-five miles, from western Connecticut into New Jersey.
3. Flexner, *George Washington*, p. 348; Heath, *Memoirs*, p. 217.
4. Robert Howe to Thomas Burke, 21 June 1779, Emmet Collection.
5. George Washington to Robert Howe, 25 June 1779, Washington Papers, ser. 4, LC; Robert Howe to Henry Laurens, 2 June 1779, Laurens Papers, Letterbook #16, p. 105; Robert Howe to Gov. Jonathan Trumbull, 2 July 1779, Trumbull Papers, vol. 9, doc. 261ab.
6. Flexner, *George Washington*, pp. 348–49. Washington had forbidden ammunition for fear that an accidental firing of a musket would alert the enemy.
7. George Washington to Robert Howe, 16 July 1779, Washington Papers, ser. 3B, LC; Heath, *Memoirs*, pp. 223–24; *Papers of Alexander Hamilton*, 2:105. At the time of the attack, Gen. Nathanael Greene observed from Stony Point that Verplanck's Point was "much more strongly fortified . . . than this, having seven enclosed redoubts." Newspaper extracts,

1779–80, Nathanael Greene to Col. Cox, 17 July 1779, *New Jersey Archives*, ser. 2, vol 3.

8. George Washington to Robert Howe (2 letters), 17 July 1779, Washington Papers, ser. 3B, LC; George Washington to William Heath, 17 and 18 July 1779, William Heath to Robert Howe, 17 July 1779, Robert Howe to William Heath, 17 July 1779, and William Heath to Robert Howe, 18 July 1779, Heath Papers, 13:214, 218, 221, 225, 234; Clark, *State Records*, 14:330–31; Heath, *Memoirs*, pp. 224–25; Robert Howe to [?], [July 1779?], Lamb Papers. It appears that Heath became incensed on 17 July at Brig. Gen. Samuel H. Parsons, who commanded one of his brigades, due to his slowness in march. After an abrupt exchange, Heath ended the matter by repeating "that the Troops must march without a moments loss of time." Heath Papers, 13:226–28.

9. Freeman, *George Washington*, 5:110–21; George Washington to president of Congress, 21 July 1779, Papers of the Continental Congress, m. 247, r. 169, i. 152, 7:503–5, NARA; William Heath to George Washington, 19 July 1779, Heath Papers, 13:244. Palmer, in *River and the Rock*, unjustifiably attributes entirely to Howe the failure at Verplanck's Point. Referring to him as a "playboy" and a "ladies' man," Palmer ignores some documentation and embellishes others in order to malign Howe.

10. George Washington to Robert Howe, 28 July 1779, Washington Papers, ser. 3B, LC; Hamilton, *Papers*, 2:115; Feb. 1778–Aug. 1779, Drew Orderly Book; Frost Orderly Book.

11. Robert Howe to Henry Laurens, 3 Aug. 1779, Laurens Papers, Letterbook #16, p. 106; Robert Howe to Γilliam Heath, Heath Papers, 13:313.

12. George Washington to Robert Howe, 9, 17, 20 (2 letters), 21, and 28 Aug. 1779, Washington Papers, ser. 3B, LC; Robert Howe to William Heath, 26 and 27 Aug. 1779, Heath Papers, 13:450, 457.

13. Elophalet Lockwood to Hon. Gold S. Silliman, 13 June 1780, Trumbull Papers, vol. 12, doc. 9a–c; Hall, *Life and Letters of Samuel Holden Parsons*, p. 300.

14. Robert Howe to George Washington, 6 Aug. 1779, Papers of the Continental Congress, m. 247, r. 169, i. 152, 7:477, NARA; William Heath to Robert Howe, 8 Aug. 1779, Heath Papers, 13:353.

15. George Washington to Robert Howe, 11 Sept. 1779, Washington Papers, ser. 3B, LC; William Heath to Robert Howe, 10 and 13 Aug. 1779, Heath Papers, 13:366, 382; Robert Howe to William Heath, 11 and 13 Aug. 1779, Heath Papers, 13:376, 393–94, 396; William Heath to Robert Howe and George Washington to Robert Howe, 15 Aug. 1779, Washington Papers, ser. 3B, LC.

16. Robert Howe to William Heath, 16 and 23 Aug. 1779, Heath Papers, 13:398, 439; George Washington to Robert Howe, 20, 21, and 28 Aug. 1779, Washington Papers, ser. 3B, LC.

17. George Washington to Robert Howe, 21 Aug. and 5 Sept. 1779, Washington Papers, ser. 3B, LC; Robert Howe to William Heath, 26 Aug. 1779, Heath Papers, 13:450; George Washington to William Heath, 29 Aug. 1779, Heath Papers, 13:465.

18. Robert Howe to William Heath, 10 Sept. 1779, Heath Papers, 14:62; William Heath to Robert Howe, 17 Sept. 1779, Heath Papers, 14:65; George Washington to William Heath, 18 Sept. 1779, Heath Papers, 14:67; George Washington to Robert Howe, 13 and 18 Sept. 1779, Washington Papers, ser. 3B, LC.

19. Robert Howe to William Heath, 23 Sept. 1779, Heath Papers, 14:78.

20. Heath, *Memoirs*, 230–34; Washington, *Writings*, 16:400–406; George Washington to Robert Howe, 4 and 9 Oct. 1779, Washington Papers, ser. 3B, LC.

21. Robert Howe to William Heath, 21 Oct. 1779, Heath Papers, 14:184.

22. George Washington to Robert Howe, 27 Oct. 1779, Washington Papers, ser. 3B, LC; William Heath to Robert Howe, 1, 4, and 5 Dec. 1779, Heath Papers, 14:315–16, 332, 348.

23. Robert Howe to William Heath, 13 Aug. 1779, Heath Papers, 13:394.

24. William Heath to Robert Howe, 4 and 8 Aug. 1779, Heath Papers, 13:339, 353; Robert Howe to William Heath, 3 Aug. 1779, Heath Papers, 13:332.

25. Robert Howe to William Heath, 26 Sept. 1779, Heath Papers, 14:89.

26. Washington, *Writings*, 15:172, 181–82.

27. *Proceedings of General Court-Martial . . . of Major General Benedict Arnold*, pp. 2–3; Washington, *Writings*, 15:206; George Washington to Robert Howe, 12 Dec. 1779, Washington Papers, ser. 3B, LC; Robert Howe to William Heath, 15, 18, and 20 Dec. 1779, Heath Papers, 14:391–93. Howe did not finally despair of receiving the countermand until 20 December, when he finally set out from the Robinson house.

28. *Proceedings of General Court-Martial . . . of Major General Benedict Arnold*.

29. Ibid, pp. 76–145; Robert Howe to William Heath, 16 Dec. 1779, Heath Papers, 14:391; Robert Howe to George Washington, 30 Dec. 1779, Washington Papers, ser. 4, LC.

30. *Proceedings of General Court-Martial . . . of Major General Benedict Arnold*, p. 167.

CHAPTER 9

1. Thacher, *Military Journal*, pp. 184–85; Heath, *Memoirs*, pp. 237, 240; Heath, *The Heath Papers*, ser. 7, vol. 4, pt. 2, pp. 334–35. The Americans were not alone in their misery, as spies repeatedly reported on the dire conditions in New York. Inhabitants were cutting up the wharves for fuel as they impatiently awaited the arrival of victualers.

2. Heath, *Memoirs*, pp. 240–43.

3. Clinton, *Public Papers*, 5:492, 541–42; George Washington to Robert Howe, 5 Feb. 1780, Washington Papers, ser. 3B, LC; William Heath to Robert Howe, 18 Feb. 1780, Heath, *The Heath Papers*, ser. 7, 5:34–36; Bradford Orderly Book.

4. Thacher, *Military Journal*, pp. 215–16.

5. Entries for 1, 2, 7, 8, and 11 Mar. and 13 Apr. 1780, Bradford Orderly Book; entry for 14 Apr. 1780, Drew Orderly Book.

6. Roberts, *New York's Forts*, pp. 98–100, 116, 118, 133, 136; Washington, *Writings*, 18:131–33; entry for 15 Mar. 1780, Frost Orderly Book; Thacher, *Military Journal*, pp. 215–16.

7. Royster, *A Revolutionary People*, p. 332; Kapp, *Life of Frederick William von Steuben*, pp. 279–80; entries for 29 Feb.–9 Apr. 1780, Bradford Orderly Book; entry for 1 Mar. 1780, Frost Orderly Book; George Washington to Robert Howe, 10 Mar. 1780, Washington Papers, ser. 3B, LC. Howe was greatly incensed that court-martial proceedings against soldiers were either too lenient in their sentences or were prone to acquit individuals that the general considered guilty. On several occasions, he criticized the court for its poor judgment, reminding them that he "is a disciplinarian by inclination, and habit has confirmed the disposition." Entry for 29 Feb. 1780, Bradford Orderly Book. Palmer, in *River and the Rock*, p. 229, used these same sources to justify his contention that Howe was a weak disciplinarian. These authors' reading of the Bradford Orderly Book does not bear out Palmer's interpretation.

8. Entry for 26 Apr. 1780, Drew Orderly Book; entries for 17 and 23 Apr. 1780, Frost Orderly Book.

9. Petition to Legislature of the State of New York, Mar. 1780, Emmet Collection.

10. Robert Howe to Gov. George Clinton, 26 Mar. 1780 and response 27 Mar. 1780, Miscellaneous Manuscripts, Robert Howe, NYHS.

11. Flexner, *George Washington*, pp. 339–42.

12. George Washington to Robert Howe, 28 Apr. 1780, Washington Papers, ser. 3B, LC.

13. Ibid.

14. Robert Howe to Gov. Jonathan Trumbull, 27 Apr. 1780, 18 May 1780, Trumbull Papers, vol. 11, docs. 162, 191; George Washington to Robert Howe, 28 Apr. 1780, Washington Papers, ser. 3B, LC; Robert Howe to Nehemiah Hubbard, 29 Apr. 1780, Emmet Collection; Robert Howe to Gov. George Clinton, 30 Apr. 1780, George Clinton to Robert Howe, 1 May 1780, Clinton, *Public Papers*, 5:661–62, 664–65; Udny Hay to Robert Howe, 10 July 1780, Papers of the Continental Congress, m. 247, r. 147, i. 136, v. 5, p. 47, NARA; Robert Howe to Samuel Huntington, 17 Oct. 1780, Papers of the Continental Congress, m. 247, r. 178, i. 160, pp. 519–21, NARA.

15. Robert Howe to Udny Hay, 17 May 1780, Papers of the Continental Congress, m. 247, r. 96, i. 78, v. 12, pp. 83–84, NARA; Robert Howe to William Smith, 17 May 1780, Revolutionary Letters, 1779–80, vol. 202, MSA; Udny Hay to Samuel Huntington, 15 Aug. 1780, Papers of the Continental Congress, m. 247, r. 96, i. 78, v. 12, pp. 77–78, NARA.

16. Robert Howe to Udny Hay, 24 June 1780, Legislative Papers, 1778–1803, vol. 10, NYSA; John Paterson to Gen. William Heath, 17 May 1780, Revolutionary Letters, 1779–80, vol. 202, MSA; Nehemiah Hubbard to Gov. Jonathan Trumbull, 29 May 1780, Trumbull Papers, vol. 11, doc. 211; Philip Schuyler, Nathan Peabody & Committee of Congress to Gov. Jonathan Trumbull, 1 June 1780, Trumbull Papers, vol. 11, doc. 231 (also Papers of the Continental Congress, m. 247, r. 46, i. 39, v. 3, pp. 81–84, NARA); Robert Howe to Gov. Jonathan Trumbull, 19 June 1780, Trumbull Papers, vol. 12, doc. 24abd.

17. William Heath to George Washington, 2 and 29 Mar. 1780, Heath, *The Heath Papers*, ser. 7, vol. 5, pt. 3, pp. 37, 42–43.

18. John Paterson to William Heath, 31 Mar. 1780, Heath, *The Heath Papers*, ser. 7, vol. 5, pt. 3, p. 44.

19. Van Doren, *Secret History*, pp. 266–67.

20. Lafayette, *Lafayette in the Age of the American Revolution*, 3:78–80; Ford, *Journals of Continental Congress*, 17:725–27, 771–73. The general officers had written to Congress the previous November complaining of inadequate pay, but Howe had declined to join in that protest.

21. Robert Howe to William Heath, 23 Sept. 1779, Heath Papers, 14:78; William Heath to Robert Howe, 25 Apr. 1780, Heath, *The Heath Papers*, ser. 7, vol. 5, pt. 3, pp. 57–58; Robert Howe to William Heath, 15 Mar. 1780, Heath Papers, 15:404.

22. George Washington to Robert Howe, 21 Mar. 1780, 1 Apr. 1780, Washington Papers, ser. 3B, LC; Robert Howe to William Heath, 17 Apr. 1780, Heath Papers, 15:455.

23. Robert Howe to Lt. Col. James Millan, 4 May 1780, U.S. Revolution Collection, AAS.

24. Entry for 20 May 1780, Drew Orderly Book; entry for 3 June 1780, Frost Orderly Book.

25. Clinton, *Public Papers*, 5:826, passim; Public Records of the State of Connecticut, 3:109–10; Hamilton, *Papers*, 2:340, 344–45; George Washington to Robert Howe, copy transmitted to Udny Hay, 23 June 1780, Legislative Papers, 1780–1803, vol. 10, no. 77, NYSA; Robert Howe to Gov. Jonathan Trumbull, 23, 24, 27, and 28 June 1780, Trumbull Papers, vol. 12, docs. 38ab, 43, 52, 55, and vol. 11, doc. 256a.

26. Flexner, *George Washington*, pp. 362–64; Boatner, *Encyclopedia of the American Revolution*, pp. 1045–47.

27. Newspaper extracts, 1779–80, Chatham, 9 Aug. 1780, *New Jersey Archives*, ser. 2, vol. 4; Robert Howe to William Heath, 23 July 1780, Heath

Papers, vol. 16, item 192; Hamilton, *Papers*, 2:372–73; Public Records of the State of Connecticut, 3:142.

28. Van Doren, *Secret History*, pp. 266–67.

29. Freeman, *George Washington*, 5:175; Robert Howe to Udny Hay, 24 July 1780, Papers of the Continental Congress, m. 247, r. 165, i. 151, p. 84, NARA; entries for 1 Aug.–3 Aug. 1780, Frost Orderly Book; Flexner, *George Washington*, pp. 381–82.

30. Van Doren, *Secret History*, p. 288; Freeman, *George Washington*, 5: 210–11.

31. Koke, *Accomplice in Treason*, pp. 38–44.

32. Koke, *Accomplice in Treason*, pp. 169, 294.

33. Richard Peters to George Washington, 18 Oct. 1780, Washington Papers, ser. 4, LC; Washington, *Writings*, 20:256–57; Freeman, *George Washington*, 5:225–26; Van Doren, *Secret History*, pp. 362–63.

CHAPTER 10

1. Washington, *Writings*, 20:272–73.

2. Tower, *Marquis de La Fayette*, 2:180–83.

3. Flexner, *George Washington*, pp. 396–97; Washington, *Writings*, 20: 405.

4. Robert Howe to [?], 17 Feb. 1780, de Coppet Collection.

5. George Washington to William Heath, 12 Jan. 1781, George Washington to Robert Howe, 22 Jan. 1781, Washington Papers, ser. 3B, LC; Van Doren, *Mutiny in January*, passim; Flexner, *George Washington*, pp. 405–7. The British did send two emissaries to subvert the mutineers, but they were promptly arrested, turned over to Gen. Wayne, and ultimately executed.

6. George Washington to William Heath, 12 Jan. 1781, Washington Papers, ser. 3B, LC.

7. After orders for 11 Jan.–12 Jan. 1781, Reid Orderly Book; William Heath to George Washington, 12 Jan. 1781, Heath, *The Heath Papers*, ser. 7, vol. 5, pt. 3, pp. 158–59. Heath reported that Howe never mentioned to him his previous discussion of the command with Washington.

8. George Washington to Robert Howe, 22 Jan. 1781, Washington Papers, ser. 3B, LC.

9. George Washington to William Heath, George Washington to Robert Howe, and George Washington to Timothy Pickering, 25 Jan. 1781, Washington, *Writings*, 21:139–42.

10. Robert Howe to William Heath, 26 Jan. 1781, Heath Papers, vol. 19, item 106.

11. Robert Howe to George Washington, 27 Jan. 1781, Papers of the Continental Congress, m. 247, r. 170, i. 152, pp. 521–24, NARA.

12. George Washington to Gov. George Clinton, 29 Jan. 1781, Washington

Papers, WH; George Washington to Nathanael Greene, 2 Feb. 1781, George Washington to president of Congress, 31 Jan. 1781, George Washington to John Laurens, 30 Jan. 1781, Washington, *Writings*, 21:161–66. Washington used the opportunity of the mutiny to appeal for better treatment of the troops by the various states. He dispatched letters to the governors of the various states in the area warning them that unless the states did a better job of feeding, clothing, and paying their troops the same could recur with disastrous results.

13. Flexner, *George Washington*, p. 414; Samuel Shaw to Winthrop Sargent, 12 Feb. 1781, *Pennsylvania Magazine of History and Biography*, 70: 317, 319.

14. George Washington to Robert Howe and George Washington to Comte De Rochambeau, 7 May 1781, Washington, *Writings*, 22:51, 53–54.

15. George Washington to Pres. Joseph Reed, 5 May–7 May 1781, George Washington to Brig. Gen. James Clinton, 7 May 1781, George Washington to Pres. of Congress, 8 May 1781, George Washington to William Heath, 9 May 1781, Washington, *Writings*, 22:45, 51–52, 59–61, 63–66.

16. Robert Howe to George Washington, 4 June 1781, Dreer Collection; Robert Howe to Col. Timothy Pickering, 5 June 1781, Miscellaneous Numbered Records, Record Group 93, NARA.

17. War of the Revolution Orderly Books, 51:134–36, NARA.

18. Washington, *Writings*, 22:199, 201–4.

19. Washington, *Writings*, 22:238–304; order of march, 30 June 1781, Hand Papers, 2:8.

20. Washington, *Diaries*, 2:235–40; entry for 17 July 1781, War of the Revolution Orderly Books, 54:42–43, NARA.

21. Washington, *Diaries*, 2:223–58; Flexner, *George Washington*, p. 430–37.

22. George Washington to Robert Howe, 24 Sept. 1781, Washington Papers, ser. 3B, LC. Washington actually had bypassed seniority by offering the command to McDougall, whose troops were to be used in Virginia, but when he declined for health reasons Washington reverted to seniority.

23. Committee Report, 5 Sept. 1781, Papers of the Continental Congress, m. 247, r. 27, i. 19, vol. 3, pp. 205–7, NARA; Robert Howe to George Washington, 19 Sept. 1781, Howe Papers, SHC UNC; George Washington to William Heath, 24 Sept. 1781, Heath Papers, vol. 21, item 10; William Heath to George Washington, 5 Oct. 1781, Heath Papers, vol. 21, item 142.

24. Robert Howe to William Heath, 6 and 25 Oct. 1781, Heath Papers, vol. 21, items 144 and 384; Robert Howe to Congress, 8 Nov. 1781, Papers of the Continental Congress, m. 247, r. 178, i. 173, pp. 523–26, NARA.

25. Washington, *Writings*, 23:374–75.

26. *Proceedings of a General Court-Martial . . . of Major General Howe*, pp. 223–27, 236–50, 285–91.

27. *Proceedings of a General Court-Martial . . . of Major General Howe*,

pp. 285–91; Ford, *Journals of Continental Congress,* 22:46, 78; Robert Howe to Continental Congress, 15 Feb. 1782, Papers of the Continental Congress, m. 247, r. 178, i. 173, pp. 527–28, NARA.

28. Robert Howe to George Washington, 8 Feb. 1782, and George Washington to Robert Howe, 10 Mar. 1782, Washington Papers, ser. 4, LC.

29. Heath, *The Heath Papers,* ser. 7, vol. 5, pt. 3, pp. 400–408.

30. Robert Howe to George Washington, 30 Oct. 1782, George Washington to Robert Howe, 30 Oct. 1782, and William Heath to George Washington, 28 Oct. 1782, Washington Papers, ser. 4, LC.

31. Robert Howe to Samuel Webb, 6 June 1782, Webb Papers.

32. Robert Howe to Henry Knox, 31 Aug. 1782, Knox Papers.

33. Thacher, *Military Journal,* pp. 310–12.

34. Thacher, *Military Journal,* p. 322.

35. Robert Howe to George Washington, 9, 10, and 25 Feb. 1783, and George Washington to Robert Howe, 10 and 25 Feb. 1783, Washington Papers, ser. 4, LC.

36. Martin and Lender, *Respectable Army,* pp. 186–93.

37. Robert Howe to Executive Council of Pennsylvania [Gov. John Dickinson], 2 July 1783, Washington Papers, ser. 4, LC.

38. George Washington to Robert Howe, 25 June 1783, Washington Papers, ser. 3B, LC; Robert Howe to president of Congress, 28 June and 5 July 1783, Papers of the Continental Congress, m. 247, r. 45, i. 38, pp. 81, 85–88, NARA; Robert Howe to Elias Boudinot, 6, 13, 15, and 23 July, 12 Aug., and 2 Sept. 1783, Papers of the Continental Congress, m. 247, r. 45, i. 38, pp. 89–123, NARA; Elias Boudinot to Robert Howe, 18 Aug. and 13 Sept. 1783, Papers of the Continental Congress, m. 247, r. 24, i. 16, pp. 242, 246, NARA; entry for 13 Sept. 1783, Ford, *Journals of Continental Congress,* 25:566–67.

39. Order from Gen. Robert Howe, 17 Nov. 1783, U.S. Revolution Collection, AAS.

40. Newburgh Orderly Book.

CONCLUSION

1. Foster, *Society of the Cincinnati,* p. 15; Davis, *North Carolina Society of the Cincinnati,* pp. 7–26.

2. Robert Howe to Benjamin Lincoln, 11 June 1783, Emmet Collection. Howe asked Lincoln to "please burn this the minute you have read it."

3. George Washington to Robert Howe, 31 Aug. 1783, Washington Papers, ser. 3B, LC.

4. Robert Howe to George Washington, 21 Oct. 1783, Washington Papers, ser. 4, LC.

5. Samuel Hodgdon to Col. Timothy Pickering, 12 Nov. 1783, Miscellaneous Numbered Records, Record Group 93, NARA. For detailed ac-

counts of Howe's claims for forage, housing, etc., for himself and his
"family," see Pickering Papers, MHS, and Timothy Pickering Papers, WH.

6. Robert Howe to Continental Congress, 10 Mar. 1785, Papers of the Continental Congress, m. 247, r. 178, i. 173, pp. 531–37, NARA.

7. Committee Report, 12 Apr. 1785, Papers of the Continental Congress, m. 247, r. 27, i. 19, vol. 3, pp. 209–10, NARA; Brunswick County Deed Books, Book B, pp. 287–88. As late as November, Howe was continuing to memorialize Congress to settle the question of his pay. Ford, *Journals of Continental Congress*, 29:871.

8. Ford, *Journals of Continental Congress*, 29:576n, 620, 650, 721, 735–36; Thomas Hutchins to president of Congress, 15 Sept. 1785, Papers of the Continental Congress, m. 247, r. 74, i. 60, pp. 189–91, NARA; Denny, *Military Journal*, 263–82; Robert Howe to Continental Congress, Papers of the Continental Congress, m. 247, r. 178, i. 173, p. 543, NARA; Hamilton, *Papers*, 3:638.

9. Hooper, "Abridgement of the Memoirs of Major General Robert Howe." Although Hooper claimed to have been an eyewitness to these events, there are numerous documented errors in his accounts of events. He credited Howe with returning during March and April of 1785; yet it is certain that Howe was in New York at that time. Also, Hooper used 1785 as Howe's death date when he actually died in 1786.

10. Archibald Maclaine to James Iredell, 6 Mar. 1786, Iredell, *Life and Correspondence*, 2:139; "Land, Estates, Boundaries and Surveys, Confiscated Lands: Return of Wilmington District," accounts of Nov. 1786, 2 Dec. 1789, Treasurers and Comptrollers Papers, Military Papers, NCSA.

11. Robert Howe to Gov. [Richard Caswell], 8 Feb. 1786, Joint Resolutions File Regarding Administration of Justice, General Assembly Session Records (Legislative Papers), Nov. 1786–Jan. 1787, NCSA.

12. Alfred Moore to James Iredell, 14 Dec. 1786, Iredell, *Life and Correspondence*, 2:154; Hooper, "Abridgement of the Memoirs of Major General Robert Howe," pp. 159–60.

13. Hooper, "Abridgement of the Memoirs of Major General Robert Howe."

14. Hazard, "View of Coastal South Carolina," p. 189; Chastellux, *Travels in North America*, 1:111.

15. Parramore, *Launching the Craft*, pp. 63–64.

16. Biddle, "Case of Major André," p. 317; Hazard, "View of Coastal South Carolina," p. 189. A French report of 1778 noted that Howe "is regarded as having some ability." Kennett, "Charleston in 1778," p. 110.

17. Higginbotham, "Military Leadership in the American Revolution," pp. 103–7.

18. "Letters of Col. William Woodford," p. 131; 4 and 20 Sept. 1776, Howe Orderly Book; Elbert, *Order Book*, pp. 8–9.

BIBLIOGRAPHY

MANUSCRIPTS

American Antiquarian Society, Worcester, Mass.
  U.S. Revolution Collection
Clement Library, University of Michigan, Ann Arbor, Mich.
  Nathanael Greene Papers
College of William and Mary Library, Williamsburg, Va.
  Tucker-Coleman Collection
Connecticut State Archives, Hartford, Conn.
  Public Records of the State of Connecticut
  Jonathan Trumbull Papers
Duke University Library, Durham, N.C.
  Robert Howe Papers
  Edward Telfair Papers
Georgia Historical Society, Savannah, Ga.
  Mortecai Sheftall Papers
Georgia State Archives, Atlanta, Ga.
  Executive Council Minutes, 1778
Historical Society of Pennsylvania, Philadelphia, Pa.
  Ferdinand J. Dreer Collection
  Frank Marx Etting Collection
  Simon Gratz Collection
  Edward Hand Papers
  North Carolina Manuscripts
  Richard Peters Papers
  Society Collection
Library of Congress, Manuscripts Division, Washington, D.C.
  Continental Congress Miscellaneous
  Robert Howe Orderly Book
  Newburgh Orderly Book (copy)
  PRO Colonial Office (copies)
  U.S. Revolutionary War Papers
  George Washington Papers (microfilm)
Massachusetts Historical Society, Boston, Mass.
  William Heath Papers

Henry Knox Papers
Timothy Pickering Papers
Josiah Quincy, Jr., Papers
Quincy, Wendell, Holmes, and Upham Families Papers
Revolutionary Letters
Washburn Papers
Whitwell Autograph Collection
Massachusetts State Archives, Boston, Mass.
Revolutionary Letters, 1779–1780
National Archives, Washington, D.C.
Miscellaneous Numbered Records
Papers of the Continental Congress (microfilm)
War of the Revolution Orderly Books (microfilm)
New Hampshire Historical Society, Concord, N.H.
George Reid Orderly Book
New Hampshire State Archives, Concord, N.H.
Executive Papers, 1776–1786
New-York Historical Society, New York, N.Y.
Sam Frost Orderly Book
Horatio Gates Papers
John Lamb Papers
Alexander McDougall Papers
Miscellaneous Manuscripts, Gov. George Clinton
Miscellaneous Manuscripts, Robert Howe
Frederick William von Steuben Papers
B. V. Vail Papers
New York Public Library, New York, N.Y.
Emmet Collection
Dr. Samuel Adams Diary
Miscellaneous Collection
New York State Archives, Albany, N.Y.
Legislative Papers
North Carolina State Archives, Raleigh, N.C.
Bladen County Tax Lists
Brunswick County Civil Action Papers
Brunswick County Deed Books (microfilm)
Brunswick County Will Books (microfilm)
Council of Safety Papers, Secretary of State Papers
Craven County Deed Books (microfilm)
Craven County Wills
English Records, Dartmouth MSS (transcripts)
General Assembly Session Records (Legislative Papers)
Governors Letter Books
Governors Papers

Military Collection
New Hanover County Deed Books (microfilm)
PRO Colonial Office (copies)
PRO War Office (copies)
Treasurers and Comptrollers Papers, Military Papers
Princeton University Library, Princeton, N.J.
  Andre de Coppet Collection
South Carolina Historical Society, Charleston, S.C.
  John Faucheraud Grimké Military Records
  Henry Laurens Papers
South Caroliniana Library, University of South Carolina, Columbia, S.C.
  Christopher Gadsden Miscellaneous
  Charles Lee Letterbook
  Miscellaneous Papers
Southern Historical Collection, University of North Carolina-Chapel Hill,
    Chapel Hill, N.C.
  Preston Davie Collection
  Robert Howe Papers
U.S. Army Historical Institute, Carlyle Barracks, Pa.
  Sol Fernstone Collection of the American Revolution
U.S. Military Academy Library, West Point, N.Y.
  Gamaliel Bradford Orderly Book
  Seth Drew Orderly Book
Virginia Historical Society, Richmond, Va.
  Francis Otway Byrd Papers
Washington Headquarters, Newburgh, N.Y.
  Timothy Pickering Papers
  George Washington Papers
Yale University Library, New Haven, Conn.
  Samuel B. Webb Papers

PUBLISHED PRIMARY SOURCES

Biddle, Charles. *Autobiography of Charles Biddle, Vice-President of the
    Supreme Executive Council of Pennsylvania, 1745–1821*. Philadelphia:
    Privately printed, E. Claxton, 1883.
Burnett, Edmund C., ed. *Letters of Members of the Continental Congress*. 8
    vols. Washington, D.C.: Carnegie Institution, 1934.
*Calendar of State Papers, Colonial Series, America and West Indies, Dec. 1,
    1702–1703*. Edited by Cecil Headlam. London: N.p., 1913.
*Calendar of State Papers, Colonial Series, America and West Indies, Jan.
    1716–July 1717, Preserved in the Public Records Office*. Edited by Cecil
    Headlam. London: His Majesties Stationery Office, 1930.

Calendar of Virginia State Papers and Other Manuscripts. Richmond, 1890. Reprint. 11 vols. New York: Kraus Reprint Corp., 1918.

Chastellux, Marquis de. *Travels in North America in the Years 1780, 1781 and 1782 by the Marquis de Chastellux*. Translated by Howard C. Rice, Jr. 2 vols. Chapel Hill: University of North Carolina Press, 1963.

Clark, Walter, ed. *The State Records of North Carolina*. 16 vols. numbered 11–26. Winston and Goldsboro: State of North Carolina, 1895–1906.

Clinton, George. *Public Papers of George Clinton, First Governor of New York, 1775–1795, 1801–1804*. Edited by Hugh Hastings. 10 vols. New York and Albany: N.p., 1899–1914.

Davies, K. G., ed. *Documents of the American Revolution, 1770–1773*. Vol. 12, Transcripts, 1776. Dublin, Ireland: Irish University Press, 1976.

Denny, Ebenezer. *Military Journal of Major Ebenezer Denny*. Memoirs of the Historical Society of Pennsylvania. Philadelphia: Historical Society of Pennsylvania, 1859.

Elbert, Samuel. *Order Book of Samuel Elbert, Colonel and Brigadier General in the Continental Army, October 1776 to November 1778*. Georgia Historical Society Collections. Vol. 5, pt. 2. Savannah, 1902.

Force, Peter, comp. *American Archives*. Fourth and fifth series. 9 vols. Washington: U.S. Congress, 1837–53.

Ford, Worthington C., ed. *Journals of the Continental Congress, 1774–1789*. 34 vols. Washington: U.S. Government Printing Office, 1904–37.

Gadsden, Christopher. *The Writings of Christopher Gadsden, 1746–1805*. Edited by Richard Walsh. Columbia: University of South Carolina Press, 1966.

Gazette of State of North Carolina. New Bern, N.C.

Gervais, John Lewis. "Letters from John Lewis Gervais to Henry Laurens, 1777–1778." Edited by Raymond Starr. *South Carolina Historical Magazine* 66 (1965): 15–37.

Gibbes, Robert W. *Documentary History of the American Revolution*. New York: N.p., 1855–57.

Grimké, John Faucheraud. "Journal of the Campaign to the Southward, May 9th to July 14, 1778." *South Carolina Historical (and Genealogical) Magazine* 12 (1911): 60–69, 118–34, 190–206.

———. "Order Book of John Faucheraud Grimké." *South Carolina Historical and Genealogical Magazine* 13–14 (January 1912–January 1913): 42–55, 89–103, 148–53, 205–12, 44–57.

Hall, Charles Samuel. *Life and Letters of Samuel Holden Parsons, Major-General in the Continental Army and Chief Judge of the Northwestern Territory, 1737–1789*. Binghamton, N.Y.: Otseningo Publishing Co., 1905.

Hamilton, Alexander. *Papers of Alexander Hamilton*. Edited by Harold C. Syrett. 27 vols. New York: Columbia University Press, 1961–88.

Hazard, Ebenezer. "A View of Coastal South Carolina in 1778: The Journal of Ebenezer Hazard." Edited by H. Roy Merrens. *South Carolina Historical Magazine* 73 (1972): 177–93.

Heath, William. *The Heath Papers.* Collections of the Massachusetts Historical Society. Series 5, vol. 4, and series 7, vols. 4–5. Boston: 1878–1905.

———. *Heath's Memoirs of the American Revolution.* Reprint with introduction and notes by Rufus Rockwell Wilson. Freeport, N.Y.: Books for Libraries Press, 1970.

Hemphill, William Edwin, and Wylma Anne Wates. *Extracts from Journals of Provincial Congress of South Carolina, 1775–1776.* Columbia: South Carolina Archives, 1960.

Hemphill, William Edwin, Wylma Anne Wates, and R. Nicholas Olsberg, eds. *Journals of the General Assembly and House of Representatives, 1776–1780: The State Records of South Carolina.* Columbia: University of South Carolina Press, 1970.

The Historical Magazine. September 1860.

Historical Manuscripts Commission Report on American Manuscripts. London: Stationery Office, 1904.

Iredell, James. *Life and Correspondence of James Iredell.* Edited by Griffith J. McRee. 2 vols. New York: D. Appleton, 1857.

Kennett, Lee, ed. "Charleston in 1778: A French Intelligence Report." *South Carolina Historical Magazine* 66 (April 1965): 109–11.

"La Carolina Meridionale: Some French Sources of South Carolina Revolutionary History, with Two Unpublished Letters of Baron de Kalb." Edited by Paul G. Sifton. *South Carolina Historical Magazine* 66 (April 1965): 102–8.

Lafayette, Marquis de. *Lafayette in the Age of the American Revolution: Selected Letters and Papers, 1776–1790.* Edited by Stanley J. Idzerda. 5 vols. Ithaca and London: Cornell University Press, 1977–83.

Laurens, Henry. *The Papers of Henry Laurens.* Edited by Philip M. Hamer, George C. Rogers, and David R. Chesnutt. 12 vols. to date. Columbia: University of South Carolina Press, 1968–89.

Lee, Charles. *The Lee Papers.* Collections of the New-York Historical Society. Vols. 4–7. New York: 1872–75.

Lee, Henry. *Memoirs of the War in the Southern Department of the United States.* 2 vols. Philadelphia: N.p., 1812.

"Letters and Documents Relating to the Early History of the Lower Cape Fear, with Introduction and Notes by Kemp P. Battle." *James Sprunt Historical Monograph No. 4.* Chapel Hill: Published by the University of North Carolina, 1903.

"Letters from John Stewart to William Dunlop." *South Carolina Historical and Genealogical Magazine* 32 (January 1931): 1–33.

"The Letters of Col. William Woodford, Col. Robert Howe and Gen.

Charles Lee to Edmund Pendleton." *Richmond College Historical Papers* 1, no. 1 (June 1915): 96–163.

McEachern, Leora H., and Isabel M. Williams, eds. *Wilmington-New Hanover Safety Committee Minutes*. Wilmington, N.C.: N.p., 1974.

McIntosh, Lachlan. "Papers of Lachlan McIntosh, 1774–1779." *Georgia Historical Quarterly* 37 (1954): 148–69, 253–67, 356–68.

Moultrie, William. *Memoirs of the American Revolution*. 2 vols. New York: N.p., 1802.

New Jersey Archives: Documents Relating to the Revolutionary History of the State of New Jersey. Edited by William S. Stryker. 2d Series. 5 vols. Trenton: New Jersey Archives, 1901–17.

"Order Book of the 1st Regiment, S.C. Line, Continental Establishment." *South Carolina Historical and Genealogical Magazine* 7–8 (April 1906–April 1907): 75–80, 130–42, 194–203, 19–28, 69–87.

Pennsylvania Magazine of History and Biography 70 (1947).

Pennsylvania Packet. 22 July 1783.

Pinckney, Thomas. "Letters of Thomas Pinckney, 1775–1780." Edited by Jack L. Cross. *South Carolina Historical Magazine* 58 (July 1957): 145–62.

Powell, William S., James K. Huhta, and Thomas J. Farnham, eds. *The Regulators in North Carolina: A Documentary History, 1759–1776*. Raleigh, N.C.: State Department of Archives and History, 1971.

Proceedings of a General Court-Martial, held at Philadelphia . . . by Order of His Excellency General Washington . . . for the trial of Major General Howe, December 7, 1781. Philadelphia: Hall and Sellers, 1782. Reprinted in *New-York Historical Society Collections . . . for the Year 1879*, New York, 1880.

Proceedings of General Court-Martial for the Trial of Major General Benedict Arnold. New York: Privately printed, 1865.

Quincy, Josiah, Jr. "Journal of Josiah Quincy, Jun." Edited by Mark A. DeWolfe Howe. *Massachusetts Historical Society Proceedings* 44 (1916): 424–81.

Revolution in America: Confidential Letters and Journals, 1776–1784 of Adjutant General Major Baurmeister of the Hessian Forces. Translated and annotated by Bernhard A. Uhlendorf. New Brunswick, N.J.: Rutgers University Press, 1957.

The Royal Gazette Extraordinary. London, 1779.

Saunders, William L., ed. *Colonial Records of North Carolina*. 10 vols. Goldsboro, N.C.: N.p., 1886–90.

Schaw, Janet. *Journal of a Lady of Quality: Being the Narrative of a Journey from Scotland to the West Indies, North Carolina and Portugal in the Years, 1774–1776*. Edited by Evangeline Walker Andrews with the collaboration of Charles McLean Andrews. New Haven: Yale University Press, 1939.

Shakespeare, William. *The Complete Works of Shakespeare*. Edited by
    Hardin Craig. Chicago: Scott, Foresman, 1951.
Shaw, Samuel. *The Life and Journal of Major Samuel Shaw*. Edited by
    Josiah Quincy. Boston: N.p., 1847.
*Sinews of Independence: Monthly Strength Reports of the Continental
    Army*. Edited by Charles H. Lesser. Chicago: University of Chicago
    Press, 1976.
Smith, Paul H., ed. *Letters of Delegates to Congress, 1774–1789*. 10 vols.
    to date. Washington: Library of Congress, 1973–.
Smyth, J. F. D. *A Tour of the United States of America*. 2 vols. London:
    N.p., 1784.
South Carolina and American General Gazette. Charleston, S.C.
South Carolina Gazette. Charleston, S.C.
Sparks, Jared, ed. *Correspondence of the American Revolution: Being
    Letters of Eminent Men to George Washington from the Time of His
    Taking Command of the Army to the End of His Presidency*. 4 vols.
    Boston: N.p., 1853.
Tarter, Brent, and Robert L. Scribner, eds. *Revolutionary Virginia: The
    Road to Independence*. 7 vols. Charlottesville: University Press of
    Virginia, 1973–83.
Thacher, James. *Military Journal of the American Revolution*. Hartford,
    Conn: N.p., 1862.
Tryon, William. *The Correspondence of William Tryon and Other Selected
    Papers*. Edited by William S. Powell. 2 vols. Raleigh, N.C.: Division of
    Archives and History, 1980–81.
The Virginia Gazette. Williamsburg, Va.
Washington, George. *The Diaries of George Washington, 1748–1799*.
    Edited by John C. Fitzpatrick. Boston and New York: Houghton
    Mifflin, 1925.
———. *The Writings of George Washington: From the Original
    Manuscript Sources, 1745–1799*. Edited by John C. Fitzpatrick. 39 vols.
    Washington: U.S. Government Printing Office, 1931–44.
Year Book: City of Charleston, S.C., 1889. Charleston, S.C.: 1890.

SECONDARY SOURCES

Adams, Douglas N. "Jean Baptiste Ternant, Inspector General and Advisor
    to the Commanding Generals of the Southern Forces, 1778–1782." *South
    Carolina Historical Magazine* 83 (October 1982): 221–40.
Alden, John Richard. *General Charles Lee: Traitor or Patriot?* Baton
    Rouge: Louisiana State University Press, 1951.
Bennett, Charles E. *Southernmost Battlefields of the Revolution*. Bailey's
    Crossroads, Va.: Blair, 1970.

Biddle, Charles B. *The Case of Major André*. Memoirs of the Historical Society of Pennsylvania. Philadelphia: Historical Society of Pennsylvania, 1884.

Boatner, Mark M., III. *Encyclopedia of the American Revolution*. New York: David McKay, 1966.

Buel, Richard, Jr. *Dear Liberty: Connecticut's Mobilization for the Revolutionary War*. Middletown, Conn.: Wesleyan University Press, 1980.

Buker, George E., and Richard Apley Martin. "Governor Tonyn's Brown-Water Navy: East Florida during the American Revolution, 1775–1778." *Florida Historical Quarterly* 58 (July 1979): 58–71.

Carp, E. Wayne. *To Starve the Army at Pleasure: Continental Army Administration and American Political Culture, 1775–1783*. Chapel Hill: University of North Carolina Press, 1984.

Cavanagh, John C. "American Military Leadership in the Southern Campaign: Benjamin Lincoln." In *The Revolutionary War in the South: Power, Conflict, and Leadership*, edited by W. Robert Higgins, pp. 101–31. Durham: Duke University Press, 1979.

Champagne, Roger J. *Alexander McDougall and the American Revolution in New York*. Schenectady, N.Y.: New York State American Revolution Bicentennial Commission, 1975.

Cheves, Langdon. "Middleton of South Carolina." *South Carolina Historical and Genealogical Magazine* 1 (July 1900): 228–62.

Clow, Richard Brent. *Edward Rutledge of South Carolina, 1749–1800: Unproclaimed Statesman*. Ph.D. dissertation, University of Georgia, 1976.

Coleman, Kenneth. *The American Revolution in Georgia, 1763–1789*. Athens: University of Georgia Press, 1958.

———. *Colonial Georgia: A History*. New York: Charles Scribner's Sons, 1976.

Davis, Charles Lukens. *North Carolina Society of the Cincinnati*. Boston: N.p., 1907.

Dawson, Henry B. *Battles of the United States by Sea and Land*. 2 vols. New York: Johnson, Fry, 1858.

Dunn, Richard S. "The Barbados Census of 1680: Profile of the Richest Colony in English America." *William and Mary Quarterly* 3d Series, 25 (January 1969): 3–30.

———. "The English Sugar Islands and the Founding of South Carolina." *South Carolina Historical Magazine* 72 (April 1971): 81–93.

Edgar, Walter B., ed. *Biographical Directory of the South Carolina House of Representatives*. Columbia: University of South Carolina Press, 1974.

Eller, Ernest McNeill, ed. *Chesapeake Bay in the American Revolution*. Centerville, Md.: Tidewater Publishers, 1981.

Ferguson, E. James. *The Power of the Purse: A History of American Public Finance, 1776–1790*. Chapel Hill: University of North Carolina Press, 1961.

"The First Governor Moore and His Children." *South Carolina Historical and Genealogical Magazine* 37 (January 1936): 1–23.

Flexner, James Thomas. *George Washington in the American Revolution*. Boston: Little, Brown, 1967.

Foster, Francis Aptharp. *The Institution of the Society of the Cincinnati; Together with Standing Resolutions, Ordinances, Rules and Precedents of the General Society of the Cincinnati, 1783–1920*. Boston: General Society of the Cincinnati, 1923.

Freeman, Douglas Southall. *George Washington: A Biography*. 7 vols. New York: Charles Scribner's Sons, 1952.

Godbold, E. Stanley, Jr., and Robert H. Woody. *Christopher Gadsden and the American Revolution*. Knoxville: University of Tennessee Press, 1982.

Greene, Francis V. *The Revolutionary War*. New York: Charles Scribner's Sons, 1911.

Greene, Jack P. *The Quest for Power: The Lower Houses of Assembly in the Southern Royal Colonies*. Chapel Hill: University of North Carolina Press, 1963.

Hast, Adele. *Loyalism in Revolutionary Virginia: The Norfolk Area and Eastern Shore*. Ann Arbor, Mich.: University of Michigan Research Press, 1982.

Heitman, Francis B. *Historical Register of Officers of the Continental Army during the War of the Revolution, April 1775 to December 1783*. 1914. Reprint. Baltimore: Genealogical Publishing, 1982.

Higginbotham, Don. "Military Leadership in the American Revolution." *Leadership in the American Revolution*. Papers Presented at the Third Symposium May 9 and 10, 1974, Library of Congress Symposium on the American Revolution. Washington: Library of Congress, 1974.

———. *The War of American Independence: Military, Attitudes, Policies, and Practices, 1763–1789*. New York: Macmillan, 1971.

———, ed. *Reconsiderations on the Revolutionary War: Selected Essays*. Westport, Conn.: Greenwood Press, 1978.

Higgins, W. Robert, ed. *The Revolutionary War in the South: Power, Conflict and Leadership*. Durham: Duke University Press, 1979.

Higham, Robin, ed. *A Guide to the Sources of United States Military History*. Hamden, Conn.: Archon Books, 1975.

Hill, George Canning. *The Life of Israel Putnam*. New York: A. L. Burt Co., 1903.

Hoffman, Ronald, and Peter J. Albert, eds. *Arms and Independence: The Military Character of the American Revolution*. Charlottesville: University Press of Virginia, 1984.

Hooper, Archibald Maclaine. "Abridgement of the Memoirs of Major General Robert Howe." *North Carolina University Magazine*. Raleigh: 1853.

Jackson, Harvey H. *Lachlan McIntosh and the Politics of Revolutionary Georgia*. Athens: University of Georgia Press, 1979.

Jenkins, Charles Francis. *Button Gwinnett: Signer of the Declaration of Independence*. Garden City, N.Y.: Doubleday, Page, 1926.

Johnson, James Michael. " 'Not a Single Soldier in the Province': The Military Establishment of Georgia and the Coming of the American Revolution." Ph.D. dissertation, Duke University, 1980.

Jones, Charles, Jr. *The History of Georgia*. Boston and New York: Houghton, Mifflin, 1883.

Kapp, Friedrich. *Life of Frederick William von Steuben, Major General in the Revolutionary Army*. New York: Mason Brothers, 1859.

Koke, Richard J. *Accomplice in Treason: Joshua Hett Smith and the Arnold Conspiracy*. New York: New-York Historical Society, 1973.

Lawrence, Alexander A. "General Howe and the British Capture of Savannah in 1778." *Georgia Historical Quarterly* 36 (1952): 303–27.

Lee, E. Lawrence. *The Lower Cape Fear in Colonial Days*. Chapel Hill: University of North Carolina Press, 1965.

Lefler, Hugh Talmage, and Albert Ray Newsome. *North Carolina: The History of a Southern State*. 3d ed. Chapel Hill: University of North Carolina Press, 1973.

Lefler, Hugh Talmage, and William S. Powell. *Colonial North Carolina: A History*. New York: Charles Scribner's Sons, 1973.

Lennon, Donald R. " 'The Graveyard of American Commanders': The Continental Army's Southern Department, 1776–1778." *North Carolina Historical Review* 67 (April 1990): 133–58.

McCrady, Edward. *The History of South Carolina under the Proprietary Government, 1670–1719*. New York: Macmillan, 1901.

MacMillan, Margaret Burnham. *The War Governors in the American Revolution*. New York: Columbia University Press, 1943.

Martin, Harold H. *Georgia: A Bicentennial History*. New York: W. W. Norton, 1977.

Martin, James Kirby, and Mark Edward Lender. *A Respectable Army: The Military Origins of the Republic, 1763–1789*. Arlington Heights, Ill.: Harlan Davidson, 1982.

Mays, David John. *Edmund Pendleton, 1721–1803: A Biography*. 2 vols. Cambridge: Harvard University Press, 1952.

Miller, John C. *Triumph of Freedom, 1775–1783*. Boston: Little, Brown, 1948.

Nadelhoft, Jerome J. *The Disorders of War: The Revolution in South Carolina*. Orono: University of Maine at Orono Press, 1981.

Palmer, Dave Richard. *The River and the Rock*. New York: Greenwood Publishing, 1969.

Palmer, John McAuley. *General von Steuben*. New Haven: Yale University Press, 1937.

Parramore, Thomac C. *Launching the Craft: The First Half-Century of Freemasonry in North Carolina*. Raleigh, N.C.: Grand Lodge of North Carolina, A. F. & A. M., 1975.

Rankin, Hugh F. *Francis Marion: The Swamp Fox*. New York: Thomas Y. Crowell, 1973.

―――. *The North Carolina Continentals*. Chapel Hill: University of North Carolina Press, 1971.

Rankin, Richard. " 'Mosquetoe' Bites: Caricatures of Lower Cape Fear Whigs and Tories on the Eve of the American Revolution." *North Carolina Historical Review* 65 (1988): 173–207.

Risch, Erna. *Supplying Washington's Army*. Special Studies Series. Washington, D.C.: Center of Military History, U.S. Army, 1981.

Roberts, Robert B. *New York's Forts in the Revolution*. Rutherford, N.J.: Fairleigh Dickinson University Press, 1980.

Rogers, George C., Jr. *Charleston in the Age of the Pinckneys*. Norman: University of Oklahoma Press, 1969.

Rossie, Jonathan Gregory. *The Politics of Command in the American Revolution*. New York: Syracuse University Press, 1975.

Royster, Charles. *A Revolutionary People At War: The Continental Army and American Character, 1775–1783*. Chapel Hill: University of North Carolina Press, 1979.

Sargent, Winthrop. *The Life of Major John André, Adjutant General of the British Army in America*. New York: D. Appleton, 1871.

Searcy, Martha Condray. "The Georgia-Florida Campaigns in the American Revolution, 1776, 1777, and 1778." Ph.D. dissertation, Tulane University, 1979.

―――. *Georgia-Florida Contest in the American Revolution, 1776–1778* University: University of Alabama Press, 1985.

Selby, John E. *The Revolution in Virginia, 1775–1783*. Williamsburg, Va.: The Colonial Williamsburg Foundation, 1988.

Sellers, John R., Gerod W. Gawalt, Paul H. Smith, and Patricia Molen Van Ee, comps. *Manuscript Sources in the Library of Congress on the American Revolution*. Washington: Library of Congress, 1975.

Sirmans, M. Eugene. *Colonial South Carolina: A Political History 1663–1763*. Chapel Hill: University of North Carolina Press for Institute of Early American History and Culture, 1966.

Smith, W. Calvin. "Mermaids Riding Alligators: Divided Command on the Southern Frontier, 1776–1778." *Florida Historical Quarterly* 54 (April 1976): 443–64.

Speech of Hon. John D. Bellamy of North Carolina in the House of Representatives, February 14, 1903. Washington: 1903.

Stewart, Catesby Willis. *The Life of Brigadier General William Woodford of the American Revolution.* 2 vols. Richmond: Whittet and Shepperson, 1973.

Taylor, H. Braugh. "The Foreign Attachment Law and the Coming of the Revolution in North Carolina." *North Carolina Historical Review* 52 (January 1975): 20–36.

Tower, Charlemagne, Jr. *The Marquis de La Fayette in the American Revolution.* 2 vols. Philadelphia: J. B. Lippincott, 1895.

Van Doren, Carl. *Mutiny in January.* New York: Viking Press, 1943.

———. *Secret History of the American Revolution: An Account of the Conspiracies of Benedict Arnold and Numerous Others Drawn from the Secret Papers of the British Headquarters in North America.* New York: Viking Press, 1941.

Vipperman, Carl J. *The Rise of Rawlins Lowndes, 1721–1800.* Columbia: University of South Carolina Press, 1978.

Ward, Harry M. *Charles Scott and the "Spirit of 76."* Charlottesville: University Press of Virginia, 1988.

Watson, Alan D., Dennis R. Lawson, and Donald R. Lennon. *Harnett, Hooper and Howe: Revolutionary Leaders of the Lower Cape Fear.* Wilmington, N.C.: Lower Cape Fear Historical Society, 1979.

White, John Todd. "Standing Armies in Time of War: Republican Theory and Military Practice during the American Revolution." Ph.D. dissertation, George Washington University, 1978.

Williams, Frances Leigh. *A Founding Family: The Pinckneys of South Carolina.* New York and London: Harcourt Brace Jovanovich, 1978.

Wright, J. Leitch, Jr. *Florida in the American Revolution.* Gainesville: University Presses of Florida, 1975.

INDEX

CG EAXY